MAP OF **PHILADELPHIA** 1900

LEGEND:

1. 19th and Walnut (John H. McFadden house), later the Wellington
2. Rittenhouse Club
3. *Billy Goat* statue
4. "Chinese Wall"
5. Pennsylvania Railroad Center City terminal
6. City Hall
7. George H. McFadden house
8. Church of the Holy Trinity
9. Edward T. Stotesbury townhouses
10. Aldine Hotel
11. JHM house
12. Land Title Building
13. Drexel Bank
14. Union League
15. Academy of Music
16. Jasper Brinton house
17. Art Club of Philadelphia
18. John G. Johnson houses
19. Philadelphia Club
20. Episcopal Academy
21. Continental Hotel
22. Geo. H. McFadden & Bro. office

JOHN H. MCFADDEN AND HIS AGE

McFadden

"A Strong Hand Uppermost"
     —McFadden family motto
     (from the Gaelic, "Lamh
     Laidir An Uachdar")

John H. McFadden and His Age

COTTON AND CULTURE IN PHILADELPHIA

RICHARD CARREÑO

CAMINO BOOKS, INC.
PHILADELPHIA

Manufactured in the United States of America

1 2 3 4   25 24 23 22 21

Library of Congress Cataloging-in-Publication Data

Names: Carreño, Richard, author.
Title: John H. McFadden and his age : cotton and culture in Philadelphia /
 Richard Carreño.
Description: Philadelphia : Camino Books, Inc., [2020] | Includes
 bibliographical references and index.
Identifiers: LCCN 2020013050 (print) | LCCN 2020013051 (ebook) | ISBN
 9781680980394 (hardcover) | ISBN 9781680980400 (ebook)
Subjects: LCSH: McFadden, John H., 1850-1921. |
 Businessmen--Pennsylvania--Philadelphia--Biography. | Art--Collectors
 and collecting--Pennsylvania--Philadelphia--Biography. |
 Philanthropists--Pennsylvania--Philadelphia--Biography. | Cotton
 trade--United States--History. | Philadelphia (Pa.)--History. | United
 States--Civilization--1865-1918.
Classification: LCC HC102.5.M346 C37 2020 (print) | LCC HC102.5.M346
 (ebook) | DDC 338.7/63351092 [B]--dc23
LC record available at https://lccn.loc.gov/2020013050
LC ebook record available at https://lccn.loc.gov/2020013051

ISBN 978-1-68098-039-4
ISBN 978-1-68098-040-0 (ebook)

Cover design: Jerilyn DiCarlo
Interior design: Rachel Reiss

Edits and additions to the endpaper maps © 2020 Joseph Gannon. Based on a map
originally published by Rand McNally, 1895.

This book is available at a special discount on bulk purchases for educational, business, and promotional purposes. For information write:

Publisher
Camino Books, Inc.
P.O. Box 59026
Philadelphia, PA 19102
www.caminobooks.com

For
Joan T. Kane

MAP OF PHILADELPHIA 1900
(See endpapers)

1. The Wellington, northeastern corner of 19th & Walnut Streets
2. Rittenhouse Club, Walnut Street between 18th and 19th Streets
3. *Billy Goat*, Rittenhouse Square
4. "Chinese Wall," Pennsylvania Railroad viaduct
5. Pennsylvania Railroad Center City Terminal
6. City Hall
7. George H. McFadden house, northeastern corner of 18th and Spruce Streets
8. Church of the Holy Trinity, Rittenhouse Square
9. Edward T. Stotesbury townhouses, 1923 and 1925 Walnut Street
10. Aldine Hotel, Chestnut Street between 19th and 20th Streets
11. JHM house, 2107 Chestnut Street
12. Land Title Building, 100 South Broad Street
13. Drexel Bank, northeastern corner of Walnut and 15th Streets
14. Union League, southwestern corner of Sansom and South Broad Streets
15. Academy of Music, 240 South Broad Street
16. Alice (McFadden) and Jasper Brinton house, 1423 Spruce Street
17. Art Club of Philadelphia, 220 South Broad Street
18. John G. Johnson houses, 506 and 510 South Broad Street
19. Philadelphia Club, northwestern corner of 13th and Walnut Streets
20. Episcopal Academy, Locust and Juniper Streets
21. Continental Hotel, 9th and Chestnut Streets
22. Geo. H. McFadden & Bro., 121 Chestnut Street

Contents

PREFACE

Beau Ideal

IN A CITY WHERE Benjamin Franklin's legacy permeates the institutional landscape, it is easy to believe that the Philadelphia Museum of Art is another of Philadelphia's ancient and legendary cultural institutions. Many of them indeed date from the eighteenth and nineteenth centuries, including the Pennsylvania Academy of the Fine Arts, founded in 1805, and the Athenaeum of Philadelphia, begun in 1814. And Franklin was in fact associated with two public institutions: the Library Company (1731) and the American Philosophical Society (1743). In contrast, the Philadelphia Museum is a mere youngblood, less than a century from its opening in 1928 as the Pennsylvania Museum of Art.

That is, if we are considering it as it is today: the majestic Greek Revival colossus atop Fairmount Hill. But the museum's roots run much deeper, to the late nineteenth century, in its first incarnation in 1877 as the Pennsylvania Museum and School of Industrial Art. By this measure, it is actually older than the iconic Metropolitan Museum of Art (1880) in New York.

The Pennsylvania Museum of Art was born in a time of tumultuous municipal transition, which tore and remade the fabric of virtually all of Philadelphia's institutions, from political to cultural, from commercial to societal. In a period of no more than thirty years beginning in the late 19th century, Philadelphia reconsidered how money changed hands, who lived where, and how immigrant Americans would shape the city's demographic landscape. The new museum, remarkably, also contributed to sounding the death knell of "Proper Philadelphia," as E. Digby Baltzell famously memorialized the city's WASP élite.

Unlike Philadelphia's other venerable cultural institutions, the Philadelphia Museum was not the product of a single visionary, nor of a coterie of affluent connoisseurs. The museum's founding was contentious, public, messy, and expensive.

One Philadelphian, among the many who figured in the museum's creation, stands out prominently in shaping its transformation. John H. McFadden, having made his fortune as a cotton merchant in England, stepped forward to become Philadelphia's singular cultural impresario.

McFadden's renown as Philadelphia's—indeed, America's—grandest cotton king has been largely forgotten. If he is known for anything nowadays, it is as the collector and donor of the John Howard McFadden Memorial Collection of British art to the Philadelphia Museum. Scant biographical resources, and no recent writing about the man's life, meant that McFadden's multitude of remarkable roles—as philanthropist, rare book collector, sponsor of exploration, real estate developer, and museum administrator—had fallen into the shadows of history.

This has been the case with many of Philadelphia's great art collectors: no "big" books have been written about such giants as P.A.B. Widener, William L. Elkins, and, most egregiously, John G. Johnson. The exception is Dr. Albert C. Barnes, the founder of the legendary Barnes Foundation.

Very little was known about McFadden: how he formed his massive wealth as a cotton trader in Liverpool; his role as an art connoisseur and collector, or as importantly, how he became Philadelphia's unofficial arts czar, overseeing—often ruling— the city's major cultural institutions.

Stipulations attached to the donation of his art trove—at the time the largest collection of British art in America—were instrumental in driving the Philadelphia Museum to reinvent itself, taking the form it has today, the world-class cultural capstone of the Benjamin Franklin Parkway.[1]

McFadden's is the donation that keeps on giving. The McFadden bequest states that the collection can never be disassembled—and despite a dreary, anachronistic gallery setting, its renditions of "Olde England"—its paean to British order, beauty, and dignity—will remain on view forever.

McFadden did not singlehandedly invent Philadelphia's great museum. John D. McIlhenny, Eli Kirk Price II, and Fiske Kimball also harnessed the mounting synergy of funds, influence, civic motivation, and artwork that finally led to the creation of the neo-Classical masterpiece in brick and mortar. But like no other early twentieth-century Philadelphian, John H. McFadden laid the museum's foundation. Even its cornerstone.

—Richard Carreño
Philadelphia, 2021

PART I

In Boston they ask, how much does he know?
In New York, how much is he worth?
In Philadelphia, who were his parents?

—MARK TWAIN

ABOVE: *John H. McFadden and grandchild,*
believed to be Florence Pamela Brinton.

Will

1917

O N AN UNUSUALLY BALMY December day in 1917, John H.
McFadden signed his will, in a moment that encapsulated the man's great success and his modesty. His valet Robert
Potts dutifully added his name as one of several witnesses. In
twenty-first century dollars, the Philadelphia cotton merchant,
landowner, and art patron was a multi-millionaire. His estate,
valued at more than $5.2 million ($73 million today),[1] was bequeathed to his "beloved" wife Florence and their three adult
children. The eldest, Philip, was a high-goal polo player. Alice,
the middle child, had a dilettante's interest in the theater. The
youngest, John H. McFadden, Jr., or "Jack," was a former U.S.
Army officer.

Despite his immense wealth, McFadden was a man of pro-
bity. He once told a friend that his aim in life was to create
"lasting good," concluding, "Then I could die happy."[2] On December 2, a day before his 67th birthday, McFadden had that
last mission in mind when he put a pen from his favorite sta-
tioner, Bailey, Banks & Biddle, to foolscap, and forever sealed

the fate of his art collection as a gift to Philadelphia's cultural patrimony. Or, so it might appear.

———✕———

JOHN HOWARD MCFADDEN was an international "cotton man."[3] Among only a handful of such commodity moguls in the late nineteenth century, he and his older brother, George, reigned over an empire that brokered and shipped raw American and Egyptian cotton worldwide. Millions of cotton bales made their way to mills in England and in New England, and millions of dollars made their way to the coffers of their family firm, Geo. H. McFadden & Bro., Cotton Merchants.[4] By the end of the Spanish-American War in 1898, the McFadden partnership, headed by George as managing director, had become the country's largest cotton trading venture.

It further established itself as one of America's first truly multinational conglomerates, with shipping and trading interests in Europe, Africa, and in South America. As the otherwise anonymous "Bro.," John McFadden headed the company's key Liverpool subsidiary. A third brother, the youngest, got no billing. J. Franklin McFadden was, like George, based in Philadelphia. Frank, as he was known, was a poloist like his nephew Philip, enjoying the sport in the city's Main Line suburbs and in Florida. Whatever their individual contributions, Geo. H. McFadden & Bro. ballooned into a prodigiously remunerative entity, making the three siblings millionaires many times over.

The Philadelphia press, never shy of hyperbole, singled out John McFadden for a most glowing superlative: "[T]he richest cotton broker in the world."[5] Actually, George edged out his brother. When George died in 1927, six years after John's death in 1921, he left an estate of $8 million ($115 million today).

———✕———

THE COTTON MAGNATE indulged in the perquisites of wealth. He was a yachtsman and epicure. He saw wealth as a means to embrace beauty in art (portraiture in particular), and as a way to forever freeze the face of nobility, accomplishment, and dignity by acquiring painted portraits, scenes, and landscapes. The canvases he collected over more than two decades idealized these virtues in the artists' painterly visions. Reflected in this glory, it seems, he saw part of himself.

McFadden maintained an almost boyish fascination with adventure and derring-do, and championed both historical and contemporary figures he saw embodying those attributes. He was an obsessive Anglophile, comforted in the knowledge that he was only one generation from being a British subject himself (both his parents were born in Great Britain). He admired a range of English personalities as disparate as the merchant prince Edward Guinness, First Earl of Iveagh, and the more rough-hewn Antarctic explorer Sir Ernest H. Shackleton.

Against a backdrop of fabulous wealth and luxury, McFadden was also a manic traveler, often undertaking six transatlantic round-trip voyages a year and spending up to two months at sea. He found validation as a compulsive joiner of clubs, even some he had no particular interest in.

In later years, he suffered from anxiety; he might well have been haunted by the sense that his prosperity bore the stain of slavery. His relations with his brothers were never warm. George and Frank were sportsmen, highly accomplished polo and racquetball players. John indulged in less strenuous pursuits. His brothers were good-looking and fit. John was fat. They were graduates of the University of Pennsylvania. With training limited to high school, John surged into the art field as an autodidact. Art set him apart in his sibling rivalry, and conferred a gravitas that neither of his brothers could project.

From his choice perch in London, the Philadelphian followed his passion, assembling the largest group of eighteenth- and nineteenth-century British paintings in private hands in the United States. The collection, twenty-five years in the making, eventually totaled forty-three pictures flowered into a multi-faceted creation. Over time, some pictures came. Some went. The fevered atmosphere of American collecting in the late nineteenth century was no deterrent in his amassing his works. In 1917, despite the dangers of a wartime sea crossing, he made the final formal addition to his holdings.

McFadden favored the most respected artists of the time in Britain, including John Constable, George Stubbs, Thomas Gainsborough, William Hogarth, and J. M. W. Turner. An inventory of his collection underscored the magnificent discernment of his "boutique" selection of drawing room-sized pictures. He left the more monumental paintings to his art-collecting competitors. Conservatively estimated, his paintings were worth more than $2 million ($29 million today).[6]

The collection's first cataloguer, the early twentieth-century English art critic William Roberts, summed up the group as the "largest" of its kind, the "most interesting," and "without a rival."[7] One of America's most widely read art critics, James Huneker, thought so much of McFadden that in 1913 he dedicated his art tome *The Pathos of Distance: A Book of a Thousand and One Moments* to his friend. The inscription read, "To John McFadden: A Lover of Fine Arts."[8]

JOHN, THE MIDDLE McFadden brother, was an unmistakable Proper Philadelphian. He was a clubman. A family man. A pillar of rectitude, who radiated confidence and an engaging, felicitous charm. He had a passing resemblance to a well-nourished, aging putto. His mustache was customary for a man of his station.

He was vain, it was said, in dress. He wore bespoke, English-styled apparel, and was considered one of the best-attired men on the Exchange Flags premises of the Liverpool cotton trade. In public, he was never seen without a silk top hat, "always carefully ironed."[9] Rounding out the "Robber Baron" look was a "fat" cigar, usually unlighted.[10]

Otherwise, McFadden conformed to Philadelphia's conservative, pecuniary, and inbred tribal ethic. His only lapse, some might whisper, was a worldly, cosmopolitan air, foreign to the city's insular élite. He was as much at home in the boardrooms of Wall Street and in the salons and galleries of upmarket Mayfair, as he was in the residences of parochial Rittenhouse Square. There was also something, in Philadelphia, at least, curious, if not downright suspicious, about his public life, that of both a mercantile power broker and, equally, an eminent art connoisseur.

DESPITE HIS PUBLIC roles, McFadden maintained a relatively low profile. In England, his home for long stretches, and during his often reluctant residence in his native America, he eschewed the celebrity that many of his art collecting contemporaries attracted. (His promotional skills were more subtle.) He left no diaries. No commentary setting forth his strategies in forming his collection. Besides his will, very little epistolary record exists. Fortunately, others have made up for his reticence.

What was previously known about McFadden, to his death at 71, has been largely confined to fewer than a dozen biographical briefs. Many of these accounts date from his own era; none amount to more than a few hundred words. Their accuracy, without confirmation from other sources, has always been in doubt.

McFadden's portrayal as connoisseur and collector has been woefully one-dimensional. It did not include the middle-aged polymath whose life was a composite of numerous interests and causes. His life tracked a public side (his art collection had renown on two continents) and a shadow existence as a virtually unknown progressive philanthropist. His advocacy of medical research and scientific exploration has been largely unrecorded. New research has also revealed his interest in rare book collecting.

Seen more fully, he defies being pigeonholed as a stereotypical period capitalist who hoarded art to engineer social acceptance and prominence. Industry and will drove him to become, late in life, one of the most prominent governing mandarins of the city's arts community. He was a board member of the Pennsylvania Academy of the Fine Arts, president of the Art Club of Philadelphia, and oversaw the early development of the Philadelphia Museum of Art, then known as the Pennsylvania Museum and School of Industrial Art.

In a mercurial time, McFadden offered the embryonic institution a steady hand and prescient guidance, holding out his art collection as a dangling, irresistible draw to drive the museum to achievement and stature. A fevered seven-year period of wait-and-see legal intrigue ensued, ending with the new art museum transformed from a prim nineteenth-century artifact to a dynamic twentieth-century cultural dynamo.

McFadden's contributions as an art connoisseur and as an unlikely real estate developer placed him in the forefront of those who managed cultural, social, and demographic initiatives in early twentieth-century Philadelphia. For a brief, fraught time, from 1917 to his death, McFadden was one of Philadelphia's chief change agents. For a first-rank Proper Philadelphian, McFadden wound up curiously enough as one of its most "improper."

A NOTE ABOUT COSTS AND MONETARY VALUES

Monetary values are listed in contemporary figures for the year cited. In parentheses, the historic values are converted to current dollars. Some caveats should be noted. Inflation in the art world is notoriously higher than that of the overall economic inflation rate for the 75-year period under study. Furthermore, prices for fine art are sometimes subject to subterfuge, manipulation, and hidden costs.

A NOTE ABOUT PICTURE TITLES

The names of paintings often vary from source to source. Titles are those cited by the Philadelphia Museum of Art.

CHAPTER ONE

Philadelphia

SEVENTEENTH-CENTURY QUAKERISM gave Philadelphia its birth name, the "City of Brotherly Love." The eighteenth-century Enlightenment gave it its lesser-known nickname, "Athens of America." The first stuck. The second vanished.

The city's reserve harked back to its founding in 1682 by William Penn, a London-born member of the Society of Friends. That quality stuck too. While the city itself took many star turns in subsequent years for its commercial and cultural innovation, its people always took pains to be plain; never flashy and never vulgar. Modesty and rectitude prevailed. It was the Quaker way.

More than two hundred years later, Henry James was still able to confirm the impression. Following a national tour that included a few days of boredom in the "Quaker City" (another, altogether more considered nickname), James declared that "Philadelphia *didn't* 'bristle,'"[1] meaning, one supposed, *bustle*. Charles Dickens, some years before, blamed Philadelphia's fusty nature on its physical layout, one attributed to town planner

Penn. "[D]istractingly regular," Dickens declared. "After walking about it for an hour or two, I felt that I would have given the world for a crooked street."[2]

Another foreign visitor, Alexis de Tocqueville,[3] praised the street grid. What others saw as monotonous, Tocqueville considered progressive, setting a municipal standard that promoted commerce, coherence, and public safety.

As he settled into middle age, John McFadden was residing in a fading American metropolis. At the turn of the twentieth century, Philadelphia's ascendancy as the country's undisputed "second city" was losing its blush. This seeming inevitability had been slow, and, for many Philadelphians, almost imperceptible. The Gilded Age had tarnished.

In the colonial era, Philadelphia wavered between being the world's second- and third-largest English-speaking city after London. (In the mid-1700s, Bristol, the English Atlantic port city with a population of about 45,000, just edged out Philadelphia, at roughly 43,000.) The Declaration of Independence, the American Revolution, and the signing of the United States Constitution all pivoted around Philadelphia. It was the nascent nation's first capital, from 1790 to 1800.

Philadelphia was a city of firsts. From its earliest days, Philadelphians staked their claim as the nation's scientific, financial, and cultural capital. Pennsylvania Hospital became the nation's first in 1748. The country's first medical school, founded in 1765, was the University of Pennsylvania Medical School. The exigencies of capitalism were recognized on the nation's first "Wall Street" (actually, at the corner of Second and Walnut Streets, near Independence Hall) when a stock exchange opened for trading in 1790. The first United States Mint quickly followed in 1792. America's first combined museum and art school, the

Pennsylvania Academy of the Fine Arts, founded in 1805, was a strong cultural linchpin.[4]

Philadelphia's grandeur was encapsulated, for the last time, in the Centennial International Exhibition of 1876, also the first World's Fair to be held in America. Sprawling over about 285 acres in Fairmount Park, in northwest Philadelphia, the fair celebrated the 100th anniversary of the Declaration of Independence. Besides the United States, thirty-seven countries participated. During a crammed six-month period from May to November, almost 10 million visitors[5] learned about such modern contraptions as the sewing machine, the typewriter, and the telephone.

And also something about art—at least, the popular kind. Of almost 150 buildings constructed on the fairgrounds, Memorial Hall, a $1.5 million, domed Beaux Arts pavilion, was a purpose-built gallery. On display were American achievements in the arts, as well as artistic bounty from represented countries.

The Centennial Exhibition was a fabulous marketing and commercial undertaking. (Its true colors were given away by its official name, the International Exhibition of Arts, Manufactures and Products of the Soil and the Mine.) The fair ended up as a nationally exhilarating feel-good exercise. An early version of American "exceptionalism" took center stage. Beneath the reflected glory, however, Philadelphia was losing its shine.

For nearly fifty years, the city's prominence in the commercial, financial, and cultural firmament of the United States ebbed. The Erie Canal, which opened on November 4, 1825, directly connected inland trade for the first time with New York City, via the Great Lakes. After this, Philadelphia surrendered its mantle as the country's key East Coast port and financial center to New York. The city began to leak population. A few short years after the canal's inauguration, Philadelphia dipped to about 160,000, conceding its eminence as the country's population center for the first time to New York, then at almost 200,000. By the time of the Centennial, New York's population had jumped to almost a million (even excluding the roughly 400,000 citizens of Brooklyn, later incorporated into New York in 1898). In 1900, Philadelphia was the country's third-largest city.

Many "Proper Philadelphians" of the city's WASP establishment were hardly miffed by the loss of supremacy. An anonymous letter writer to *The New York Times* in 1850, citing a recent visit, noted that New York was welcome to its "dust," a nasty byproduct of its "business and bustle." He preferred, he told the *Times*, "the Quaker neatness and the Quaker quiet of most Philadelphia thoroughfares."[6]

As a city of tradition, with a long memory, Philadelphia was forever mindful of its stolid cultural legacies, many of them of significant renown. These included the Walnut Street Theatre (founded in 1809); the first women's arts college, the Moore College of Art & Design (1848); the country's first subscription library, the Library Company (1731); and two amateur art associations, the Art Club of Philadelphia (1887) and the Philadelphia Art Alliance (1915). Lacking was the crown jewel, a fine arts museum. Preferably a big one. That looked like the Pantheon.

Some brasher, smaller cities had already recognized the importance of a large public art venue in a fully formed municipal infrastructure. Almost as one, emerging social élites in many of the nation's legacy cities cast an admiring and envious eye to London's established art shrines. Many viewed the South Kensington Museum, founded in 1852, and later rechristened the Victoria and Albert in 1899, as an international model of art diversity, showcasing pictures, sculpture, and textiles. The National Gallery (established in 1924), however, famously restricted itself to Classical and fine art.

America in the meantime experienced increasing concentrations of wealth in the hands of its plutocracies. Power brokers, sometimes aligned with old moneyed Brahmins, set their sights on art connoisseurship.

From Michigan Avenue in Chicago, and Back Bay in Boston, to Fifth Avenue in New York, captains of industry—many of them now elevated to generalissimo status—lived large and thought big. As they built their fine homes, they both emulated and surpassed the opulence of London's South Kensington. They looked acquisitively toward another European model, considered fittingly palatial, embodied in the Musée de Louvre in Paris, former home of another art patron, Louis XIV. And they invited such comparisons.

In the American iteration of that monument to art, as exemplified at the Metropolitan Museum of Art in New York, the first *encyclopedic* behemoth was launched. A Medici complex was born. Immortality would surely follow.

In marshaling civic forces, building America's great museums was fraught with clashes of egos and vision. Harnessing charitable commitment was left to the few who could rally disparate interests. No one was more forceful in coupling the virtues of giving and public service than Joseph C. Choate, who brought his Harvard and Boston Brahmin background and temperament to bear as the Metropolitan's most robust supporter. At its opening in 1880 in its iconic Central Park location, Choate, a trustee, turned his inauguration address into a *cri de coeur* to "men of fortune and estate."[7]

Choate's appeal for private largess foreshadowed what became the prescriptive model in funding America's great public arts institutions. He added a dash of self-interest:

> Think of it, ye millionaires of many markets—what
> glory may yet be yours, if only listen to our advice,
> to convert pork into porcelain, grain and produce

into priceless pottery, the rude ores of commerce into sculptured marble, and railroad shares and mining stocks—things which perish without the using, and which in the next financial panic shall surely shrivel like parched scrolls—into the glorified canvas of the world's masters, that shall adorn these walls for centuries. The rage of Wall Street is to hunt the philosopher's stone, to convert all baser things into gold, which is but dross; but ours is the higher ambition to convert your useless gold into things of living beauty that shall be joy to a whole people for a thousand years.

After several permutations, the Art Institute of Chicago welcomed visitors to its neo-Italianate building on Michigan Avenue in 1893, a year after its founding. In Boston, then about a third of Philadelphia's size, the Museum of Fine Arts had opened in 1876, the same year the nation was celebrating its 100th anniversary in Fairmount Park. Even Cleveland, the country's seventh-largest city at about 400,000 in 1900, could celebrate its Museum of Art's début in 1916.

Public Philadelphia had hardly inched forward since the Centennial Exhibition, a spectacle more of commercial showmanship and jingoism than any commanding commitment to fulfilling the city's cultural destiny. While great public works rose elsewhere, no great cultural monuments rose in Philadelphia. One sensed, as in 1850 when the anonymous Philadelphia letter writer declaimed to *The New York Times* on "Quaker neatness" and "Quaker quiet," that Proper Philadelphians believed such futuristic flights of folly were best left to the crass "business and bustle" of that place north of the city.

Joseph C. Choate's call on behalf of the Metropolitan—really, for public funding in the arts everywhere—had resonated through the country. But it largely fell on deaf ears within hearing distance of Proper Philadelphia's home ground, Rittenhouse Square.

THE PENNSYLVANIA ACADEMY of the Fine Arts, the city's premier
picture gallery, was also hoping to expand. Despite its inclusive
name, the Academy was really the exclusive repository of American works. Its constitution prevented it from ever becoming
the universal fine arts museum championed by Joseph Choate.
Still, PAFA knew how to exploit a public relations moment, and
timed the début of its new home on North Broad Street, designed
by Frank Furness, with the opening of the Centennial.

Less than twenty years later, in 1892, Furness's stone fortress
came under withering criticism as "a heavy tomb" and as "a
deep and chilling recess, a prematurely old ruin." That blistering
appraisal came from no other than Harrison S. Morris, the Academy's managing director and the country's first professional
arts administrator. Several years later, in a memoir, Morris took
aim at Proper Philadelphia for leaving the academy financially
bereft. His remarks were muted, but equally piercing. "There was
little money to go on," he lamented. "The structure we had built
of friendship and patronage was not any too strong."[8]

In the rarefied precincts of Rittenhouse Square, sustenance
was found in the past. Its denizens lived frugally. They gathered,
in worship and in other forms of fraternal order, within a frame-
work of interlocking, close-knit family units. Marriage within
their milieu was encouraged: many young marrieds were only a
single or double bloodline away. Most Proper Philadelphians were
on a first-name basis with each other. Almost all were "cousins."

Not mincing words, E. Digby Baltzell attributed this
upper-class web to tribalism.[9] Proper Philadelphians fostered,
he argued, a clan culture with "family values"..."not too different from those of the Italian-American family portrayed in
The Godfather."

Proper Philadelphia circled the wagons around Rittenhouse
Square. From there, they were the keenest surveyors in drawing

the boundaries of their ancestral patch, roughly circumscribed by Chestnut Street to the north; Broad Street to the east; Pine Street to the south; and the Schuylkill River to the west. North of Market Street and south of Pine were *terra incognita*, inhabited by the unfamiliar: immigrants from Ireland, Italy, and Eastern Europe.

North Philadelphia was on the wrong side of the tracks—literally, those owned by the powerful Pennsylvania Railroad. Its Center City hub was Broad Street Station, a massive terminal facing City Hall. After a final expansion in 1893, the rail hub became another landmark by local architect Frank Furness. The station followed Furness's signature, idiosyncratically neo-Gothic style. It could have easily doubled as a Transylvanian Railroad station.

A stone viaduct along Market Street that supported tracks to a 30th Street connector drew criticism almost from the start. Tunnels allowed for north-south street traffic. But trains above were a noisy, sooty nuisance. In no time, the causeway was belittled with a popular pejorative, the "Chinese Wall."

Proper Philadelphia, on the other hand, looked kindly on the wall as a physical barrier, as well as a psychological one. Such snobbism had unintentional, negative consequences. The imaginary line of geographical acceptability singled out several of Philadelphia's most prominent art collectors as outliers. Two, the renowned lawyer John G. Johnson, who lived in South Philadelphia, and industrialist P.A.B. Widener, a North Philadelphia resident, did not take their rejection lightly. Whether their artwork would join the city's cultural patrimony would become problematic.

THE CENTENNIAL *DID* endow the city with an "art" museum, albeit a humble one. The Memorial Hall gallery, as intended, had been rechristened the Pennsylvania Museum and School of

Industrial Art. The Fairmount Park Commission was overseer. Nobler consciences, outside the orbit of patrician Philadelphia, could at least soothe their misgivings in the belief that the new gallery might be only a temporary substitute. The Memorial Hall museum, it was rationalized, might wind up as just an ersatz stop-gap, a way-station to its proper destination as a high-minded institution of fine art.

Some years later, no less a figure of Proper Philadelphia nobility than George Wharton Pepper, a former U.S. senator, had a sharp word for his own kind. Philadelphia, he declared, was tarnished by "provincialism." A less charitable barb, *philistine*, also cropped up.[10]

The Pennsylvania Museum was never supposed to be temporary; from the start, it represented an earnest effort at channeling the eclectic virtues of London's Victoria and Albert Museum. Chartered on February 25, 1876[11] by the Pennsylvania Legislature, the Pennsylvania Museum and School of Industrial Art would feature, according to its mission statement, a "Museum of Art" and "practical schools, special libraries, lectures, and otherwise" to develop "Art Industries of the State" and provide "instruction in Drawing, Painting, Modeling, Designing, etc." The charter advised that the Philadelphia institution would be "similar in its general features to that of the South Kensington Museum of London."

Unlike the Louvre-like Met in New York, the Pennsylvania Museum was a high Victorian paean to democratic values in a working-class city. There was something telling in the class consciousness each museum evoked. In its formal age, the Met's self-image required a dress code. More relaxed and welcoming, the Pennsylvania Museum had none.

Full of optimism, the Pennsylvania Museum's first public day was May 10, 1877,[12] one year after the Centennial Exhibition's opening. Yet the launch was halting. One barrier to immediate success was the Museum's location. The Fairmount Park grounds had been filled with crowds for the vast Centennial extravaganza. But once the fair ended, Memorial Hall remained as the only physical reminder; virtually all other exhibit spaces were razed on schedule. It was left a lonely outpost in the Park, difficult to reach by public transportation. The art school's classes were held in Center City.

The museum also suffered from the awkwardness of its name. Some grumbled that the new museum could be too easily confused with the archaeological museum at the University of Pennsylvania. Founded in 1887, the museum changed its name in 1894 from the Museum of Archaeology and Paleontology, nomenclature that clearly separated the two institutions, to the Free Museum of Science and Art.

The museum itself was the occasional target of scorn, even by those in the arts community who might have welcomed its appearance: its capacious halls housed less fine art than had been hoped for. Some holdovers remained from the Centennial exhibit, including paintings of the mid-nineteenth century French Barbizon School (or "sweet French," as S. N. Behrman ridiculed the genre).[13]

In 1893, sixteen years after its début, the museum finally received its first substantial bequest of artwork, the W.P. Wilstach Collection, assembled by William P. Wilstach, a rich saddler who had died twenty-three years before.

Wilstach's widow, heir, and donor, Anna Wilstach, had added to their cache during the years since her husband's death. Much of it was of the second rank, mainly German pastorals and American landscapes. Interestingly enough, one of the few examples of an American work, Thomas Sully's *Gypsy Woman and Child*, wormed its way into the Wilstach group. In all, about 150 objects were deposited in Memorial Hall, including a bust of the great man Wilstach himself. Most important, Anna Wilstach had the foresight to establish an endowment for the collection's perpetual maintenance and for new purchases. She allocated the enormous sum of $500,000 ($13 million).

Whatever its artistic merits, the Wilstach accession served as a long-awaited mid-course redirection. Plaster sculptural casts, second-rate substitutes for the original ancient marble sculptures, and antiquated vitrine displays started being consigned to storage. For those who wished the Pennsylvania Museum to be more Louvre-like, the collection became a harbinger of better things to come. A new museum would be born. But it would be a breech birth.

CHAPTER TWO

Cotton Man

1820–1881

J OHN HOWARD MCFADDEN WAS born a Proper Philadelphian. But barely.

In the mid-nineteenth century, Philadelphia's patricians— many of the great and wealthy industrial and financial tycoons of the age—took a dim view of Catholic immigrants, especially Irish interlopers. They were viewed as maids and workmen, hardly the sort for their posh residential precinct of Rittenhouse Square. There were exceptions to the "No Irish Need Apply" dictum: Protestant Irish. People-Like-Us Irish. And, of course, moneyed Irish.

John's father, George McIntosh McFadden, slipped through the cracks. As for affluence, not so much. He managed moderate success as a scrappy cotton merchant. He was also Protestant, and "Scotch Irish," descending from Scots who emigrated to Ireland. Also in the People-Like-Us category, it probably helped that he somehow managed to show up in Philadelphia sporting a coat of arms. The family's motto in Irish Gaelic, eventually emblazoned on notepaper, was "Lamh Laidir An Uachdar" ("A

Strong Hand Uppermost"). That John's mother, Charlotte, had English roots, was another salubrious leg up. George McIntosh McFadden was a striver.

George McIntosh was born in 1806, in Coothill, a small market town in County Cavan in northern Protestant Ulster. Like all of Ireland at the time, the town was part of the United Kingdom. To this small extent he could also claim British ethnicity, a fortunate class signifier. In 1820, when George McIntosh was fourteen years old, he immigrated with his father, Samuel McFadden; his mother, the former Lydia Stafford; and his siblings to America. Thousands of other Irish were also leaving their homeland, but most were fleeing less fortunate circumstances in the south. And they were Catholic.

While most southern Irish immigrants secured only a toehold on the lowest rung of their American experience, Samuel McFadden, thanks to his family's means, eased into more favorable circumstances. His family lineage also helped. His father, George McFadden, was a prominent Coothill burgher who had further caught his stride after marrying Isabella McIntosh, the daughter of a local landowner and merchant, James McIntosh. (In some references, James McIntosh is referenced with the almost certainly fanciful title of "Sir.")

Samuel's path to affluence, and that of successful immigrant, took some twists and turns. Like many seekers of fortune from Ireland, he sailed from Liverpool to Philadelphia. After a few months, he and his family proceeded west, winding up in the small eastern Ohio town of Cadiz. There, surrounded by Lydia and his sons George McIntosh, Henry Stafford, and daughter Letitia, he committed to setting down roots. A family history flatly recorded: "They bought a house and built a warehouse and went into the business of wool buying."

Over time, George's siblings also prospered. Letitia married Joseph Hunter, a Cadiz businessman. Henry Stafford married and became a lawyer, banker, and the founder of a local general store.

Their father, on the other hand, was restive and, with his two older children, Letitia and George McIntosh, Samuel returned to Philadelphia. In the process, he altered the course of his family's fortune—from wool to cotton. Success seemed to come easy. Thanks to his wool business in Cadiz and his trading experience, Samuel walked into a cotton firm partnership, soon titled Graham, McFadden. Thus the family reputation, as cotton traders and as an anchor in early nineteenth-century Philadelphia mercantile history, was established.

The growing business required a presence in the American South for buying ginned, raw cotton and for arranging the shipment of the compressed bales to the North. In time, Samuel opened a branch "house" in Memphis, Tennessee, and hired a representative to oversee those aspects of the trade. In Philadelphia, George McIntosh also joined Graham, McFadden.

In 1845, George McIntosh McFadden married Charlotte Elliot, 22, a native of Ripon, Yorkshire, and transplant to Virginia. Charlotte was the daughter of a journeyman architect and engineer, in the manner of fellow Virginian Thomas Jefferson. She was well-born. George, 39, had married up.

The age difference between the newlyweds drew little attention. If anything, it would have been gossiped about on its positive merits, an older man having the good fortune of pairing with a wife with many childbearing years ahead. Charlotte's fecundity was soon proven. The union produced, in quick succession, seven children, five of whom did not survive childhood. Two boys did. George Henry was born early in the marriage, on July 24, 1847; John Howard, on December 3, 1850. An eighth child, a son, James Franklin, was born twelve years later, on November 17, 1862. They called him "Frank." Later in life, the young man styled himself, for public consumption, as "J. Franklin."

Like his father Samuel before, George McIntosh became restless and began to chafe under Samuel's thumb. Surprising for a well-settled, middle-aged man, at fifty-two, he distanced

himself from the familiar. In 1858, after resigning his partnership at Graham, McFadden, George McIntosh sought new
fortune—and a new future in cotton—in Memphis. If anyone
had known that the outbreak of the Civil War was only three
years away, George McIntosh's striking out might have been
branded as foolhardy. A Northerner had it hard enough adjusting to the region's slave society.

George McIntosh might have had a premonition. He kept
his Philadelphia house, and George Henry and John remained
behind with their mother. If the transition went well, no doubt
Charlotte and boys would have been called to Memphis. She
was hardly abandoned. Within four years, on a visit to Philadelphia, George learned that Charlotte was pregnant with
Frank; she gave birth later in the year. George McIntosh was
fifty-six.

Serendipity was at hand. Following in father Samuel's foot-
steps when he initially landed in Philadelphia, George found a
partner who could smooth his way into the sinews of local business. Whether his new local contact was arranged with the help
of his father's local representative or was simply good fortune,
George went to the top with an associate surnamed "Boyle."
Boyle's first name has been lost to recorded history. But not his
family's eminence in Memphis history. The Boyles were among
Memphis's first families, joining Andrew Jackson as founders
of the city in 1819.

With two male heirs, George McIntosh took yet another step,
in 1858, to confirm his family's commitment to cotton and the
McFadden family's future business legacy. The undertaking
was hardly seamless. With Boyle's support, George backed his
way into cotton trading. According to an insert in *The Memphis
City Directory*, what George rolled out was, in fact, a dry goods
concern. The shop was housed just west from Front Street (otherwise "Cotton Row"), at the northeast corner of Main Street and
Pontotoc Avenue, in a low-slung building sided in red brick and

fronted in cast-iron.[1] Cotton trading received no billing in business notices. An associate, an employed agent, did.

> Geo. McFadden
> Wholesale Dealer in Drygoods
> 299 Main Street
> Ignatius W. Mattingly, Agent

His brief quickly changed. Starting out selling "notions" and "variety" items, to the public, George McIntosh also found footing as a factor, serving in an often-complicated relationship as a combined banker and wholesale grocer to planters. He financed the growers and advanced them supplies (all at fixed interest rates) during the growing season, later receiving their cotton on consignment in the fall. The cotton would then be sold to local brokers at commission, usually at two and a half percent.[2]

The setting was raucous. Hundreds of thousands of cotton bales (a standard size was 28 inches by 54 inches) would crowd the docks on the Mississippi River. Most arrived by rail. Most departed on steamboats for mills in the North.

The Memphis location was choice. As a riparian seller and distributor, George could also count on a constant flow of commercial goods, headed North through to the Ohio River and South to New Orleans. *The Memphis Appeal*—no doubt to the local business community's delight—encouraged the river commerce by regularly reporting the arrival of new shipments. The public, in turn, would rush to snap up the latest, and smartest, goods, from as far away as New York City.

George McIntosh had hit upon a successful, remunerative formula. Just before the Civil War, there were less than thirty factors in Memphis. At a time when planters could not draw on regular banking credit, demand for the wildcatting services of factors was high. All of this crashed when news reached the city that the Union's Fort Sumter in Charleston Bay had been fired upon by Confederate artillery on April 12, 1861, igniting what George's patriotic neighbors in the South were now calling the "War Between the States."

McFadden, again, relied on instinct. He left Memphis. Carefully. He arranged to have the business managed as best it could during the coming war years by his agent, Ignatius Mattingly. Avoiding the Mississippi, McFadden rode by horseback north through Kentucky, finally booking passage by steam packet, probably at Cincinnati, Ohio, to Pittsburgh, then east by coach to Philadelphia. Whether George's return to Philadelphia could be attributed to Union sympathies, a desire to be out of harm's way, or a calculated understanding that King Cotton would be demoted to serf status during the war, is unknown.

As a full-fledged cotton man, there was little alternative than to wait out the conflict.[3] The war's first year was also fateful for another reason: Samuel's death at 79. (His remains were returned to Ohio where he and Lydia, who died five years later in 1866, were both buried in Old Cadiz Cemetery.) Without his father to partner with, George McIntosh found a powerful ally in another Philadelphia cotton firm, Randolph & Jenks.

John Story Jenks's progress as a cotton man followed a similar career trajectory as George's. Jenks had also joined his father's Philadelphia cotton firm, and father and son catapulted to success in the antebellum years. George and John shared much in common, though John Jenks was nearly a generation younger. Like George McIntosh, John Jenks lacked an identifiable Philadelphia pedigree. One strike against him was his status as an alumnus of Central High School, a public school. That putative black mark was notable for its egregious irony, a fact ignored by his "betters." Down-market Central competed on par academically with the city's élite private schools.[4] Jenks finally jumped up a peg or two on the social ladder when he married socially prominent Sidney Howell Brown. It was an advantageous union. Like the McFadden family, the Jenkses over time seeped into Proper Philadelphia's bloodstream.

After aligning with Randolph & Jenks, George McIntosh pivoted to reestablish his business bona fides in Philadelphia, albeit in a market of erratic wartime uncertainties. In the short term, he sold whatever raw cotton that he could get his hands on to finishing mills in New England. Mattingly, George's Memphis associate, maintained McFadden's tenuous toehold in that city's riverfront "Cotton Row."

In the war's aftermath, the numbers were not good. At its start, the South's overall cotton crop was already a dismal 4.5 million bales annually. More than half this output was shipped, through northeastern and southern ports, to Liverpool, for sales to the world's largest mill market, located around Manchester in Lancashire. Access to these shipping lanes quickly became perilous after a Union blockade of all Confederate shipping. Bilateral relations between Great Britain and the Confederate States, which had a strong diplomatic presence in Liverpool, and between Great Britain and the United States, the likely victor, further complicated trade.

How well business fared during these troubled years has no clear narrative. But George's and Charlotte's private life seemed to be unaltered from the normal rhythms—and struggles—of their workaday Philadelphia life. These included the vicissitudes of a home life with a youngster underfoot and two boisterous teenaged boys. Still, the McFaddens were presumably doing well enough financially to decide that George Henry would enter, when the time was right, a private high school. If anything, the McFaddens were aspirational.

The site of the family's residence revealed another, less sanguine, side of the McFadden household, one that rubbed disturbingly close to a hardscrabble environment. Their dwelling at 613 North 8th Street, as it was listed in city directories for the period,[5] was in a working-class neighborhood known as

Northern Liberties. The area had few bragging rights. For the predominantly German immigrant population, there was at least one notable exception: the massive brewery of the Christian Schmidt Company, the maker of the nationally popular Schmidt's lager. Beyond that, the area was a warren of apartments, single-family tenements, and boarding houses. The place was rough, gritty, and light-years away from Rittenhouse Square.

⸻✕⸻

RITTENHOUSE SQUARE ITSELF was still a generation from ascending to its zenith as the city's most desirable residential neighborhood. As more and more fashionable Philadelphians moved westward, arterial streets such as Chestnut, Walnut, Locust, and Spruce became feeder channels to the seven-acre bucolic square.

Sealing the square's status as Philadelphia's patrician ground-zero were two landmark churches, magnets for the upper-class faithful. Not surprisingly, both were Episcopalian, the denomination that was upstaging Quakerism as the religion of the city's patrons. Each congregation harbored a twist to its denominational theme. St. Mark's, in the 16th Street block of Locust Street, opened first, in 1851. It was High Church, more Anglican, almost Roman Catholic, in its commitment to formalized ritual. The Church of the Holy Trinity, at the northeast corner of Rittenhouse Square, was Low Church, less strait-jacketed by liturgical rigor.

The two parishes shared, nevertheless, a style of worship that owed nothing to the stripped-down simplicity of Quakerism, the spiritual nourishment of the city's founders that led to Philadelphia's "Quaker City" nickname. The churches had more in common. Both were finely decorated houses of worship, consecrated on behalf of the rich select—at least those hoping to slip through the proverbial needle's eye.

The square itself had a practical side. For area children, it served as their neighborhood playground. Spinning tops after school was all the rage. If their play fell on a special day or on Sunday, these same children of privilege, when called home, dressed the part. Eton-collared suits were customary for dinner. Boys chafed, embarrassed by their "Little Lord Fauntleroy" outfits. Mothers swooned as they contemplated their prettified offspring.

Simply known as Southwest Square since the American Revolution, the park had adopted its august name, in honor of David Rittenhouse, a noted astronomer, only a quarter-century before, in 1825. In less than two decades, the rude park, originally part of William Penn's five-square city plan, would become the indisputable parade ground of the Great and the Good.

AWAY FROM BUSINESS, George McIntosh was attending to family affairs. He had arranged George Henry's secondary-school years to be at Friends Central School, then located north of Market Street near Independence Hall. Friends Central, as its name indicated, was affiliated with the Society of Friends, or Quakers, whose core values were simplicity, peace, and social justice. How much the senior George shared these principles is unknown, but they must have been close enough to those of his own Presbyterian faith. At any rate, the school was not public.

George Henry soaked up enough formal education that, upon graduation in 1864, he marched into the University of Pennsylvania, founded in 1740 by Benjamin Franklin and in later years stamped with Proper Philadelphia's imprimatur.

The senior McFadden's business fortunes were improving. In addition to George Henry's tuition fees at Penn, John's upcoming private education would also dent the family budget. Nevertheless, George McIntosh decided on a grander secondary school experience for John, and on September 11, 1865, he enrolled his middle son in the city's flagship patrician school, Episcopal Academy. That choice was probably a bow to Charlotte's ancestry as an Englishwoman and Anglican. According to the school's records, the family was still living on 8th Street.

All-male Episcopal, founded in 1785 as the Academy of the Protestant Episcopal Church, was then on Locust Street, at Juniper, a small street just a block east of South Broad. In the 1860s, the school had about two hundred students in its ornate neo-Gothic, Victorian building. Its appearance could encourage visions of dungeons in the basement. Instead, there was a large chapel there, fitted with an organ and more than thirty wooden pews, ample enough seating for required attendance. The pews, perhaps meaningfully, lacked cushioned kneelers. The boys' knobby, bare knees would do nicely.

Alumni did not remember chapel services with fondness. William W. Newton, a new boy in 1855, recalled that a proctor "watched as well as prayed, and the boys who misbehaved during prayers were left solitary and alone, squirming in their seats, to settle their accounts with the Principal, after the service was over...."[6]

Individual prayers were concluded with a solemn "Aw-men," intoned with a "profundity I have never since heard equally," Newton went on. Hymns never varied. "There were just two, *'Alas! what hourly dangers rise'* and *'Lord, forever at Thy side.'*"[7]

A self-confessed "bad boy," one Burnett Landreth, recalled other mischief, releasing "crows from Jersey, Bumble bees, snakes, frogs...."[8] He added, laconically, "[A]ll of education is not the three r's."[9]

Outside of chapel, the school's religious training was informed by "the doctrine of the Protestant Episcopal Church as contained in the Book of Common Prayer."[10] Maybe teachers had better luck at instruction in the classroom setting.

Tuition fees seemed within the means of the academy's largely affluent clientele, at $60 ($875 today) per annum, payable in advance half-yearly. "[B]esides which there are no charges whatsoever," an academy advertisement assures parents of prospective students, somewhat over eagerly. "Music, drawing, fuel, the French language and the Gymnasium being included in the one price named."[11]

The curriculum was classical: Latin studies in Horace, Cicero, and Virgil were served up. Depending on the grade level, courses included algebra, American history, geography, mathematics, and French. Lots of French. Taught by "none other but a native of France."[12]

Science study received a boost, in 1861, when a loan of $2,500 ($66,000 today) financed the completion of a new west-wing laboratory. The Reverend James Wiltbank Robins, headmaster during the years of John's matriculation, supported the expansion. His reasoning implied his pessimism regarding the school's student college-bound success rate. The expanded science program was important, Robins argued, because "a very large proportion of the [academy's] pupils do not intend to go to College but receive their Academic education here."[13]

Students who did graduate, or, at least, moved on, were quick to return to lives of privilege and culinary enjoyment. The school's alumni group, the Association of Old Members of The Protestant Episcopal Academy, liked to provide hardy banquets, including, on one occasion in 1864, one that would have made Henry VIII blush. The menu included oysters on the half shell, partridges, pheasant, grouse, corn, potatoes, French peas, spinach, boiled oysters, fried oysters, and croquettes, followed by desserts of Charlotte Russe, vanilla and strawberry ice cream, almonds, raisins, English walnuts, and prunes. Wine and coffee washed everything down.[14]

Episcopal Academy introduced John to fine art and medical science, at least one biographical note claimed. School records show that his last day was June 30, 1868. His graduation is presumed, but not certain, according to the school.

FOLLOWING GRADUATION FROM Penn, in 1868, George Henry joined the family firm as an apprentice. His grooming in the fundamentals quickly turned into a crash course, and his acquired lessons were put in practice far faster than anyone had expected. His father George McIntosh died in 1868, leaving a 55-year-old widow; a young son, Frank, 6; 17-year-old John, finishing at Episcopal; and a business with no executive head. Twenty-one-year-old George Henry, who had just reached his majority, stepped into the breach. Fortunately, with the Civil War having ended three years before, business was picking up. Soon enough, George Henry refashioned the brand to "Geo. H. McFadden, Cotton Merchant." Not for the first time, there was no mistaking who was in charge.

Just a few years later, when John reached manhood, circumstances changed, requiring a tweaking of the company name. George Henry rolled out "Geo. H. McFadden Co. & Bro., Cotton Merchants." The "Bro.," of course, was John. George Henry's authority as the elder brother was unchallenged.

John's official hire date was January 1, 1872, twenty-nine days after his twenty-first birthday. John had skipped Penn. No record explains the three-year hiatus following his departure from Episcopal. (The Reverend Robins had been right about Episcopal's spotty college enrollment rate.) Besides his lack of academic training, John was also a novice cotton man, known in industry parlance as a "squidge." George Henry could afford to tutor his younger brother. Business was expanding. In the same year that John joined the firm, George Henry expanded his reach in the Cotton Belt, aggressively acquiring agencies and correspondents to handle their cotton purchases.[15]

Expansion also meant new office space. There was no skimping.

Like the owners of other Philadelphia-based shipping and maritime firms, the McFaddens searched for permanent quarters in the cobblestone-paved byways near Front Street, hard by the Delaware River. The area teemed with grocers, taverns, shipwrights, ropewalks (rope makers), boarding houses, cordwainers, blacksmiths, and carpenters. And, at night, ladies of questionable virtue. The siting was happily completed: the brothers had found a four-story brick building at 121 Chestnut Street that would become the company's permanent head office through the next century. The building plot was an ample 1,640 square feet.

The real estate deal between the McFaddens and Mr. and Mrs. David M. Chambers was struck on April 27, 1878, according to records filed with the city's Recorder of Deeds. No financial figures were mentioned.[16]

The new headquarters were ensconced in Philadelphia's version of "Cotton Row," the 100 block of Chestnut Street. More than a dozen other cotton brokers and merchants lined both sides of the street. Next door, at 116 Chestnut Street, was another aspiring cotton trading firm, Joseph H. Coates & Co., whose fortunes, as time would tell, were not as sanguine as the McFaddens'. Randolph & Jenks, the McFaddens' friendly rivals, occupied another four-floor building at 115 Chestnut Street.[17]

BY THIS TIME, George Henry had married. With his prospects seemingly more secure, George had begun courting Emily Barclay Kennedy, also of a Protestant Irish background. Of no less importance, Emily was the daughter of John R. Kennedy, a director of the powerful Pennsylvania Railroad. George Henry was lean and dashing. He was an accomplished polo and racquetball player. With clean-shaven, marquee good looks, not to mention his financial security, his attraction to the opposite sex was a given. Emily and George married on April 20, 1871. The couple moved to a brownstone townhouse at 2044 Chestnut Street, at the corner of 21st Street. They became congregants of the fashionable Second Presbyterian Church, just south on 21st at Walnut Street. Though residing several streets from Rittenhouse Square, they were still within the square's gravitational pull. Like his father before him, George Henry, at 24, had made a sagacious match.

In the years immediately following George's marriage, John still lived at the family home at 613 North 8th Street. George's upwardly mobile move to Chestnut Street had put distance between himself and his brothers, John, as well as J. Franklin. It came in a form both physical and social, and both distinctions were not lost on John—whose aspirations and growing income were beginning to match those of his older brother.

Given that reality, John also set his sights on another upwardly mobile move: the courting of the well-situated Florence De Witt Bates. At age twenty-eight and nearing, for those times, spinsterhood, Florence was likely as eager as charmed by the attentions of the younger man.

Younger, yes. But John was hardly the swain of a young woman's romantic dreams. He was already working his way to his roly-poly physique. He took no exercise; he was no sportsman like brothers George Henry and J. Franklin. Florence was a buxom young woman, born in Cincinnati, Ohio on August 7, 1848, and a member of the Daughters of the American Revolution. Her eligibility was based on her lineage through a New Jersey Revolutionary combatant, Captain Jacob Piatt. Her D.A.R. "National Number" was 3776. Other than this, there is little to be gleaned from available records about Florence, though one striking fact—for a single lady in Philadelphia—was that her parents lived in Paris. Her father, Samuel Reeves Bates, was a Bostonian. Her mother, the former Hannah McCullough Grandin, was a Cincinnati native.

It was in Paris, then, on January 18, 1876, that John and Florence married at the fashionable American Church of the Holy Trinity, located at 23 avenue d'Alma (now avenue George V) about halfway between the avenue des Champs-Élysées and the Seine. The church was primarily a universal place of worship for Protestant Americans in Paris. Officially, it was an Episcopalian refuge.[18] In the church Wedding Register, Florence wrote "of Cinncinnati," suggesting that her official residence was still in Ohio. John signed "of Phila."

The newly minted John McFaddens honeymooned in Paris, if not also elsewhere in France. Whether they shared the luxe quarters of Florence's parents is not known. But they could not have asked for a better address, at 5 rue de Castiglione. In the prestigious 1st Arrondissement, the Bates apartments were in a lavish, colonnaded building between Place Vendôme and the Tuileries Garden. If John was then the budding art maven, he only needed to satisfy an itch to see the *Mona Lisa* and works by other Masters by going down the street to the Louvre Museum.

The McFaddens returned to Philadelphia just in time to find the city absorbed in its Centennial celebration. The newlyweds moved into a house at 506 North 18th Street, in a neighborhood of working professionals. Their new home was four blocks west of Broad Street, Philadelphia's north-south main thoroughfare. At the southwest corner of Spring Garden Street, a wide avenue known for its median greensward, John and Florence were edging closer to Rittenhouse Square.

On December 5, 1878, at No. 506, the McFaddens celebrated the birth of their first child, Philip Grandin McFadden. His middle name honored Florence's mother. His surname stamped him with the McFadden imprimatur as another male heir in the family cotton dynasty. Florence was 30 years old; John, 28.

From No. 506, John soon hopscotched to Rittenhouse status. Just a year later, he mounted a penultimate rung: a perch in the 1900 block of Chestnut Street. Just around the corner from the square itself, the sine qua non brass ring, McFadden arranged for a short stay at the Aldine Hotel, one of the area's few commercial premises.

The six-floor hotel, on the south side of Chestnut between 19th and 20th Streets, was also an anomaly. Its provenance was striking in a number of ways. The hotel had started out as the private residence of James Rush, a medical doctor and bibliophile, and was never really in keeping with Proper Philadelphia's unstated, and understated, building code. The building was massive; 800 guests could be accommodated in its ballroom. In other words, the place dripped with ostentation.

The Rush house's later life had a curious twist. Its conversion to a commercial property was engineered by the least likely of change agents, one of the most proper of Proper Philadelphians: Joshua Bollinger Lippincott, founder of the city's fabled publishing company. The hotel was both expensive and exclusive. It also bore an esoteric name that undoubtedly appealed to high-minded residents, "aldine" being a reference to the 15th-century Italian printer Aldus Manutius.

The McFaddens' stay at the Aldine was short-lived. By the next year, in 1880, they had moved up to 2107 Chestnut Street, fully entering into the Rittenhouse Square mainstream. If there had been any competition with brother George Henry over social standing (George Henry had a leg up on John by moving to 2044 Chestnut Street sometime before), their domiciles were no longer part of the equation.

———— ✕ ————

AFTER THE CIVIL WAR, King Cotton entered a new commercial realm. Arguably, never before in modern history has a single industry been so upended, losing such a significant portion of its workforce in such a short period. The capitalist engine of profit had to convert virtually overnight from the unpaid labor of millions of enslaved people to a wage-based economy populated by sharecroppers. There were winners and losers. At the top of the heap were the cotton men, who were beginning to trade the commodity for fabulous gain.

The McFadden brothers made quick work in adjusting to new conditions, including one that no one had anticipated—a futures market in cotton. Moving cotton as it had been done before, on a commission basis, quickly fell away.

The new futures market was made possible by a leap forward in the speed of communications. By the time George and John began revamping their firm, the benefits of the first transatlantic telegraph cable, vastly improved since it was first laid in 1866, allowed cotton men to expand their portfolios with a new, wildly profitable source of revenue. Previously, any hope of tracking and exploiting increases in the commodity's price points relied on dubious information contained in written exchanges between company representatives and transported by steamship. Even in the fastest ship crossings of a week to ten days, these exchanges were hopelessly dated. Even more unreliable, but still part of the information flow, was gossip by steamship captains.

The new opportunity in futures trading "straddled" markets in New York and Liverpool. Cotton was purchased—often sight unseen—from growers in the New York market, and sold at a later date, or in the future, upon delivery in Liverpool to mill owners, or their brokers. Success in such an endeavor, of course, as is the case in any commodity deal, required buying low and selling high. Fast access to market data was essential. The Atlantic cable cut direct communication to seventeen hours. At this early point, the amount of communication was restricted: even by Morse code, only eight words per minute could be conveyed. By the early twentieth century, the speed of communication had improved to 120 words per minute.

George Henry understood the importance of international networking, and he and a consortium of other Philadelphia textile brokers joined in sponsoring an International Cotton Exposition in the city. The firm contributed $500 ($11,500 today) to the event.[19] George also realized that breaking into the futures market—early and aggressively—required that Geo. H. McFadden & Bro., Cotton Merchants, deploy representatives, or "correspondents," to New York and to Liverpool. In that latter capacity, George decided, in 1881,[20] that his younger brother John would do nicely.

CHAPTER THREE

Liverpudlian

1881–1902

J OHN MCFADDEN ARRIVED IN a city booming with commerce, shipping, and mercantile expansion. By the late nineteenth century, Liverpool thrived as the United Kingdom's largest overseas transportation hub, bearing such corporate legends as Cunard and White Star. Its port bustled with tons of imports and exports. Its ocean liners were crammed with the poor immigrating to North America. Above decks, thanks to speeds afforded by modern, steam-driven vessels, a glitterati of wealth, privilege, and power linked an Old World of cultural grandeur to a New World craving a purpose-built pedigree. Immigrants sought something more—economic freedom.

Liverpool found its provident siting, at a narrow neck of the River Mersey, just a few miles from the Irish Sea. There was no mistaking the city (with a population of 611,000 in 1881) for anything but a seaport. The Mersey, though inland from Liverpool Bay, flowed with brine. Seagulls' cries carried even to the city's center, and flocks perched on Liverpool's metropolitan colossus, St. George's Hall. Two hundred and twenty miles from London and about four and a half hours away by rail, Liverpool had become, as some were proud to say, the Empire's "second city."[1]

Its trade was massive and, as often as not, rough and tumble. A history lustily described the scene: "The docks and wharves of the Liverpool waterfront stretched along the eastern shore of the Mersey River for more than five miles, and were still expanding.... Every day the docks were crowded with an amazing array of coastal traders, packets, steamships, clippers, tenders, and barges, collected from all over Britain, Europe and the United States.... Crimps [the kidnappers of shanghaied civilians] and longshoremen, sailors and beggars, rubbed shoulders with emigrants, ship owners, businessmen, and ships' captains, on crooked, narrow, muddy streets that were lined with shops, boardinghouses, chandlers, pubs, hotels, whorehouses, and factories."[2]

As in most cities, the poor coexisted with the rich, the coarse with the refined. The Liverpool McFadden encountered in 1881 was far removed from any reverie of a "green and pleasant land." As much as the city was defined by the wealth and power of its shipping, it also reflected the squalor and cruel class and economic inequities of Victorian Britain.

Wealth inoculated McFadden from this urban underbelly. In his stratum, McFadden discovered the city to be a feverish nexus of capitalism and culture, unmoored from the tribal pieties of his native Philadelphia. Mean streets aside, the 31-year-old Philadelphian, in the prime of early manhood, sensed the city's underlying dynamism.

McFadden's transformation from a callow "squidge" was powered by a Midas-like wealth creation process engineered by a small band of Liverpool-based international cotton traders. Over a period of just twenty-five years, about 560 registered traders—mostly from the United States—were able to exploit modern communications to bend the world's cotton market to their will, to their own immense gain. Apart from their profit motive, they also helped clothe people around the world with a versatile, lightweight, affordable fabric. For the first time, cotton became a popular, widespread alternative to year-round heavy woolens. At the turn of the twentieth century, about 4.5 million bales of the staple annually turned up on Liverpool docks.

Cotton reigned as king. Liverpool was its court. McFadden quickly became one of its princely courtiers. Rich when he arrived, he became within ten years, almost like no other among his peers, very rich. A colleague remembered the "sheer force" of McFadden's character. "[H]e enjoyed to act the part of the American millionaire," added the associate, who knew the transplanted Philadelphian from charitable work. "He was a daring speculator, being usually 'bullish' when others were 'bears'...."[3]

With fabulous newfound wealth, the cotton magnate was soon trading anew: this time, swapping the proceeds from raw cotton for a finer commodity, rare art.

ACCOMPANYING MCFADDEN IN the move to Liverpool were Florence and Philip, still just a toddler at three. Given the urgency for immediate accommodation, the newcomer had arranged for a suite at the Adelphi Hotel, an imposing Victorian pile down the street from St. George's Hall. The "Grand Duchess," as it was known, was an easy choice. It was the best in Liverpool, and some said it rivaled London's grandest hotels. (Like other Americans, McFadden learned that Liverpudlians called the place the Ah-DEL-fee.)

The McFaddens already had experience with hotel living, from their year-long stay at the Aldine in Philadelphia. But in keeping with Philadelphia's manner, hospitality at the Aldine had been more provincial than posh.

The cosmopolitan Adelphi hummed with wealthy transients, connecting from London to Liverpool by the Boat Train.

Many settled in, as was the custom, for a few days to take care of pre-departure arrangements in the offices of the Cunard and White Star lines near George's Pier Head. Whatever their station, from merchant prince to exalted prince, they shared anticipatory jitters. Their luggage, in particular, required much forethought, and tons of their belongings had to be sorted and loaded on the right vessel.

The Adelphi was McFadden's temporary housing solution, and an easy one to get used to. In its second reincarnation, the "new" hotel had opened only five years before, in 1876, and now featured three hundred rooms and a ration of one hotel worker for each two rooms. Rooms had modern, en-suite tiled bathrooms almost the size of some shipboard staterooms. *Modern* also meant huge porcelain fixtures with hot and cold running water and the latest plumbing, a marked difference from the shared privies of the more widespread English public accommodations. The dining room was acclaimed for its turtle soup. (It was always *fresh*. The turtles were raised in the hotel's basement.)

From Liverpool's *best* hotel, the McFaddens moved for permanent housing to Liverpool's *best* neighborhood, Prince's Park in southeast Liverpool. McFadden's neighbors were other cotton traders, ship-builders, and transportation moguls.

Worsley House at 4 Croxteth Road, the McFaddens' new home, was nestled on several acres behind brick walls, facing the park's main promenade. The house was only yards away from the elaborate, sunburst entrance gates to Prince's Park. At the Prince's Gate roundabout, a divided, tree-lined mall, The Boulevard, extended a half-mile to the city's center. (The green space could have reminded the McFaddens of the flowery median of Spring Garden Street in Philadelphia.) By horse-drawn phaeton, the trip downtown was under thirty minutes.

Their new house was more than large enough for the McFaddens, as well as Philip's new governess, Miss Jane Jones, and an ample household staff. Often enough, based on an income in

McFadden's range, a family could count on at least a half-dozen permanent live-in servants, including a butler, or a manservant out of livery; a coachman or groom; one or two housemaids; a cook; and a lady's maid.[4] In other words, it was a world away from the more casual domesticity they had known in Philadelphia, most recently at 2107 Chestnut Street.

Early years in Liverpool were busy with settling in and arranging staff at Worsley House. About a year later, Florence was pregnant with the couple's second child. The McFaddens returned to Philadelphia in time for the birth of Alice Bates on March 25, 1883. John's mother, Charlotte, helped during Florence's *accouchement* and post-partum confinement. Florence's parents, Hannah and Samuel Bates, remained at their home in Paris.

Within four years, Florence suffered the loss of both parents. The expatriated pair was visiting in Philadelphia when Samuel died on March 6, 1886, at the age of sixty-seven. (He was laid to rest at The Woodlands, an historic West Philadelphia cemetery.)

On December 4, 1890, her sixty-five-year-old mother died at home in Paris. The McFaddens traveled from England to attend Hannah's funeral Mass on the following Saturday, December 6, at the American Church. They skipped any activity on December 5, Philip's twelfth birthday. Mrs. Bates, too, was interred at The Woodlands.

It was a bittersweet two years. On a happy note, Florence gave birth to Jack earlier in 1890, on April 15—in Liverpool. The delivery was almost certainly at home. (The only lying-in hospital at the time, the Liverpool Maternity Hospital, served, in the main, charity cases, and even these were few. Most women were attended by midwives.)

Miss Jones had traded home-schooling duties with Philip for Alice, then seven. The year before, in 1889, eleven-year-old Philip left home for Loretto, a well-respected public school in Scotland near Edinburgh. Philip boarded at "The Nippers," as the junior school was nicknamed, for a year, then moving up to the senior school, where he studied until he was eighteen. He subsequently entered Oxford University, at Pembroke College, where his proclivity for polo was born. In club applications and similar paperwork, Philip listed 1899 as his Oxford graduation year. After Oxford, Liverpool became an afterthought for him—just in waving distance.

WHEN MCFADDEN ARRIVED from New York, he was already closely tethered to Frederic Christian Zerega, the immensely rich scion of a New York ship-owning family. He was also a cotton trader in his own right.

Zerega, born in 1836 in New York and fourteen years John McFadden's senior, was the most improbable of cotton men. The partnership between the McFaddens and Zerega was an "invention" of brother George, who knew him as a colleague on the New York Cotton Exchange. Frederic also sold coffee, owned ships, had a French wife, and operated his various ventures under the business moniker Frederic Zerega & Co. He was treasurer of Renwick C. Hurry & Co., a real estate company that had *Social Register* connections.

His colorful and international life (he had lived in England and France) was set on its course by his ship-owner father, the "stirring and adventurous" Augustus Zerega (born in Martinique, and educated in England and France), and his mother, Eliza M. Van Vytendaele, the daughter of a German baron. *The New York Times* gleefully accented Augustus's "venturesome and romantic career as Captain of sailing vessels, plying the Spanish Main when it was scoured by countless pirates and buccaneers."[5] Augustus wound up in New York, died at 85, and left a $2 million ($50.6 million today) fortune. In dollars, not doubloons. Frederic inherited.

The New Yorker's connection—at least, his family's connection—to Liverpool was not new. Augustus's shipping and trading interests went back as far as 1850.

John McFadden's relationship with Zerega formed a complicated, tangled web. Zerega was a business partner, mentor, and friend, and the association evolved to become an existential factor in transforming McFadden's family fortunes in Liverpool from merely successful to fabulously so.[6] Once in Liverpool, John established a new outpost for Geo. H. McFadden & Bro. Frederic created Frederic Zerega & Co., of which John was promptly named a "senior partner." Diving into business, the partners joined the Liverpool Cotton Association, each taking the pledge: "I, the undersigned, solemnly undertake to abide by and conform to all the Articles of the Association, Bye-laws, Brokerage and other rules of the Liverpool Cotton Association, Limited, now in force, or that may hereafter be enacted." Their individual entrance fee of £20 ($3,000 today) was deeply discounted since each had been "brought up in the Market." Annual subscriptions were £3.3.0 ($386 today).

Their subsidiaries, agencies, and "correspondents," subsidized by McFadden capital, fanned out from there and Philadelphia, establishing a worldwide trading network from Boston and Montreal to Copenhagen and Milan. In Bremen, Germany, they formed McFadden, Zerega & Co. In Lima, Peru, George H. McFadden South American Co. was the local subsidiary.

A few years after their arrival in Liverpool, the partners expanded their presence in France by joining the Reinharts, a well-known French cotton family, to create Société d'Importation et de Commission. The company's reach was as far-flung as Japan. In 1896, the McFaddens assigned the Japan Cotton Company as their agent in the region.

The firm's roots in the Mississippi Delta in the American South were not forgotten. A shingle for "Geo. H. McFadden & Brother" was still affixed to the company's office at 299 Main

Street in Memphis, the same place where George M. McFadden, the brothers' father, had founded the company in 1858. In its post-bellum return to Memphis, the firm was among the first to join the Memphis Stock Exchange, founded in 1873. No longer factors, the brothers maintained a Memphis buying office for years after the war. So did Weil Brothers Cotton Inc. and Anderson Clayton & Co., Southern firms which also wielded power in Liverpool.

The McFaddens conducted most, if not all, of their major transactions through the New York Stock Exchange. Nevertheless, following advances in telegraphic messaging, McFadden and Zerega were also able to track Memphis's quotations while stationed in Liverpool.

John, George, and Frederic, the newly minted international cotton moguls, had unknowingly wrought what may have been the first truly global conglomerate—well before the term was actually coined in the late twentieth century.

CHAPTER FOUR

Trader
1881–1902

W ITHIN TWENTY YEARS, AS the nineteenth century waned, Geo. H. McFadden & Bro. had become the world's largest cotton firm and likely its most profitable. *The New York Times* reported that more than $10 million ($280 million today) worth of cotton annually was under McFadden control, most of it purchased in America's South for trading overseas, principally in Liverpool.[1] The firm's yearly volume was unmatched. On this world stage, Weil Brothers Cotton Inc., of Montgomery, Alabama, was thought to be a runner-up.

In Liverpool, a similar story prevailed—with a twist. There the partnership between the McFadden brothers and Frederic Zerega wielded the most muscle. The Zerega & Co. alliance was dominant: from September 1893 to March 1894, for example, the London-based merchant bankers, Baring Brothers, reported that 215,311 cotton bales entered Liverpool under the Zerega aegis. The second-largest import firm, Paton, Maclaren & Co., another American company, trailed by more than 50 percent during this same period, at 85,166 bales.[2]

Buttressing their success was a nuanced communication model engineered by McFadden and Zerega, in Liverpool, and George McFadden, in New York and Philadelphia. New technology in undersea telegraph and overland telephone use was exploited. A rapid electronic response resulted in the commodity being brokered in virtually all international markets.

It was easy to understand McFadden's growing fealty to a life in England. Though certainly never a "scouser" (the term for a Liverpudlian whose residence went back several generations), McFadden easily acclimated to being an adopted Liverpudlian. He quickly dropped any local residential reference in the comprehensive *Gopsill's Philadelphia City Directory*. During his years in England, McFadden successively cited his domicile as "Europe," "England," and finally "Liverpool."

WHEN HE DISEMBARKED at the English seaport in 1881, John McFadden arrived as a cotton merchant: in essence, he and his firm would buy "spot" cotton (mostly from the American South, but from Egypt as well) at a fixed cost, later take possession of physical bales, and sell the raw commodity to the Liverpool-based buyers of Lancashire mills. The process was riddled with inefficiencies, irksome costs associated with middlemen, and the volatile fluctuations of shipping and storage fees. Furthermore, profit margins were not assured.

Cotton storage also meant investment in real estate, or fees when space was rented. Bales were housed in vast warehouses along the River Mersey shoreline. McFadden-Zerega owned a facility in Sparling Street, south of central Liverpool, and another one, in Toronto Street, in Wallasey, across the river. Another wild card was the all-too-frequent risk of fire. At 8:25 p.m. on October 22, 1891, a spark ignited the highly combustible cotton in the Toronto Street warehouse. The Fire Brigade fought the blaze for almost three hours. By then, 1,176 bales had been consumed. (Buildings and their contents were insured.)[3]

"Trading" cotton was another alternative. Liverpool-based cotton men would act as third-party intermediaries, representing cotton growers (and their merchants) in the cauldron of Liverpool spot marketing. Shipping and storage charges would be eliminated, as owners would assume these. Traders would profit by charging commissions, but these too swung unpredictably high and low depending on bullish or bearish market forces.

As new communications tools were introduced, the Liverpool cotton market adopted yet another twist, with the introduction of a futures market. The Liverpool Cotton Association called it a "vogue." The group was slow in recognizing the innovation. Failing to keep up, its advertising slogan remained: "Liverpool—the Greatest Spot Cotton Market in the World." Be that as it may, trading in futures contracts was, well, the future, especially for well-informed, well-capitalized risk-takers. Profits soared.

Backed by a free flow of corporate funds, the McFaddens' cotton firm was among the first to expand this "futuristic" model in the Liverpool Cotton Exchange. Research and intelligence were company bywords, contributing to an insider grasp of market fluctuations. The McFaddens were soon recognized as "sound judges of economic conditions." Many industry stalwarts were impressed by the firm's statistical library in Philadelphia, "second only to that of the U.S. Department of Commerce...."[4]

Futures contracts were free of nettlesome complications. Besides the elimination of shipping and storage costs, brokers never actually had to see a cotton bale. (Attendant costs were picked up by sellers and buyers.) Deals were conducted on paper; sales and purchases confirmed by telegraph. The idea was to buy cotton from growers at a guaranteed "future" price at destination, regardless what the actual market value was on the day of arrival and transfer to a buyer. If higher, the brokers could sell at that inflated price and make out handsomely. If lower, disaster could strike—especially if the future price was guaranteed on margin, that is, on borrowed money.

The McFaddens were flush with cash; margin transactions could be covered in-house. It was unlikely that the McFaddens ever needed financing from the most prominent local sources of capital, the Liverpool Union Bank or the North & South Wales Bank, or from the venerable London merchant bank Baring Brothers, when others were beating down their doors.

If futures trading was not in itself an avenue to riches, the path was further paved by "hedging," a process by which brokers "bet" against themselves in a combined transaction—say, in which they purchased physical cotton at one price and a futures contract on that same purchase at another price.

The cotton historian Nigel Hall explained, "Should prices change, the gain in one transaction would be balanced or canceled out by a loss in another, thus obviating the risk inherent in a fluctuating market."[5] Hall elaborated: "By trading actual cotton in tandem with [their] Liverpool futures, cotton importers and holders of cotton stocks in Liverpool could guard, or 'hedge,' themselves against the price of cotton falling, [thus] devaluing the physical cotton they owned. For speculators, the fact that one was [also]...trading paper [future] contracts, not [only] the bulky, physical cotton, [meant] they were in the perfect medium for speculating on both a rising ('bull') market, or a falling ('bear') market."[6]

Due to its prominence as Liverpool's premier firm, Zerega & Co.'s influence was so significant that the merchant bankers Kleinwort, Sons & Co., Ltd. noted in 1904: "Their [Zerega & Co.] transactions are so large that they can at times make the futures market improve or decline according [to] how they are acting."[7]

For brokers like McFadden and Zerega, trading in these future contract schemes became more profitable than con-

ventional deals in spot cotton. "An American," claimed the
Porcupine, a satirical publication based in Liverpool, "fresh over
from the other side, with scarce enough credit at home to buy
a 'a suit of clothes' can promenade our [Exchange] Flags within
four-and-twenty hours after his arrival the owner of some thousand bales of cotton."[8]

Still, risks were large. Some speculators were walking a tight-
rope, their exposure more precarious because cotton traders, as
was the norm, were mostly without the protection of "limited"
incorporation. This was the case with Weil Brothers Cotton, for
example. If bankruptcy struck, it was of the most devastating
kind, wiping out personal assets.

In the year that McFadden and Zerega arrived, Morris Ranger,
a fellow American and one of the world's most daring speculators, was on the way out—as a bankrupt. His debts in Liverpool
alone finally reached £400,000 ($68.1 million today). The vast-
ness of his transactions contributed to a rogue atmosphere in
some trading circles. Nigel Hall, in a treatise on the cotton market during this period, noted, "[H]e spent about £100,000 [$17
million today] per annum in brokerages and commissions, and
in the year of his failure turned over nearly £1 million [$170
million today]."[9] Ranger was also known, according to the 1906
edition of the *Jewish Encyclopedia*, for his "great benevolence"
and support of Liverpool University.[10]

Margin account holders were particularly vulnerable to
wild swings in values, some manipulated by speculators' she-
nanigans. Bulls sought to push prices upward. Bears sought the
opposite. Depending on their stake, nefarious members of either
group were not above misrepresenting market conditions to suit
their financial interests. Bears attempted to suppress prices by
forecasting high crop yields. Bulls foretold low yields, just short
of blight conditions. Just as McFadden and Zerega were find-
ing their stride in Liverpool, Daniel J. Sully, the poster child for
market corruption, was losing millions in New York, the prey of

other speculators who outfoxed him. The following figures underscore how the futures traders were playing with fire:

In September 1902, a cotton bale sold at its highest in New York for $8.75 ($246), with a forecast "future" price in May of $8.55 ($240), a dip of 20 cents ($6). By year's end, the December price had dropped to $7.95 ($223), a fall of 80 cents ($22) from September, and to $8.40 ($236) in May, a 15-cent ($4) decline.[11] Wits, clarity, and guts were called for when these per-bale costs were transformed into trades of stratospheric millions.

Even for traditional spot traders, drastic fluctuations had their own dangers. In Philadelphia, the venerable firm of Joseph H. Coates & Co. slowly slid into bankruptcy in 1892. The Coates concern, at 116 Chestnut Street, had been a neighbor of Geo. H. McFadden & Bro. since both companies started out, and it had grown, according to *The New York Times*, to be "one of the oldest and largest houses in the business."[12] Yet their promissory notes, for as little as $5,000 ($132,000 today), could not be met. "Among the trade in general," *The Times* reported, "the greatest surprise was manifested at the firm's embarrassment, and the prevailing opinion was the heavy decline in the prices of cotton was responsible for the misfortune."[13]

Profits could skyrocket—especially if a company could rely on a soothsayer such as Zerega to forecast market forces. McFadden himself believed that the pace from crop to trading was governed by a kind of synchrony, an almost mystic force. He once said that his decisions were informed by what he *heard* almost audibly from the market. "You know, the markets can speak as well as men," he told *The Times*.[14]

Price volatility produced a jocular refrain, ascribed to a jaded broker cabling advice to colleagues: "Some think it will go up. Some think it will go down. I do, too....Act at once!"

A form of ersatz cryptology entered the picture. Competitive futures trading (Weil Brothers Cotton Inc. was always looking over the McFadden shoulder) relied on understanding market trends and acquiring insider information, especially from New York. To establish what their offers would be, the McFadden and Zerega operation, in Liverpool, New York, and Philadelphia, set about protecting proprietary details with a seemingly unique code. What resulted was a kind of gobbledy-gook that kept private deals private. A typical telegram arriving in Liverpool from Philadelphia would start out: "whinfad cables rigorous accumulate more diatonic stroking difficult to say what tantalidae yet skimmings depend action manipulators new york cotton exchange..."[15]

While the messages had the tantalizing appearance of the kind of clandestine communication normally associated with espionage agencies, the abbreviations and coding were really a cost-saving measure. Savings could be significant. Firms usually sent and received dozens of daily telegrams, and all were priced by the word. In addition, while each firm simply adopted its own terminology, safeguarding the privacy of their telegrams as much as they could, the codes themselves were available publicly. Code translations were often stated in advertising and in "code books" that were commercially printed for public consumption.[16]

Liverpool trading was really a combination of secrecy, privacy—and, perhaps, just bureaucratic confusion. The lack of transparency was often simply attributed to sloppy documentation and the capriciousness of the market.

Among those most confounded, for whatever the reason, was the correspondent for the Bank of England's Liverpool branch, who worked from a massive Neo-Grec structure up the street from the Flags at the corner of Castle and Cook Streets. Each day, he tried to unravel the market's machinations in a letter to the bank's head office in London.

Brother George, maybe to John's annoyance, was hands-on. At least once a year, usually in the summer months, his elder brother traveled to Europe, invariably making a stop in

Liverpool. One of the first crossings, in 1886, was described by
George's daughter Ella Louise many years later. At the time, Ellie,
as she was known, was nine. Their traveling party included her
mother, Emily; a nurse, who they called "Old Annie"; Ellie's
brother George; and the McFaddens' brother, J. Franklin. (From
time to time, Frank would stay on.) "As usual, we sailed the Cunard Line for Liverpool because Frank and Father wanted to do
business there with Uncle John and Frederic Zerega," Ellie recollected in an unpublished memoir.

Ellie remembered another sojourn at the English port in
1888, and one more in 1890. During yet another, in 1891, Ellie
said, "We went, of course, as usual to Liverpool. I think this time
on the *Etruria*, a very modern ship. It had a built-in cover over
the decks and canvas around the decks and electric lights so
you couldn't see the sea. We arrived in Liverpool, and from Liverpool we didn't take any special trip that year...."

John and Florence surely used the family's extended stay
in Liverpool to entertain at Worsley House—although in mod-
eration, no doubt. Emily was known for a weak disposition,
once so severe that she was hospitalized in "critical condition"
after "overtaxing her strength" from robust partying. *The New
York Times* reported, in a story sporting the deadpan headline,
"PHILADELPHIA'S LIVELY PACE," that she fell ill to "the strain
of social activities" during "the merry whirl of the society season."[17] Emily was not the only society doyenne stricken. Four
other "prominent members of Philadelphia's social set" were
also hospitalized or treated at home for conditions "brought on
by social strain." The family did get to meet one-year-old Jack
for the first time.

Ellie was an enthusiastic traveler, and an equally enthusiastic McFadden. She opined, "It was due to Father's trips abroad
and my Uncle John and Mr. Frederic Zerega being willing to live
in Liverpool that a great cotton business was built up, the greatest one in the world."

George saw to it that the Philadelphia operations contributed to success, as well. With an eye to cutting out the middleman— as had been the case in futures trading—George decided that eliminating ships owned by others to transport the commodity from American ports would be another streamlining, cost-cutting bonanza.

This would, of course, require them to own their own ships. In 1901, with an infusion of $1 million ($28 million today), George created the "McFadden Line," a freight steamship company chartered in New Jersey and based in the state's capital, Trenton. The Ocean Steamship Company, when fully operational, would primarily collect cotton cargoes in New Orleans and in other Gulf of Mexico ports, for transport to Liverpool and additional foreign destinations. George would handle the details in Philadelphia. Some of those details, it would seem, would involve adding zeroes to profit lines in ledgers.

George had another reason for the creation of the steamship company. While initially it would provide cheaper delivery of McFadden goods, the company would also in time increase business and profits by funneling "deflected" cargo from other shippers through Philadelphia onto the McFadden-owned vessels. The venture got off to a good start, *The New York Times* reported, with the "promised support" of "several commercial organizations" in Philadelphia.[18]

John also struck out on his own. His new venture was far afield from cotton, but connected to shipping. In July 1890, McFadden and a coterie of London-based bankers and businessmen joined forces—with a shared investment of £200,000 ($33 million today)—to launch an innovative information-sharing business, the District Messenger and News Company, Ltd. Seven directors, including McFadden, shared the risk.

The startup was rolled out later in the year, working from street-level offices at 2 Cockspur Street, near Trafalgar Square in London. In an age before social media, much less the internet, the company's forward-looking business plan detailed the creation—maybe the first of its kind—of a one-stop-shop clearinghouse for tourist-related travel information. This would be a kind of updated, expanded version of Thomas Cook, an English travel agency founded about fifty years before. In fact, the two companies might have competed head-to-head. Thomas Cook's Fleet Street office was not far away.

District Messenger, according to details in the *Truth*, a business publication, delivered numerous services, from shipping news, schedules, and ticketing to telephone, telegraph, and post. A reading room (with "American, Continental and English Newspapers"), international cash exchanges, and luggage storage, would be included. Access to the company's myriad offerings would be by membership: $1 ($26) for two weeks, $2 ($52) for two months, and $10 ($260) for a year.

For his part, Frederic Zerega never abandoned his own family's interests in New York. There he developed a sub-rosa relationship, involving spot cotton, with well-connected rogue dealer Daniel J. Sully. (He was the father-in-law to actor Douglas Fairbanks, Sr., and grandfather to Douglas Fairbanks, Jr.) Zerega even drew the McFaddens into a putative subterfuge, carrying out consignment sales on Sully's behalf. The arrangement was contrived and suspicious. At worst, it might have involved money laundering.

The scheme required that Zerega sell Sully's consignments in Liverpool. After accounting for his commission, he would transfer the remaining cash to Geo. H. McFadden & Bro.'s Philadelphia account. Acting then as Zerega's factors, the McFaddens paid Sully in New York.[19] In such deals, the McFadden name was powerful and respected and carried weight.

Despite their indirect dealings with Sully, the McFaddens managed to keep a public distance. But in 1904, the brothers were peripherally ensnared. The action played out at the New York Cotton Exchange. In late March, Daniel J. Sully &

Company went bankrupt, with spectacular repercussions for the cotton industry as a whole. Sully had almost cornered the commodity market in cotton, meaning his holdings and purchasing power had an inordinate control over trading opportunities. Finally, he overextended himself, and his house of cards came crashing down. McFadden was coincidentally visiting New York at the time, and he and J. Temple Gwathmey, a former exchange president, were tasked by the exchange board to deliver some bad news to Sully—that his "assignee" personally designated to untangle his financial affairs would not be acceptable to his creditors.[20]

In Philadelphia, George was also getting out from underneath Sully-related rumors:

> George H. McFadden, the leading cotton broker of this city, did not visit Sully yesterday and aid the New York speculator in trying to straighten out his affairs. Detailed rumors of such a visit were in circulation all day, but were flatly denied by J. Frank McFadden, who said that the local firm has no connection with Sully from his rise to his downfall, and are not concerned whether he resumes or not.[21]

Zerega equally evaded any bad consequences from Sully's financial collapse. He simply shifted his operational base from New York to Liverpool. Like George McFadden, Zerega also moved to attain independence from the costs of shipping by third parties. For bookkeeping purposes, his shipping entity, the Oriel Steamship Co. Ltd., and its principal vessel, the *Oriel*, were set apart from his McFadden interests. He also owned the steamers *Boliviana* and *Cebriana*. Was there a conflict of interest? If so, it was probably mitigated by John's position as a Zerega & Co. senior partner. By the early years of the new century, Frederic Zerega & Co. was importing annual cotton cargoes

to Liverpool—independent of Geo. H. McFadden & Bro.—of
£10,500 ($1.2 million today).[22]

THE LIVERPOOL COTTON Exchange had not yet shed its idiosyn-
crasy as an outdoor bidding market. From informal beginnings
on Castle Street, near Town Hall, trade moved in the early
nineteenth century to a square behind Town Hall, between
Dale and Chapel Streets. It was thought the brokers would go
indoors when the first exchange building opened in 1808. Crea-
tures of habit, they were disinclined to make a change. Instead,
flagstones were laid down in the square, and the brokers, who
found face-to-face personal contact invaluable, continued business "on the flags." Except for office needs, a reading room, and
commonsense shelter in inclement weather, the building, Exchange Flags, was largely redundant.

Technically, McFadden joined the horde "on the flags,"
however an unlikely setting that might be for the Proper Philadelphian. More to his liking was the Albany, a four-story office
block in nearby Old Hall Street in the city's Exchange Ward.
He and Zerega shared quarters at No. 56 South Corridor. Their
second-floor office overlooked an open-air atrium. McFadden
was a Cotton Association "member," never a "ring trader." This
meant his transactions were conducted through his representative stationed at the ring at Exchange Flags, or—as would be the
case in futures deals—by pre-negotiated settlements. The Albany suited him just fine.

The Liverpool Cotton Brokers' Association, founded in 1841,
finally managed to get the unruly, single-minded brokers under
cover in 1896[23] in a gaudy French Renaissance-styled structure
that fronted three sides of the square. Besides the obvious—protection from the elements—the brokers were encouraged to
recede indoors as the new exchange building became increas-

ingly wired with vital communication advances. By then, the Brokers' Association had reconstituted itself as the Liverpool Cotton Association, Limited.

Most traders preferred the bustle and hustle of their new quarters. One visitor around this time remembered:

> As you converse with [a trader] you become aware that his office is the medium of strange currents of business flowing in and out, and extending from "the flags" [nearby] to transatlantic distances. Now it is the telephone that is at work, then messengers pop in and out with verbal quotations relating to the state of the market; next comes a cablegram from New York which you are told left that city only a few minutes before. The air seems electrical, and as an illustration of the rapidity with which the transactions are sometimes effected, you are informed of one in which a message, involving a purchase, was sent from the office to New York, an answer received, and the business satisfactorily completed in fifteen minutes.[24]

The brokers had something else to protect by seeking shelter—their dapper appearances. Of all the sartorial peacocks of Victorian England, the cotton brokers were among the most finely feathered—attired in well-ironed silk top hats, cutaway jackets, and colorful vests and cravats. Many carried walking sticks. Some inspected bids squinting behind monocles. Though in a cutthroat business, they at least looked like gentlemen. A "cartoon" of McFadden, drawn by J. Wallace Coop, an illustrator for *The Liverpool Courier,* depicted the Philadelphian in a grand manner, an arm cocked on his left hip, an unlighted, blunt-shaped cigar projected forward in his right hand. His eyes gleam. His mouth attempts a smirk. His top hat is tilted dashingly to the right. In all, a pose of self-satisfied composure emerged.[25]

McFadden's trading activity was confined to the new exchange building for less than half of the roughly twenty years
that he resided in Liverpool. Though he maintained his Albany quarters, he also had assigned space in the Brown's
Buildings. His office was designated "H, Exchange Building";
cable address, "Macfadden."[26]

At day's end, the stylish brokers spilled into the byways of
Exchange Ward, comprising the Town Hall area. The streets
were clogged with horse-drawn vehicles, omnibuses, motorcars,
and pedestrians, all seeming to go their way at cross purposes.
There was no comparison to anything like it in Philadelphia.
McFadden was on top of his world.

THE McFADDEN TEAM was periodically reinforced, with Frank
McFadden arriving from Philadelphia. John's son Philip would
drop in from time to time, visiting from New York. Their material contribution seemed desultory. Corporate notices in *The
London Gazette*, a trade publication, always carried John's and
George's names, in signature form. From time to time, Philip
also got billing. Also usually listed was William E. Whineray,
who joined forces with Zerega and McFadden as a formally designated Zerega partner. Within a few years, a local Liverpool
newspaper was referring to the Zerega firm, one of the newest
enterprises doing business "on the flags," as the "influential
house of Messrs. Frederic Zerega and Company."

Together, the McFadden-Zerega enterprise expanded in size,
and staffing needs increased accordingly. The firm was able to
field a twenty-two-member cricket team, divided between office and sales workers. (A regulation team numbers eleven.)[27]

Zerega was generous: at Christmastime, 1894, he donated
£2.2.0 ($336 today) to the Liverpool Christmas Hot Pot Fund.
Still later, he gave £25 ($4,000) to the Head Constable's Fund,

£152.10.0 ($24,000) to the Indian Famine Fund, £100 ($16,000)
to the Lord Mayor's Fund, and £50 ($8,000) to the Ottawa Relief
Fund. His charitable spirit—and wealth—even allowed him to
match donations from such high-profile players as Cunard and
White Star.[28]

McFadden was also in a position to be generous. Everyone
called him "John." Prominence and popularity were not cheap.
In 1882, a year after McFadden arrived in Liverpool, association membership was limited to firms capitalized by at least
£60,000 ($9.5 million today) with 600 share distribution at £100
($15,900) each. Thirty-nine shares had to be surrendered to the
association; the remainder, 561 shares for a total of £56,100 ($8.9
million), was retained by the member firm. McFadden went on
to become a director of the Liverpool Cotton Association, and
one of its "most prominent and popular members." By the time
that McFadden left Liverpool in 1902, each share of his company
approached £1,000 ($158,600), for a total of £561,000 ($89 million).[29] The McFadden brothers made another killing. Zerega
shared the joy.

CHAPTER FIVE

Connoisseur

1892–1902

JOHN McFADDEN BECAME AN art connoisseur first; collecting came later. Like many wealthy Americans in Europe, he turned to art as a way to refine and define his tastes—and eventually, spend his money, otherwise destined to gather mold in standard investments. By happenstance, McFadden found Liverpool to be at a point of convergence between Europe's wealth and culture. Cotton, corn, and shipping accounted for the first. Two arts institutions, almost unique outside of London for their stature and size, underscored the second. Both showcased British art. McFadden quickly became an admirer.

The Walker Gallery, founded in 1877, was still in its infancy when McFadden arrived from Philadelphia as an art novice. But a previous earlier version of the museum had already been well stocked with British art, acquired when the Liverpool Academy and the Liverpool Society for the Fine Arts were forced to sell their individual collections. The Royal Institution at 24 Colquitt Street, established in 1814 as a learned society, wound up by the late nineteenth century primarily as an art museum. McFadden haunted both places, making them sites for his continuing education. In addition, the Art Gallery of Manchester (founded 1823), located in the heart of Lancashire mill district, was only about an hour away by the Liverpool & Manchester Railway.

McFadden was well aware of the recent début of the Pennsylvania Museum and School of Applied Art back home, although the public controversy over its collections had not yet bubbled up. It would be many years before he became involved in the development of the city's arts infrastructure. His attentions—both business and socially—were focused on Liverpool. In time, he became an arts maven.

Liverpool's wealth conspired with the city's cultural and commercial demographics to create a social destination. Thousands of rich transatlantic voyagers regularly descended on the city for days on end. Like many of those travelers with time on their hands, McFadden also found his way to the showrooms of Thos. Agnew & Sons, a branch of a popular and well-respected Manchester-based art firm. The travelers were a captive audience, and Agnew's tempted them with the comfortable artwork of the Old Masters (with the firm's gold standard imprimatur) as well as "modern" British pieces by Gainsborough, Romney, and Reynolds, for those with more singular tastes. Though he did not enjoy mass appeal at the time, even a masterwork by the Liverpool-born horse painter George Stubbs might appear in the gallery.

Agnew's also knew a thing or two about marketing. After opening their Liverpool branch in a showroom at 2 Duke Street, on the edge of the city's downtown, the firm moved to 1 Castle Street, at its intersection with Dale Street in the most fashionable environs in the city center. That northeastern corner site was, not so coincidentally, just across from where cotton traders gathered in Exchange Flags behind the Liverpool Town Hall. The streets were packed with businessmen and merchants. Affluent travelers, on an outing from the gilded confines of the

Adelphi Hotel, joined the crush. Many had little more to do than shop while awaiting embarkation to New York.

———✕———

AS HIS INTEREST in the realm of fine art and the finer things grew, McFadden's visits to London increased. The trip was four hours by train, from Lime Street Station, across from St. George's Hall, to St. Pancras Station, London. Aided by this manageable commute, McFadden edged his way into London's cultural life. Only after about ten years from his arrival in Liverpool in 1881 did his artistic sensibility fully evolve—along with his financial state, thanks to his firm's success on the flags.

McFadden's London was circumscribed. Much as he had lived in a Philadelphia within the precincts of Rittenhouse Square, McFadden confined himself mainly to a posh patch in central London, known as St. James's. It resembled his familiar Philadelphia domain, at least in size. He took an interest in the Victoria and Albert Museum and the National Gallery; these institutions would become reference points when in later years he returned to Philadelphia as a civic and cultural pillar. His growing interest in exploration drew him as a visitor to the Royal Geographical Society.

Like Rittenhouse Square, St. James's was informally defined by a confining rectangle of four streets. Piccadilly, once home to preening Regency boulevardiers, lay roughly to the north; Regent Street, to the east; Pall Mall, to the south; and St. James's Street, to the west. Its nucleus was St. James's Square, a Georgian version of Rittenhouse Square.

McFadden fell in quickly. For an aspirational American, happily expatriated in the country of his dreams, St. James's was cosmopolitan, sophisticated, and steeped in imperial history. (St. James's Palace dead-ended St. James's Street.) As important, it boasted a shopping preserve of goods and services drawn from the Empire's wealth, for the Empire's wealthy—the very wealthy.

Despite the city's otherwise immense size, St. James's was McFadden's London. Leave others to think of the Victorian metropolis as the center of Empire, even, arguably, the commercial and financial capital of the English-speaking world. McFadden had an eye for other things, and his appetite for art, as noted, had been already whetted in Liverpool.

From an occasional habitué from Liverpool, McFadden quickly became a part-time Londoner. He adopted local coloration. He patronized elegant shops. He dressed with the top-hatted formality befitting the neighborhood. He frequented bootmakers and hat makers in St. James's Street, and booksellers in Piccadilly. He joined, as was de rigueur, a men's club: the Junior Carlton, located across the street from the mammoth-sized Royal Automobile Club that dominated Pall Mall.

McFadden maintained his Liverpool preserve in Prince's Park. But he also purchased a London pied-à-terre, in the form of a fifty-share interest in the newly opened Carlton Hotel,[1] in nearby Haymarket. Built in 1899, the luxury hotel's association with hotel nobility surely did not escape the new shareholder's attention (the place was managed by César Ritz, and Auguste Escoffier was its chef). Nor did its favored status with the Prince of Wales, later King Edward VII, drawn to the hotel's Louis XVI interiors "especially designed to appeal to the [prince] who dined publicly in the restaurant."[2] On a more ambitious level, McFadden also bought a "country house" in Kent, southeast of the city.[3]

Thus ensconced in town, McFadden was only a stone's throw from sought-after art galleries in Old Bond Street, off Piccadilly. The art dealers, jewelers, and tailors in nearby Mayfair streets (Savile Row among them), and in arcades (early-day shopping malls), tucked behind Piccadilly, formed a matrix of high-end shopping like none other in the world. For the well-heeled, a bespoke lounge suit could be had for the equivalent of about

$1,400; a silk top hat from Lock's, the hatters in St. James's Street, for $350; and a well-furled umbrella for $175. Like McFadden, American "royalty" flocked. So did the real thing.

And McFadden was also no stranger to the London galleries of Thos. Agnew & Sons. In London, in the firmament of the art world and its feverish high-end trading, financial stakes were high. Agnew's had laid claim to being one of Britain's premier art dealers and a top marquee brand, flourishing with an international client roster including some of the world's richest art collectors. As early as 1882, a decade before McFadden caught the bug, Philadelphia art mavens John G. Johnson; P.A.B. Widener, his son, Joseph E. Widener; William L. Elkins; and Edward T. Stotesbury were also among Agnew's "new American clients," according to Geoffrey Agnew.[4] "Towering over all our clients," Agnew noted, was J. P. Morgan.[5]

Closer to home, the firm catered to the London branch of the Rothschild family. Memorably, it was also the gallery of first choice of Edward Cecil Guinness, First Earl of Iveagh, the founder of the Kenwood House art collection.

Agnew's was not alone in catering to America's fearsome art collectors. Around the corner was the Grosvenor Gallery, where Pre-Raphaelite and other contemporary, non-mainstream artists countered the conservative dictates of the Royal Academy of Art. Most significant was Colnaghi & Co., trolled by the noted art historian and connoisseur Bernard Berenson on behalf of his patron, Isabella Stewart Gardner, the Boston socialite.

Agnew's ascendancy, from its earlier incarnation in 1835 in Manchester, was swift, expedited by the move of its head offices to London in 1860. Besides its northern branch, at 1 Castle Street in Liverpool's commercial district, the gallery also maintained a robust presence, during McFadden's years abroad, in Paris and Berlin.

Agnew's harbored an almost paranoid aversion to providing monetary figures for what its firm paid for pictures. (Entries in original Stock Books, written in hand by a dutiful scrivener, were coded.)[6] Such reticence did not apply to its sales. In an unusually candid privately published corporate history, *Agnew's, 1817–1967*,[7] author Geoffrey Agnew reported typical prices in the early 1900s (the years McFadden was buying) that have a remarkable 21st-century ring. Examples varied from £7,500 ($1,259,000 today) in 1901 for an Alma-Tadema; £10,500 ($1,743,000) in 1906 for a Millais; £57,500 ($9,450,000) in 1911 for two Turners; £63,000 ($10,133,000), in the same year, for a Rembrandt; £59,000 ($9,295,000) in 1913 for another Rembrandt; to £50,000 ($7,873,000) in 1917 for a Hals. In McFadden's particular interest area, that of late eighteenth-century British pictures, a Reynolds could (and did) fetch, in 1913, up to £55,000 ($8,665,000).

At the time, Agnew's principal showroom was located in a four-floor former townhouse at 39 Old Bond Street, London.[8] Inside could be found paintings by an army of greats such as Rembrandt, Caravaggio, Rubens, and Titian—artists whose works were just beginning to reach American shores. The neophyte McFadden was smitten. This was helped along by a cordial, even warm, relationship McFadden developed—he would later refer to it as a "friendship"—with W. Lockett Agnew, a son of the founder. Born in 1858 and thus eight years younger than McFadden, Lockett was depicted at age forty in an 1898 painting by Sir Luke Fildes, as lean, appropriately mustachioed, and finely dressed. His charisma won over the American. Lockett Agnew continued to hold McFadden's affection until his death in 1918.

Lockett was responsible for the most iconic portrait of McFadden, by society artist Philip A. de László. Agnew's represented de László, and Lockett arranged the commission. McFadden appears in all his glory, equal parts capitalist, bon vivant, and art connoisseur. (His countenance, however, lacks the puckish glint captured by J. Wallace Coop's portrait in *The Liverpool Courier*, later republished in a book about the Liverpool Exchange, *Bulls and Bears*.)

The Philadelphian's first acquisition, cutting his eye-teeth, as it were, occurred on 15 September 1892 at 1 Castle Street in Liverpool when he picked up an oil, *An Alexandrian School*, by a Victorian contemporary, J.C. Horsley. It was a safe buy. He combined the purchase that same September day with a "drawing" by R. Anderson.[9]

That introduction begat an earnest commitment. With gusto. On the following day, no less, McFadden returned to shop some more. Overnight, he had become emboldened enough to set out to buy five more works on paper, including a watercolor by J.M.W. Turner, *London from the South*. On September 22, three more drawings joined McFadden's fledgling collection, including what was, in hindsight, a maverick choice for what would become a collection of solely British art: a print of the wildly popular *The Horse Fair* by the French artist Rosa Bonheur. (Had McFadden seen an original oil, the smaller of two versions of this work, in the National Gallery?)

In London, McFadden wasted no time. On January 30, 1893, while down from Liverpool, McFadden met Lockett in the Red Gallery, as the principal upper-floor sales room was dubbed. The room's walls and ceiling were wood-paneled, and light flashed through windows of leaded panes. The room had a faux Restoration-era feel.

With McFadden duly impressed, Lockett embarked on a charm offensive, coaxing the Philadelphian into what would become a formidably committed venture in high-stakes art acquisition. As was the case with the Horsley piece he picked up in Liverpool (in effect a kind of "starter kit"), Lockett presented McFadden with another comforting choice. *Girl Crossing Rustic Bridge* by David Cox, a mid-nineteenth-century landscape painter, was meant to ease McFadden with a work of soothing familiarity, down a path to an acquisitive fervor soon to be unleashed in full measure.

That time came less than six months later, when the Philadelphian laid the bedrock of the nascent McFadden Collection.

It has never been established how long McFadden had been yearning for Sir Thomas Gainsborough's *Lady Rodney*, a life-sized, three-quarter-length portrait of Henrietta, the wife of Sir George Brydges Rodney (Lord Rodney). As it was later learned, it depicted a different Lady: *Lady Anne*, the wife of Rodney's eldest son, another George and, after his father's death, another Lord Rodney. McFadden never knew; the updated identification came well after his death. The luminous, starry-eyed subject, committed to canvas by Gainsborough during 1781 and 1782, was also the mother of one daughter and eleven sons.

Given her fecundity, that Gainsborough captured her cradling her stomach, a protective pose often adopted by women in the later stages of pregnancy, was not surprising. Had McFadden been drawn to this understated nod to motherhood?

Gainsborough's study of *Lady Rodney* compares favorably with his portrait of Jonathan Buttall, famously known as *The Blue Boy*, purchased by American mega-collector Henry E. Huntington. Both shared a captivating use of turquoise and a similar composition. Gainsborough committed his last brush strokes to *The Blue Boy*'s canvas about the same time *Lady Rodney*'s was still drying.

The two paintings differed notably in two ways. The first was size: McFadden's Gainsborough was about a third smaller than Huntington's. The other was price. McFadden entered the Gainsborough market at a propitious time, and thanks to Lockett, got a deal—relatively speaking, at least. On June 5, 1893, he purchased *Lady Rodney* for the mere sum of £2,677 ($469,425 today). Two decades later, in 1922, Huntington paid its then-owner, famed New York dealer Joseph Duveen, nearly $730,000 ($10.8 million today).

Lady Rodney/Anne became the "mistress" of his collection, and her countenance presided as the centerpiece of McFadden's prized paintings, from exhibition to exhibition, to his sitting-room in Philadelphia, to, finally, a place of pride in his fully formed collection. Interestingly, the only photograph of any McFadden purchase to be found in Agnew's current in-house archives is that of *Lady Rodney*. McFadden had commissioned Chappell Studio in Philadelphia for the job.

————※————

FOR MOST OF his remaining years in Liverpool—McFadden returned to Philadelphia in 1902 as a first-time homeowner there—the increasingly savvy collector added to his art cache. (Presumably, crowding his house as he did so.) His purchases were regular, but slowly paced. That is, for an American. His American compatriots sought immediate gratification, and their tastes in art drew them toward big, bigger, and biggest. Through 1902, McFadden logged a near-perfect record of annual buys from Agnew's, in terms of regular quantities and quality. The exceptions were the years 1894, 1897, and 1898, when for reasons probably linked to his company's cash flow and profits, he made none. In all, he acquired forty-three pieces, virtually all oil paintings.

Of these, just fourteen, including *Lady Rodney*, ultimately found their way to the Philadelphia-based collection: George Romney's *Mrs. Finch* (purchased May 4, 1895); Henry Raeburn's *Lady Elibank* (May 20, 1895); James Stark's *Landscape with Cattle* (May 20, 1895); Raeburn's *Lady Belhaven* (May 25, 1895); John Crome's *The Blacksmith Shop near Hingham, Norfolk* (May 9, 1896); Romney's *Miss Tickell* (June 13, 1899); John Constable's *Branch Hill Pond, Hampstead Heath* (February 6, 1900); David Cox's *Going to the Hayfield* (February 19, 1900); George Morland's *The Stagecoach*[10] (February 19, 1900); Romney's *Mrs. Crouch* (May

10, 1901) and *Mrs. Champion de Crespigny* (June 1, 1901); Constable's *A Boat Passing a Lock* (June 14, 1901); and Raeburn's *Charles Christie, Esq.* (August 1, 1902).[11]

Twenty-nine to go.

The burgeoning collection was taking shape in the form it was eventually known for—small, jewel-like portraits by late eighteenth- and early nineteenth-century British artists. But as was the case in his acquisition of Rosa Bonheur's *The Horse Fair*, McFadden could stray well off the reservation. Most memorable was a purchase, on May 20, 1895, of *Infanta María Anne of Austria*—by Diego Velázquez. For that, McFadden handed Lockett a check for about $160,000.

Eventually, McFadden realized "without regret" that the Velázquez had to go. "[I]t did not 'belong,' however valuable in itself, to the plan he had in mind," a cataloguer of the collection would later say.[12]

Like most collectors—though he was never credited as such—McFadden was a willing seller. Lockett served him well, though many of the fabulous pictures that he bought and later, presumably deaccessioned by sale, might now be thought of as part of McFadden's "shadow collection." Included were Joshua Reynolds's *Nellie O'Brien* (purchased May 4, 1895); John Crome's *Household Cottage* (May 7, 1895); Reynolds's *Children in the Wood* (May 25, 1895); John Constable's *Canfield Valley of the Stour* (December 3, 1895); J.M.W. Turner's *The Nore;* Reynolds's *Miss Mary Palmer* (February 28, 1896); John Hoppner's *The Sisters Frankland* (May 9, 1896); Francis Wheatley's *George III with Children* (June 11, 1896); and Thomas Gainsborough's *View Near Ipswich* (February 12, 1900).

The pictures' resale values were generally high; their deaccession to raise cash to purchase other works was understandable. McFadden paid more than $1 million for Turner's *The Nore*, and about $545,000 for Reynolds's *Miss Mary Palmer*.

The deaccessioned paintings can now be considered "the ones that got away." In the following years, other prized acquisitions also came and went.

Velázquez's *Infanta María Anne of Austria* (or, now, simply, *María Anna*) is believed to be in the Prado in Madrid. McFadden resold Reynolds's *Miss Mary Palmer* to Agnew's on November 22, 1909. No one knows where it is today. He returned to Philadelphia with Bonheur's *The Horse Fair*, and displayed it there to appreciative audiences, principally at the Pennsylvania Academy of the Fine Arts. It, too, is untraced.

CHAPTER SIX

Collectors

BERNARD BERENSON, THE CONFIDANT of many of the most avid early twentieth-century collectors, called his patrons, cheekily, "squillionaires." Literary lion S.N. Behrman referred to the era's fine art tycoons as "American Monarchs."

The Gilded Age, in the late nineteenth century, was marked by the excess and faux grandeur adopted by the country's wealthiest captains of industry. Fine art "harvesting" by the most serendipitously fortunate—sometimes staged with a kind of primitive lust as large as their louche corpulence—played out in power centers of concentrated lucre, greed, and idleness, from London to New York.

Art mandarins J.P. Morgan in New York, P.A.B. Widener in Philadelphia, and other hunter-gatherers amassed their holdings as if they were mining a rich gold vein, stacking and hoarding their tons of art "bullion." Despite fabulous success in other endeavors (for example, Henry Clay Frick, in industry; William L. Elkins, in oil and mass transit; and Isabella Stewart Gardner's inherited wealth), they and a handful of other

late-nineteenth-century gentry sought another kind of long-
term validation in art's ageless permanence and cultural luster.
To shore up their own legacies as art patrons, they often built
opulent go-for-Baroque mansions that rippled with yawning
wall space. Work and investment endowed them with worldly
riches. Art harvesting promised a kind of immortality. Their
baronial follies usually went bust—their massive wealth turning to dust within two to three generations.

In Philadelphia, hurt feelings were also at stake.

On the whole, the art collectors were right. Who today re-
members other Gilded Age one-percenters—the likes of William
Weightman, Philadelphia's billionaire chemical manufacturing
mogul; or C.K. Billings, a Chicago gas fortune heir, best known
for a dinner party he hosted in 1903 at Sherry's Restaurant in
New York? (The all-male guests arrived at Billings's dinner in
white tie *and* on horseback.)

THE GRAND COLLECTORS looked upon their gains with dewy-
eyed desire, often glazed over by the blush of first acquisitive
lust. They sought a hodge-podge of works by Old Masters, comfortable in the knowledge that the marketplace had stamped its
approval on their purchases. Even if that meant they often had
to rely on frequently spurious advice, proffered by dealers and
consultants of questionable, even deceitful, character.

In that buccaneering age, the most legendary rascal of the art
world was Lord Joseph Duveen, an erstwhile Dutchman who became New York's heralded art impresario. His sales tactic, in the
words of his biographer S. N. Behrman, consisted of persuading
clients "they were fellow-epicures at the groaning banquet table
of culture."[1] Other, less showy yet important players included
the art guru Berenson, Isabella Stewart Gardner's personal tutor; and the German-born Wilhelm Reinhold Valentiner, a New

York-based art dealer, consultant, and former textile curator at the Metropolitan Museum of Art. All played significant roles in crafting the Philadelphia collections of P.A.B. Widener (Duveen, Berenson), John G. Johnson (Duveen, Berenson), Edward T. Stotesbury (Duveen), and early twentieth-century newcomer John D. McIlhenny (Valentiner).

John McFadden proceeded with a cooler head. With only a few forays elsewhere, his singular mission remained British art. He preferred his decisions to be informed by experts, not driven by the hired paladins who helped others build their collections. As detailed in Chapter Five, Thos. Agnew & Sons, one of Britain's oldest and most respected showrooms, was most often the font of that guidance.

Culture critic James Gibbons Huneker portrayed McFadden, a friend, as a precisionist. He was quick to praise "such collections as the Morgan, the Frick, the John G. Johnson," as being "catholic in their variety; different schools are represented. [McFadden's] is small [and] choice."[2]

Largely excluded in these art barons' portfolios were American artists. (Johnson made exceptions.) Cultural snobbery and misconceptions relegated American artists to second-class standing, even in Philadelphia, where one of the country's greatest practitioners lived and worked under their noses. Thomas Eakins's house and studio was not far from Rittenhouse Square, at 1729 Mount Vernon Street. In London, the expatriate American painter John Singer Sargent was making the rounds in the West End, McFadden's upscale London haunt.[3]

JOHN PIERPONT MORGAN's business interests in railroads, and especially his banking ties, bridged his native New York and his adopted Philadelphia. In 1871, Morgan rose to financial prominence in Philadelphia in his own right by taking the vows of partnership in freshly arranged corporate "nuptials." The financial newlyweds were known by their married name, Drexel, Morgan & Company. Housed within a Florentine-like stone palazzo in Center City, facing 15th Street at Walnut, the powerful bank was run by its founder and managing director, Anthony Joseph Drexel. It was a marriage of near equals; the Philadelphian's wealth and stature was almost akin to Morgan's.

Drexel's death in 1893 set the scene for a thirty-year drama in Philadelphia art collecting. It would unfold with a histrionic rollout of score-settling and one-upmanship, back-stabbing, financial scandal, and ruin, and two millionaires dying on the doomed *R.M.S. Titanic*. The drama would have at least one salutary effect: it would lead the parties involved to forge a tentative commitment to create Philadelphia's first fine arts museum. Almost everyone agreed the new museum would replace the Pennsylvania Museum and School of Industrial Art at Memorial Hall. And that it would be Philadelphia's new "Louvre."

With Drexel gone, Morgan split the bank into two retail divisions. J.P. Morgan & Company in New York, and Drexel & Company, in Philadelphia, overseen by Edward Townsend "Ned" Stotesbury as Morgan's local partner. Stotesbury, once Drexel's earnest office boy, was a born banker. He was a scrupulous record-keeper and a penny-pincher. For more than thirty years, after his wife Frances's death in 1881, he remained a bachelor, abiding by his frequently voiced dictum, "Keep your mouth shut and your ears open."

In 1912, smitten with the widow Eva Roberts Cromwell, he broke his pledge with the fateful utterance of the words "I do." The head-over-heels-in-love couple soon settled into multiple lavish love-nests, including Whitemarsh Hall, an estate in the Philadelphia suburb of Springfield, and others in Palm Beach and in Bar Harbor, Maine.

The pennies that Stotesbury had so faithfully pinched had accumulated. The floodgates of profligate spending opened.

Besides real estate, Stotesbury also learned, thanks to Eva's tutoring, to appreciate fine art. Lots of it. And which Joseph Duveen was always ready to deliver—at "enormous prices."[4] Duveen sold him portraits by Romney and Thomas Lawrence and soon after, a Raeburn. It was a "magnificent" entry, a portrait of Mrs. Andrew Hay.[5]

In the end, the investment banker established himself as an art collector extraordinaire and as a VIP in the city's cultural world. After marrying Eva, his civic involvement included becoming a trustee at the Pennsylvania Museum, acting as a Fairmount Park commissioner, and taking the role of a director of the Pennsylvania Academy of the Fine Arts. He liked to frolic at social fêtes at the Art Club of Philadelphia. (His friend, John McFadden, was president of the club.)

However, the ultimate brass ring of social arrival, a membership in the Philadelphia Club, eluded him. Try as he might to escape it, Stotesbury spent most of his life as an outsider. Even the townhouse he owned at 1923 Walnut Street, and yet another next door at 1925 Walnut Street (with an interior designed by Duveen), both across the street from Proper Philadelphia's principal house of worship, the Church of the Holy Trinity, were not enough for social salvation. Philadelphia's memory was long. Stotesbury's beginnings as Drexel's earnest office boy would not be forgotten.

PERHAPS NO ART rivalry could match that of the Philadelphia Three: renowned lawyer John Graver Johnson, and transportation czars Peter Arrell Browne Widener and William Lukens Elkins. The trio were fervent art patrons, good friends, and deeply embedded in Philadelphia's folklore and what would become its commercial and legal history. They were men of achievement, nationally known for immense success in law, transportation,

and finance. In the annals of American art collecting, they secured an equally legendary perch.

New York's Metropolitan Museum of Art recognized Johnson's fame, acumen for collecting, and wealth by appointing
him a museum trustee, one of the few from outside New York.
The Fairmount Park Commission similarly honored him,
appointing him as principal trustee of the W. P. Wilstach Collection and overseer of its Croesus-like $500,000 ($13 million
today) endowment.

Spending their own money was equally easy. Centuries-old
European art was plentiful—and affordably priced, well within
reach of any covetous grasp. Canvas after canvas sailed across
the Atlantic. Achieving social status and recognition for their
refined good taste as newly minted culture mavens was a different matter. Like Stotesbury, the trio was damned as simple
arrivistes. Widener and Elkins, more than Johnson, were particularly doomed to the status of outsiders. Proper Philadelphia,
from its inner sanctum of clubs and ballrooms, had spoken.

The Three were also judged wanting for where they lived—
outside the imaginary confines of patrician residence. For
reasons best known to himself, Johnson lived and practiced
at 506 South Broad Street, in déclassé South Philadelphia. Still
later, he doubled down, consolidating his real estate with an
adjacent four-story townhouse at 510 South Broad Street. For
Proper Philadelphians, that meant *two* black-balled houses.

Johnson's chumminess with Widener and Elkins made Rittenhouse patriarchs twist their upturned noses further out of
joint. The distinguished lawyer cast their sniffing aside. Loyalty
meant more to him: Johnson's friendship with Widener dated to their student days at Central High School, Philadelphia's
most meritorious *public* high school.

The self-made men devoted most Saturday nights to poker
at Widener's brownstone mansion at 1200 North Broad Street, at
the corner of Girard Avenue, in another putatively undesirable

neighborhood. Elkins lived next door. Art appreciation, that is, the appreciation of its acquisition, laced their conversation. The moguls later removed themselves from their under-appreciated domiciles to country estates in Montgomery County, in Elkins Park, which Elkins named for himself. (For Proper Philadelphia, such celebratory hubris was not a good sign.)

Soon after Johnson died in 1917, tongues started wagging about the contents of his yet-undisclosed will. Would he bequeath his vast art holdings, totaling about 1,200 objects and worth a staggering $7 million ($176 million today) in all, to the Pennsylvania Museum, as William P. Wilstach had? Would his premises on South Broad Street be designated a private museum, replicating a model established by Boston doyenne Isabella Stewart Gardner? Or, though it seemed almost inconceivable, would the Metropolitan Museum of Art win his favor?

———✕———

PETER A.B. WIDENER and William L. Elkins were a matched set. Both born in the early 1830s, they shared similar neuroses about social status, wealth, and self-worth. They were business partners: together, they owned and operated local inter-urban transit systems. Widener (1834–1915) also invested in steel mills, while Elkins (1832–1903) preferred power plants. They were also in-laws. Widener's eldest son, George D. Widener, married Elkins's younger daughter, Eleanor. Their stupendous art collections, according to plan, would ensure glorious destinies in forever-lasting art legacies.

As fate would have it, Widener's and Elkins's heirs-presumptive would not be the ultimate legatees. In Widener's case, tragedy struck. His oldest son, George D. Widener, never inherited his cache of Titians, Van Dycks, Holbeins, Raphaels, Millets, and Rembrandts, because George and *his* son, Harry Elkins Widener, drowned in the sinking of the *R.M.S. Titanic* in 1912. Their deaths stunned Philadelphia, and mourning ensued. At the Union League, John McFadden was part of the house committee that "out of respect" to their memory "indefinitely postponed" an exhibition of works contributed by the senior Widener.[6]

Three years later, in 1915, P.A.B. Widener died. His younger son, Joseph E. Widener, an esthete and a thoroughbred enthusiast, wound up as the collection's seigneur.

The disposition of the William L. Elkins Collection, as it was known, also fell to another generation. William's eldest son, George W. Elkins—a voracious art collector in his own right—died in 1919, and *his* son, William M. Elkins, became the executor of the William L. Elkins Collection *and* the George W. Elkins Collection.

Through these twists and turns, death after death, generation after generation, will after will, the blackballing of the Widener and Elkins patriarchs resulted in unsettling consequences for Philadelphia's great art collections, affecting how they became or did *not* become part of the city's lasting cultural legacy. Because of who they were—*and* what they controlled—Joseph E. Widener and William M. Elkins became prominent figures in the formation of Philadelphia's public art trove. If need be, smoldering personal scores would have to be settled.

CHAPTER SEVEN

Anglomane

1902–1913

JOHN MCFADDEN'S PHILADELPHIA WAS not dissimilar to the British capital he came to know so well. Philadelphia's legacy as Britain's premier colonial outpost and the second largest English-speaking city had deep roots. For McFadden, the two cities' mutual connections were familiar and comforting. After more than two decades in England, since his first posting there in 1881, the Proper Philadelphian had evolved into a quintessential Anglomane.

Philadelphia had a deep, embedded memory of its pre-Revolutionary Englishness. Some of this longing was expressed in architecture. Parts of the city, particularly around Washington Square and Rittenhouse Square, exuded a distinct English flavor, manifested in Georgian and late Victorian architectural styles, the kind seen in some of London's upmarket precincts. Place names were evocative: neighborhoods like Oxford Circle, Mayfair, Richmond, and Southwark just appropriated the names of old London boroughs. The British presence was so strong in Kensington, a north Philadelphia neighborhood, it was dubbed "Little England."[1]

Some day-to-day terminology, oddly, did not deviate from the city's English past. Philadelphians were the only Americans to refer to their sidewalks as "pavements," a British usage that still persists. Cricket was popular, even among the working classes.

Around Rittenhouse Square, a historian writes, "Visitors... notably Britishers, came, saw, and were impressed by the nostalgically English atmosphere of the tree-lined streets where the artistic and the properly descended lived in urban harmony."[2]

English ties were so close that, even well into the early 1920s, Philadelphians could sail directly to Liverpool. Such service was not new. In the early nineteenth century, financier Thomas Pym Cope, a rival of mega-banker Stephen Girard, had developed a packet line serving the two cities on an unscheduled basis.[3] In the late nineteenth century, until 1887, the American Line sailed the *S.S. Pennsylvania* on weekly Atlantic crossings. The *S.S. Haverford* and the *S.S. Swarthmore* subsequently picked up weekly service in 1903, until 1914 when New York City usurped service. After a six-year hiatus, Philadelphia demand went up again, and the *S.S. Haverford*, now owned by the White Star Line, returned to Pier 53 on the Delaware River for a reinstated Philadelphia-Liverpool run. The steamship was decommissioned four years later, in 1924, abruptly ending all scheduled sailings to England.[4]

PROPER PHILADELPHIANS, IN religion, were Episcopalian, or at least Protestant. In ethnicity, Anglo-Saxon; in the US, they were Anglo-Americans.[5] Otherwise, they were famously rich and powerful—and masters of the city.

Philadelphia's working class and a growing torrent of immigrants acquiesced to the status quo. Social historian John Lukacs concluded, "There was less radical agitation, less evidence of hatred against the upper classes in Philadelphia than in any comparable city in the United States; just as England, the very country whose aristocracy was socially more influential and widespread than that of any other country in Europe, experienced no revolution during the nineteenth century, alone among the great nations of the Old World."[6]

Like English aristocracy, Philadelphia's Rittenhouse patricians maintained their pedigrees by ruthless vetting. The men's club network in Philadelphia, like that in London, was stratified and unforgiving in exercising its admission rites. Almost exclusively, members were drawn from that geographic inner sanctum surrounding Rittenhouse Square. Due to a consanguinity of many first-family relationships, some were cousins by marriage. Others, in keeping with their tribe's legendary insularity, were at least friends from childhood. All were listed in the *Philadelphia Social Register*. Stuffy and conservative were just part of the air they breathed.

McFadden looked the part of a fully paid-up clubman. His attire included natty English-made suits—a swallow-tail, pin-striped morning suit was a favorite—cravat and stickpin, watch and chain secured by a pocket fob, and, *de rigueur*, a silk top hat. He wore, in the English manner, a gold signet ring on his right ring finger. Photographs show a wedding band on his left ring finger. McFadden cut a figure that would not have been out of place strolling in St. James's or Pall Mall, the heart of London's Clubland. An ivory-topped walking stick, another favored accoutrement, and an occasional carnation in his left lapel contributed to his appearance as the aristocratic toff. Full regalia included spats, striped trousers, and if the weather was right, a velvet-lapelled Chesterfield topcoat. Based on photographic comparisons, McFadden was of average height, under six feet.

His speech was most likely dominated by a mid-Atlantic or transatlantic accent, linguistic terms that described an acquired cadence popular among upper-crust Americans at that time. In McFadden's case, just back from a long residence in England, some Oxbridge-posh might also have been detected. That he likely spelled "cheque" and "colour" in the English form were affectations adopted by many in blueblood Philadelphia. In an eerie parallel, McFadden could have been a character who walked off the pages of his London-based contemporary, Anglo-American author Henry James. Elegant. Effete. Patrician.

McFadden's formality did not extend to certain forms of address. In business and on the Liverpool Exchange "flags," he was "affectionately" known as "John."[7] How affectionate he was with his wife Florence has never been described. The closest public indication was a 1901 reception, in Philadelphia, celebrating the couple's twenty-fifth wedding anniversary. "Invitations have been sent out," a society columnist informed Philadelphia's newspaper readership.[8]

Reliable descriptions of McFadden are hard to come by. Glowing, even hagiographic exaggerations in contemporaneous accounts are suspect. Still, they offer a glimpse into how the highly private McFadden was perceived after passing through a public media filter. McFadden struck local journalist Charles J. Cohen, who documented many Rittenhouse swells in a series of biographical vignettes, as "modest and unassuming."[9]

J. St. George Joyce, in his day a notable Irish-born journalist, celebrated McFadden for being "a man of many parts, a man of affairs and of the world, a good citizen and a credit to Philadelphia." There was more in the same vein. McFadden, Joyce gushed, possessed "an inherent urbanity, a rare personal magnetism, a wide and varied knowledge of men and things, a cultured mind, a charming manner and an almost inexhaustible fund of humor and that sense of humor so typical of the Irish race, and one from one of the most prominent northern septs [clans]...."

Commerce and Finance, a cotton trade journal, lauded him as "a man of great versatility and broad sympathies, always willing to help those who were in distress or lend his aid to a deserving cause."

As with most things, the truth probably was somewhere in between.

McFadden's British tendencies—almost a gravitational pull—were never in question. Son Jack was born in England. Son Philip was schooled there and in Scotland. Until she married, daughter Alice had spent more time in England than in Philadelphia. Florence developed friendships there. (A close friend was Mrs. William Lowes Rushton, wife of a court magistrate and English Shakespearean scholar, and they socialized in Liverpool and in Philadelphia.) As previously noted, in Chapter Five, John and Florence owned a country house in Kent, and they usually spent their summer holidays there. Throughout their stay in England, they also maintained their "handsome residence" at 4 Croxteth Road, Liverpool, reported *The Philadelphia Inquirer*.[10] While in London, if they gadded about the five-star Carlton Hotel (a Victorian pile in the heart of the West End) like they owned the place, it was because they actually did. At least fifty shares worth.

Being well-tutored in all things British, John and Florence would never have skipped a chance to witness a king's coronation. Fortunately, the elevation of George V, father of the future rogue prince, the Duke of Windsor, was scheduled for June 22, 1911 in Westminster Abbey. It seemed that almost all of Philadelphia's rich, famous, and notorious planned to show up. The Wideners were staying *en famille* at the Ritz, not far from Buckingham Palace. McFadden had constituted his own coronation party, including the dodgy Philadelphia millionaire financier Edward T. Stotesbury, an important art collector in his own right; Stotesbury's daughter Frances, and her philandering husband J. Kearsley Mitchell, who, several years later, would be implicated in "The Butterfly Murders" of two Broadway showgirls. Of course, the Carlton was the Philadelphia holidaymakers' home away from home.

McFadden was accustomed to five-star service. When on land, at the Carlton. When by sea, to use nautical parlance, it was always "first class." His line of choice was the English Cunard Steamship Company, in a class of its own, whose motto was high-flown braggadocio: "Going Cunard is a State of Grace." McFadden graced Cunard with an average of six annual round trips, or twelve Atlantic crossings, for a total of up to sixty days at sea each year. Despite the accumulated time away from home and office, Cunard's most favored passengers found their journey less than arduous. For most, it was time for catching up on business, on-board social engagements, or, simply, rest and relaxation. Others engaged in romantic interludes. And on arrival, there was no jetlag.

McFadden was loyal in particular to the *R.M.S. Mauretania*, part of Cunard's first-tier Olympic Class fleet, from its launching in 1907. The sea-going pleasure palace frequently counted the Philadelphian among its 563 first-class passengers. (More than 3,000 mail sacks were also usually aboard.) The ship's décor was accented by "warmly wood-toned interiors" in oak, maple, mahogany, and walnut. In the First Dining Room, all eyes looked to the Captain's Table, encompassing an area opened to a floor above. In the First-Class Lounge, many passengers, wanting natural light for better reading, jockeyed to sit under or near an oval skylight. McFadden and his fellow passengers also had their pick of multi-roomed suites, decked out in several King Louis styles (XIV, XV, or XVI), or in Georgian or Regency themes.[11]

Lucius Beebe, the journalist, author, and social arbiter nonpareil, told how the passengers of the *Mauretania* usually headed to New York from Southampton, its English home port, "with vastly more luggage and motorcars than they started out with."[12] First-Class passengers thronged the ship bow to stern. Cunard advertisements touted a Who's Who of the rich and famous who traveled the company's steamships. These commercial blandishments cynically targeted passengers in below-decks Second and Third Class, who would never see, much less rub shoulders with, these upper-tier notables. For starry-eyed

First-Class voyagers, legendary movie stars of the day such as
Charlie Chaplin, Clara Bow, Stan Laurel and Oliver Hardy, Tal-
lulah Bankhead, and Douglas Fairbanks Jr. (disgraced cotton
broker Daniel J. Sully's son-in-law) and his wife, Mary Pickford,
were frequently on offer.[13]

Beebe recounted how the behavior of some "patroons" approached the freakish. "They went with valets and maids,
hatboxes and shoe trunks, jewel cases and, in some fastidious
instances, their own personal bed linen. Invalids brought their
doctors and nurses, dog lovers traveled with mastiffs and St. Ber-
nards. Occasional magnificoes or eccentrics brought their own
barbers, and food faddists carried their special rations..." No
doubt McFadden subscribed to Beebe's *pronunciamento,* "How
You Traveled Was Who You Were."[14]

McFadden preferred the four-smokestack, turbine-driven
Mauretania for another reason—speed. A swift run in 1913 averaged five days. Eventually the ocean liner pared the transatlantic
crossing to four and a half days, a record held until 1937. That
was important to McFadden, whose frenetic crossings would
qualify him today for frequent-traveler status. His schedule was
hectic, even harried. In less than a month, on one occasion, Mc-
Fadden set out from Philadelphia to Atlantic City and finally to
New York for a sailing to Southampton. On another, he arrived
in Liverpool in May, and less than a month later was en route
to New York. One head-spinning round-trip, rivaling the peregrinations of a modern-day road warrior, involved an arrival on
the *Mauretania* on a Friday. "But will return by the same boat on
Wednesday," he said matter-of-factly in a letter to a Philadelphia
correspondent.[15]

AFTER MORE THAN twenty years abroad, McFadden was an
American with an English core. He readily adopted English

manners and mannerisms. He was never an expatriate; no disaffected rich American in the mold of socialite-artist Gerald Murphy. Rather, he had become a gentleman. Later, he evolved into its sub-species, a Victorian idealist.

Since attending Episcopal Academy, his interest in art history had been juxtaposed with a keen respect for science. Thirty years later, as he did in art collecting, McFadden eagerly sought to put his personal stamp on that other interest.

He was a late bloomer. But the time was ripe, as scientific mysteries in Victorian-age Britain were increasingly being unraveled. McFadden recognized his role was on the sidelines; he pulled out his checkbook.

McFadden thought himself different from the raw capitalist stereotype that tarred many of his contemporary—and far wealthier—peers like J.P. Morgan and John D. Rockefeller Sr., whose reputations for unfettered ruthlessness became the public face of American capitalism.

He felt more akin to Andrew Carnegie, the Pittsburgh coke titan, and George Peabody, the Massachusetts-born financier—known for their public spirit, qualities not normally associated with America's mega tycoons. Both men, neither of whom was a significant art collector, had also extended their good works to England. The Scottish-born Carnegie funded new libraries. Most were in the United States, but many, too, were scattered in Britain. Five libraries alone rose in Liverpool, one in McFadden's own "neighborhood" near Prince's Park. Peabody spent on housing estates for "the poor and needy" in London. McFadden hoped to ease into the ranks of these high-minded donors.

McFadden's awareness of the plight of the downtrodden must have been tinged with guilt. Surely he understood that the roots of his family wealth, especially during the early stages of the McFadden cotton empire, were sullied by the inhuman expediency of slavery. Sounding very much like Carnegie, McFadden reasoned in a conversation with a friend that his wealth counted for nothing unless it enabled him to do some "lasting good." This sentiment eerily paralleled Carnegie's famous public statement, "My business is to do as much good in the world as I can."[16]

Perhaps this revealed a genuine humanitarian streak; perhaps, an impulse to make penance for a life of providential affluence based upon the cruel exploitation of others. Whatever the inner psychological motivation, McFadden's civic turn fit well within the ethic of the Victorian Modern figure: a champion of duty and innovation on behalf of the commonweal. Reason and will, according to this worldview, would transform primitive beliefs, bringing the world to a transcendent enlightenment—all in keeping, of course, with the primacy of the British Empire. The public lauded the inventiveness of its Industrial Age, and Queen Victoria's subjects were proud that her Empire was leading the way in industry (iron-hull steamships, for example), communication (the telegraph), transportation (the world's first subway in London), and medicine (the hypodermic syringe). And, of course, in supplying cotton fabric to the world.

The public imagination was animated by the "Rational Man," even if its most prominent exponent, Arthur Conan Doyle's Sherlock Holmes, was fictional. Jules Verne's peregrinating personage, the upper-crust clubman Phileas Fogg in *Around the World in Eighty Days*, exemplified Britain's wild affection for the amateur, the adventurer, and the dilettante. In real life, no better exemplar could be found than in Edward Guinness, First Earl of Iveagh, who embodied the virtues of a merchant prince (he was the heir of the world's largest brewery) committed to compassionate societal advancement.

McFadden was affected by Iveagh's standard, and wished to make it his own. The two men had striking similarities—as art collectors, as supporters of medical science, and as moneyed men behind the derring-do of polar exploration. As patrons of the latter, they might have crossed paths at the Royal Geographical Society, or quite possibly at Thos. Agnew & Sons, where Iveagh was also a customer. If the neophyte did not know Iveagh personally, he would have been certainly aware of his British counterpart's reputation—and his purchasing habits at Agnew's. Like Iveagh, McFadden shared a taste for British portraits. In one case, he indulged in an exercise in reflected glory by association. McFadden bought Raeburn's *Portrait of Lady Belhaven* from Agnew's—*after* it belonged to Iveagh.[17]

McFadden directed his philanthropy to disease prevention. Within the newly founded Lister Institute of Preventative Medicine in London, McFadden launched a special-interest charity, the "John Howard McFadden Research Fund," to study cures for measles (then without a vaccine) and cancer. He was the sole patron and was appointed the fund's director. During a shipboard interview at New York, the Philadelphian said if more money was needed, he would provide it. He denied, however, that he was financing a cancer "cure." With typical optimism—albeit tinged with naïveté—McFadden confided:

> I have been to London to visit the Lister Institute there where experiments are being carried on to discover the cause of cancer in which I am taking a deep interest. The scientists engaged on the work were confident that good results would be obtained, and when the cause has been found it will be easy to get a remedy. It was a simple matter to cure yellow fever and malaria when the causes had been determined.[18]

In addition, in his adopted Liverpool, he donated to the pioneering Liverpool School of Tropical Medicine, and was a director of special researches at the Royal Southern Hospital, a Liverpool teaching hospital. He also partnered with the British Home Office to research the cause of "industrial cancer at briquette works," and received an official recognition for "spade work" in the project.

McFadden made the cause personal, supporting Dr. Hugh Campbell Ross, an eminent English cancer specialist, and his assistant, Dr. John Westray Cropper, in their study of cell reproduction and growth. His backing was "carte blanche," Ross said.

The Royal Society of Medicine threw its weight behind what were known as "The John Howard McFadden Researches." In 1912, London publisher John Murray published Ross's and Cropper's groundbreaking studies, *The Problem of the Gasworks Pitch Industry and Cancer,* and *Further Researches into Induced Cell-Reproduction and Cancer* (Volumes 1, 2). Distribution of the Ross and Cropper studies in the medical community was not confined to Britain. Volume 2 of *Further Researches* was also published, in the same year, by P. Blakiston's Son & Co. in Philadelphia.

No city in America depended on club membership as a totem of social acceptance and civic stature as did Philadelphia.

The pinnacle was the Philadelphia Club, founded as America's first men's club in 1834. Like some of its London confrères, the Philadelphia began as a coffeehouse, finally moving to its Center City townhouse in 1865. In a red-brick corner neo-Georgian at 13th and Walnut Streets, legions of society potentates—Drexels, Cassatts, Lippincotts, and Peppers among them—smoked cigars and partook of fine food and wine. Almost equal in social cachet was the Rittenhouse Club, established in 1875. Its home was a stately late Victorian on the north side of Rittenhouse Square.

"The primary function of the Philadelphia and Rittenhouse clubs is the ascription of upper class status," E. Digby Baltzell, Philadelphia's eminent social critic, has explained.[19] He added, "On the whole, pedigree and fashionable background is more highly valued at the Philadelphia Club...."[20] And, "members of the Rittenhouse Club are somewhat more intellectually inclined...."[21]

McFadden's social sphere, as evidenced by his club affiliations, was a widespread affair. In Philadelphia, his memberships included the Racquet Club, the Union League, the Philadelphia Geographical Society, and the Pennsylvania Society, a Republican association that held its politically charged annual meeting in New York. He was an officer and sometime president of the Art Club of Philadelphia, a nationally recognized group promoting Philadelphia artists. He also branched out—in a most un-Philadelphian way—to social perches in other cities. In New York, he rubbed shoulders at the Metropolitan Club, founded by J.P. Morgan in 1891; at the New York Yacht Club; and at the Players. In London, he clubbed at the Junior Carlton, at 30 Pall Mall.[22]

One membership was conspicuous by its absence. McFadden never bothered with the Old Hall Club, a popular venue of Exchange Flags traders, and just a stone's throw from his Albany building office. The club had become an ostensible refuge, where the ruthlessness of trading could be set aside under the assumed guise of collegial civility. McFadden's soft-edged temperament had little tolerance for business friction, nor much less the fiction of comity. Son Jack, on the other hand, *was* a member.

His National Geographical Society membership, like that in the Philadelphia Geographical Society, underscored his commitment to exploration. His dedication to medical science found expression in his trusteeship at Thomas Jefferson Hospital.

He was also a mainstay of the Radnor Hunt Club, though there is no record of McFadden ever mounting a horse, much less foxhunting. The club's foxhunting "country" in Philadelphia's Main Line suburbs, according to *Bailey's Hunting Directory*, was "rather rolling," "good" for galloping, and "principally fenced with post-and-rail." In 1897, when the Huntington Valley Country Club got its start, he became a member there as well. The record does not reveal whether he participated in typical recreational activities there.

In one way, however, McFadden did indulge in the sporting life—as an ocean-going yachtsman. His New York Yacht Club membership was not all window dressing. By all appearances, he fancied the life at sea as the owner of a steam-powered yacht. At least one hundred fifty feet, fitted with double masts and a single funnel, the craft resembled more a seaworthy steamer. Its crew, accordingly, needed to be sizable. As for the price tag of such playthings for the rich, J.P. Morgan famously remarked, "Nobody who has to ask what a yacht costs has any business owning one."

While it would be almost unimaginable (given his portly dimensions) to envision McFadden in tight-fitting hunting garb, his plump frame filled out nautical attire with jaunty élan. Family photographs from 1907 show him in full commodore's regalia, his captain's cap tilted to an insouciant angle, and pipe in hand. The ladies were pictured in straw boaters, reading and knitting. An unidentified youth sports a sailor's outfit, a beret atop his head.

The old salt, the father of an expanding family, also demonstrated his fondness for the sea by buying a vacation house on New Jersey's Shore, in Ventnor, then a district of Atlantic City. McFadden and other area residents called their dwellings "cottages." They were not.

McFadden's beachfront property, at Montgomery Avenue and the Boardwalk, was big enough, and the Philadelphian rich enough, that several servants were employed to maintain it. McFadden's property was long ago demolished. But based on still-standing houses that followed in the teens, it was probably a massive, two-story structure topped with a gabled roof and outdoor porches, suitable for enjoying sea breezes. Other Philadelphia swells lived in the area. Rodman Wanamaker, a sometime Pennsylvania Museum trustee and the son of the legendary Philadelphia merchant, John Wanamaker, was a

neighbor. McFadden's yacht was also probably moored somewhere nearby.[23]

McFadden had no usual hobbies and few friends, certainly
none who can be identified from childhood.[24] Club affiliations,
support of medicine and exploration, book collecting, and
yachting encompassed McFadden's day-to-day existence—apart
from buying and curating his art. His interest in art expanded
into official roles at the Pennsylvania Museum and at the Pennsylvania Academy of the Fine Arts. Florence and the children
never seemed to interfere with his solitary, introspective pleasure. Because he was never reluctant to exhibit his collection in
its finest settings, those joys might have extended to the niceties
of framing and hanging of pictures.

Florence liked to play euchre, akin to whist or contract
bridge. She was a charter member of the Card Club, "founded
a trifle over six years [ago] by Mrs. John Kink Van Rensselaer,"
The Philadelphia Inquirer reported.[25] She was partial to opera,
and attended the newly opened Philadelphia Opera House (later the Metropolitan Opera House) on North Broad Street, where
she took in *Carmen* and *Rigoletto* in its early years. Whether her
husband had to be coaxed along is unknown. On Wednesdays,
an "open house" afternoon tea was served at home by Florence
and Alice. Only "friends" needed to show up.

For his part, McFadden began dabbling in real estate. Besides
his one-third interest in the Geo. H. McFadden & Bro. building at
121 Chestnut Street and his interest in the London-based Carlton
Hotel, Ltd. (fifty shares), he had acquired 770 shares in the Land
Company of Canada, and an equity interest (all of ten shares) in
the Philadelphia Ritz-Carlton Hotel, on the west side of Broad
Street at Chestnut Street.[26]

Of greater consequence was an outstanding $75,000 ($1.9
million today) mortgage he held on properties at 1411 and 1413
Locust Street. The buildings and lots were acquired in July 1910
for "a consideration exceeding $100,000" ($2.5 million today).[27]

McFadden converted everything into a multilevel parking garage. It was an astute investment. The garage was across the street from the Academy of Music, and was a magnet for parking-hungry attendees of the Philadelphia Orchestra.

IN 1911, MCFADDEN became entangled in a four-year public spectacle involving, as it turned out, a naïve commitment to medical research into pellagra, a skin disease that at the time was often fatal. McFadden's leap into the medical maelstrom was uncharacteristically reckless. For a private man, the way the episode backfired and spilled into national newspaper headlines must have been humiliating.

Pellagra was rampant among poor farmhands, primarily in the American South. Women were most afflicted. The timing of its increased incidence, in the early part of the twentieth century, meant that those suffering most from the disease were former plantation slaves or children of slaves. Many worked as cotton farm workers, and now as sharecroppers were still subject to economic servitude, albeit of another kind.

For a man who liked to guard his privacy, McFadden showed an uncommon openness in the anti-pellagra cause. Aside from an occasional reference in a shipping news brief in *The New York Times* (which, like other New York newspapers, covered the comings and goings of shipboard passengers with breathless rigor), McFadden rarely received mention in the press. In his advocacy of a pellagra cure, McFadden went public.

McFadden's curiosity about the causes and prevention of infectious diseases was not new. Defeating pellagra fell in line with this long-held interest, and in 1911 he joined the philanthropist and political conservative Robert Means Thompson in forming the New York-based Thompson-McFadden Commission. Unusual for the time, the commission was what we would now call a quasi-autonomous non-governmental organization or QUANGO, staffed by U.S. Army and Navy research personnel, but privately funded. McFadden contributed $15,000 ($377,000 today). McFadden knew Colonel Thompson, as he styled himself, from the Pennsylvania Society, a Republican-leaning lobbying and advocacy group that McFadden had joined the same year he and Thompson created the commission. (The Pennsylvania-born Thompson was a former president of the group.)

Like many of his generation, McFadden had a predilection for linking disease to infection. While the commission was still up and running, McFadden had, in 1913, established an independent body to study infectious diseases, the John H. McFadden Research Institute in Liverpool. The Thompson-McFadden Commission's findings, after years of investigation at South Carolina cotton-mill villages, were perhaps not surprising. *The New York Times* headline, on March 15, 1914, summed up:

PELLAGRA CALLED INFECTIOUS DISEASE
Thompson-McFadden Commission Discounts Maize Theory and Blames Stable Fly

The commission's report summed up:
    [O]bservations strongly suggest that unsanitary
    methods of sewage disposal have an important rela-
    tionship to the spread of pellagra. If these indications
    can be confirmed in other places, we feel that the
    proper correction of these conditions by the installa-
    tion of water carriage systems of sewage disposal will
    go far toward restricting the spread of the disease.

The report's author, W.W. King, acknowledged a bias, however. "Infectiousness of the disease and its transmission by blood-sucking insects were assumed, purely as a necessary basis for our work.[28]

A few months later, the Spartanburg County Medical Society called for South Carolina to appropriate state funding to expand the commission's brief. "It is said that it would be an irretrievable loss to the state to lose the work of [the] commission," reported *The Journal of the American Medical Association* on October 10, 1914.

Pellagra's *actual* cause was uncovered a few months later by Dr. Joseph Goldberger, a U.S. Public Health Service physician. Goldberger's discovery was not what politicians wanted to hear. Nor, probably McFadden. Rather than being an infectious disease, the illness was linked to a poor, unvaried diet, especially one lacking in niacin. "Goldberger was able to prevent and induce pellagra by dietary modifications, a landmark event in the annals of medicine, nutrition, and epidemiology."[29]

Not wishing to admit that poor South Carolinians were suffering from human-caused malnutrition, rather than infection spread by the stable fly, political supporters of the Thompson-McFadden Commission came away discredited.

Why did McFadden throw himself so passionately behind this research project? Here as elsewhere, he was reluctant to expound on his personal motives. One might speculate, however, that the man who, along with his family, had profited so handsomely from the cotton trade, may have been motivated by the prospect of improving the living conditions of those whose lives had been brutally exploited in that same venture.

CHAPTER EIGHT

Philadelphian

1902–1918

PREPARING FOR HIS PERMANENT return to Philadelphia, John McFadden sold his long-time Liverpool residence, Worsley House, to Sir Edward Richard Russell, the editor of the Liverpool *Daily Post*. He kept his shares in London's Carlton Hotel and his ownership of the family's summer retreat in Kent, south of London.

The move to America, in 1902, was timed to the opening of the first New York-based office of Geo. H. McFadden & Bro., and John was tasked with managing the rollout. Ironically, the brothers maintained no official presence in New York, even though so much of their work arose there; until then, they had worked from the Cotton Exchange. George had been one of the first elected members of the New York Cotton Exchange, since 1881, the year he dispatched John and Frederic C. Zerega to Liverpool. Despite his long-time membership, George remained at 121 Chestnut Street in Philadelphia, and the firm's interests in New York were represented by acting brokers.

Liverpool's cotton trade dwarfed that in Philadelphia. George was one of about 100 brokers in Philadelphia, compared to more than 500 in Liverpool. Back home, the McFaddens were on the top of the smallish heap: *The Philadelphia Inquirer* always referred to George H. McFadden & Bro. as the city's "leading" broker.

Like the McFaddens, many of their colleagues had offices around the Delaware River port. Others maintained premises in the Bourse, Philadelphia's commodities exchange near Independence Hall, where spot-cotton brokers bid and tracked prices on worldwide markets.

John's resettlement turned awkward, as it actually involved two moves—one to New York and another to Philadelphia. For about two years, while establishing himself in New York as a resident partner, he lived on a part-time basis in midtown Manhattan. His office was in Lower Manhattan, near Wall Street at 56 Beaver Street, the same building that housed the famous Delmonico's steakhouse.

John reckoned the New York relocation to be only temporary. He had in mind that Philip, who had already relocated to New York, would take over. Still, New York had its benefits, including a respite from joyless commuting by rail to and from Philadelphia. Sailing to England was also made easier. Between trips, sometimes with almost back-to-back schedules, he favored the company of the like-minded at the Metropolitan, the Players, and the New York Yacht Club. Living in New York also eliminated the pesky extra cost of his frequent overnight stays at the five-star Waldorf-Astoria Hotel.

As he had in England, McFadden easily adapted to his new surroundings. His residence, a townhouse on the south side of East 55th, between Fifth and Madison Avenues, was near his clubs. The neighborhood was posh enough that some Vanderbilts lived nearby, and William Avery Rockefeller Jr., a co-founder of Standard Oil, lived up the street. He persuaded Florence, a born-again Philadelphia homebody, to join him. Alice, in her early twenties, also came along. So did two maids. The premises were furnished "handsomely," with a "considerable sum" spent on decorations. The McFaddens "lived in a style and after a standard commensurate with the value and character of the house."[1]

In 1904, life in the McFadden household came crashing down. Literally. The cause involved the construction of the luxury St. Regis Hotel, an 18-floor high-rise going up on a building lot just west of the McFadden property.

Perhaps McFadden had a premonition of trouble; he had sold his house the year before providing that he could remain as a lease-holder through 1904. Annual rent would be $6,000 ($160,000).

"Crashing down" came in the form of about two tons of plaster dropped in an air flue. Soon after, the building's roof was smashed "so that a gentle rain blew in upon the upper part of the house. Next the sewer was stopped up with the aid of a few loads of bricks, and water began softly trickling over the McFadden floors as the sewage rose in every pipe in the house."[2]

The "once happy household" began living through a year of rental hell. McFadden first called the hotel's building contractors, Thompson-Starrett Co., to settle the matter amicably. When that failed, he gathered up the household, and on February 22 "sought shelter" in "modest accommodations" for two months at the Waldorf-Astoria Hotel. He took a parlor suite of five bedrooms.

Naturally enough, Florence was distressed. "We simply had to move," she said. "The builders dumped plaster, brick dust and all kinds of things down our cold air flue, so that we could not heat the house. Then a big piece of the roof was knocked off, so that the water ran in, but what made living there absolutely impossible was that the builders stopped up the sewerage pipes in some way and broke others, so that water began running up the sewerage pipes and overflowing and we could do nothing with it."[3]

McFadden sued in New York State court, Appellate Division, for $12,000 ($313,000 today) in damages. He won, though not until 1906.[4]

Florence was still unnerved. Newspapers had feigned horror on how much the McFaddens were reportedly reimbursed by Thompson-Starrett for food, said to be $79 ($2,000) per day. In fact, Florence declared, the two maids were dining comfortably enough on about $4 ($104) a day. Their own daily food bill for three was "only something like $20 [$522] a day."

"I would like to know where that story came from that we paid $79 a day for food," Florence wrote. "It was nothing like that, and I do hope the newspapers are not going to try to make a sensation out of it."

Upending Florence's hope, back in Philadelphia, the press was having a front-page field day.

McFadden had a softer landing in Philadelphia. While still in New York, in 1902, McFadden had also, at long last, established his bona fides as a Rittenhouse Square property owner. He entered the market in a splashy way, buying a marquee house on the northeast corner of 19th and Walnut Streets. Corner properties—there were just twelve on the square—were always the most desirable. The house's location, just down the street from the Rittenhouse Club, was an extra plum.

An early twentieth-century chronicler described the McFadden "mansion" as "a fine brown-stone," built in the mid-century by a namesake of Samuel Powel, Philadelphia's first mayor after the revolution.[5] The three-story house had a Walnut Street frontage of fifty feet, and was 235 feet deep along the 19th Street side north to Sansom Street. Its Walnut Street address was No. 1829. However, the McFaddens always referred to the house's address as the "N.E. Cor." of 19th and

Walnut Streets, never bothering with any numerical designation. Nor a house name. On engraved stationery, they
referenced the address in a small, upper case heading: "N.E.
COR. NINETEENTH AND WALNUT STREET, PHILADEL-
PHIA." It sounded fancier.

The house had a Proper Philadelphia provenance. In 1860,
ownership of the Powel "mansion" (as opposed to the Powel
"house," the former mayor's dwelling in Society Hill) had passed
to Alexander Brown, the Finance Committee chairman of the
American Sunday School Union. His bushy mutton-chop mustache made him a distinctive sight out and about the square.
Brown died in 1893. His heir, John A. Brown, Jr., a founder of the
merchant-banking firm Brown Brothers & Co.,[6] sold the premises nine years later to McFadden. The deed was signed on April
24, 1902. No price was mentioned in city land records.

At the time, the youngest McFadden, John Jr., was twelve
years old. Alice, nineteen. Philip, twenty-four, a bachelor who
had joined the family firm the year before, was living in New
York, assigned, as his father wished, to the Geo. H. McFadden &
Bro.'s office there.

The McFadden house was an architectural pastiche: a faux
Italian-like structure, with Palladian windows *and* English-
style quoining. The top floor, featuring ecclesiastical lancet windows, consisted of utility and servant rooms. Provisions were
made for McFadden's valet, Robert Potts, and the household
chauffeur, who was known by his surname Dowling. (The family sedan, a Packard, was garaged in the rear, off Sansom Street.)

The third floor was about half the height of the lower floors,
where the McFaddens themselves lived and entertained. The
total floor space was massive, about 33,000 square feet. Interestingly, the house's entrance was up several steps from Walnut, on
19th Street. The exterior itself was sparsely landscaped. Just two
bushes stood guard on the Walnut Street side, behind a decorative stone balustrade.

For all its outward commonality with other Rittenhouse Square properties, the McFadden house was nevertheless distinct from them. The conversion of the interior into an art gallery—a *fine* art gallery—marked it for special attention. Three principal ground-floor rooms—the drawing room, dining room, and library—were jammed with McFadden's pictures. So were walls in adjacent halls. Additional artworks came pouring in, as they were shipped from the collection's former Worsley House showcase.

A laudatory appraisal of the new installation came from the influential *American Art News,* a New York-based weekly with a large number of national and European subscribers. Permanent correspondents contributed news and reviews from New York, Boston, Chicago, Philadelphia, London, Paris, and Berlin. One of the journal's art critics in New York, Helen W. Henderson, wrote glowingly: "The rooms are sumptuous in a style thoroughly consistent with the works of art displayed—the whole suggesting the comfort and elegance of an old English manor house."[7]

Not quite. Actually, the interior was dark and almost funereal, typifying an overstuffed, late Victorian look. Tables and chairs were in the Louis XV style. Mammoth damask draperies outlined the doorways. The décor exuded a woman's touch, underscored by the porcelain bric-a-brac that appeared throughout and the chichi furniture. The overall effect was Victorian bourgeois (otherwise known at the time as *good taste*), however much that period look and somber formalities were actually slipping away. A foretaste of the new century was just a ring away: the household telephone number was 2144 Spr.

McFadden scattered paintings throughout. Most were positioned at eye level; in some cases, their placement seemed random. One notable exception was Thomas Gainsborough's representation of Henrietta Rodney in his portrait *Lady Rodney,* the collector's first acquisition (1893) and subsequently his most-prominently featured piece.[8] The painting took center stage in the library, the house's most luxurious room. Even with deference to Florence, the picture channeled her husband's first love (at least, pictorially).

The music room contained ten pictures: two by Hogarth, one by Reynolds, two by Raeburn, two by Hoppner, one by Harlow, and two by Romney. For good measure, a Steinway grand piano also found its way there, though there was no record that McFadden nor anyone else ever bothered with it.

The drawing room featured, as revealed in a family photograph, at least four (unidentifiable) landscape paintings. McFadden reserved the dining room for Henry Raeburn's *Master John Campbell of Saddell*, Gainsborough's *A Pastoral Landscape*, and Thomas Lawrence's *Miss Harriott West*. Hanging as a companion piece was what would become the ill-fated *Portrait of Miss Nelthorpe*. The pièce de résistance was J.M.W. Turner's *The Burning of the Houses of Lords and Commons*. A hall doorway was straddled by George Romney's *Lady Hamilton as Miranda*.

Other paintings were haphazardly scattered about: John Singleton Copley's *Portrait of George Beaumont, Esq.*; two "tall" pictures by 17th-century English court painter William Dobson; and two canvases by David Cox, *Going to the Hayfield* and *Girl Crossing a Rustic Bridge*. The drawing room was a repository for more than a half-dozen other works, including John Constable's *The Lock*; John Crome's *The Blacksmith Shop near Hingham, Norfolk*; and Romney's *Mrs. Champion de Crespigny*.

In a hall leading to the library, McFadden hung John Watson Gordon's *Sir Walter Scott*, Romney's *John Wesley*, Joshua Reynolds's *Edmund Burke*, and other like gems. In another hall was "a small landscape" by the Philadelphia artist Thomas Doughty (1793–1856).[9] In the library itself, not far from *Lady Rodney*, stood a prominently situated globe and stand, always a favorite conversation piece.[10]

Those who knew McFadden were not surprised that the Philadelphian also gave a nod to his French hero. A print of the

Emperor Napoleon's portrait hung over the marble fireplace and mirror in his master bedroom. Another anomaly was a print of *The Horse Fair* by the French artist Rosa Bonheur, an early purchase made in Liverpool.

As described by contemporary newspaper accounts and visible in family photographs, the arrangement was a work in progress. Time and time again, pictures ascribed to the formal collection eventually fell by the wayside. McFadden, meanwhile, was still actively scooping up canvases in London. Through the mid-teens, McFadden was creating not only a setting, but a mood. His pictures needed to harmonize.

Some years later, another visitor to 19th and Walnut, believed to be the ubiquitous and prolix arts writer Harvey Maitland Watts, noted how the paintings possessed "a certain eloquent memory of their friendly association with the collector in his own home amid the tasteful and sympathetic accessories of hangings, furniture, rugs, and all those 'personalia' that gave them their proper frame and made them live."[11]

The house doubled much as a museum—albeit a very private and peculiar one.

McFadden was not averse to seeing 19th and Walnut in this light. In fact he encouraged it, as he began to nurture inchoate plans to raise the public profile of his creation. How that would eventually play out was still several years away; it would not resolve until his association with the Pennsylvania Academy of the Fine Arts, in 1916, crystallized his mission. Meantime, McFadden was happy to entertain celebrity journalists, particularly New York-based scribes with national followings.

When the *American Art News* came calling in May 1912, McFadden scored an attention-getting coup. The weekly newspaper devoted almost three pages, about a third of the total publication, to "The John H. McFadden Collection," and included seven photographs. One, of Sir Henry Raeburn's *Lady Elibank*, was billboarded on the front page.

The famed art critic and friend, Philadelphia-born James Gibbons Huneker, a sometime visitor to 19th and Walnut, was also impressed with what McFadden had wrought—so much so that he honored his friend with a book dedication. That came in a 1913 first edition of *The Pathos of Distance: A Book of a Thousand and One Moments*: "To John Howard McFadden / A Lover of the Fine Arts."[12]

Stray visitors were also welcome—as long as they came from the Proper Philadelphia caste. And, hopefully, were able to advance the merits of the McFadden Collection by word of mouth. Philadelphian Edwin AtLee Barber, an expert on pottery and porcelain, eminently met that means test, especially since he was also the director of the Pennsylvania Museum and School of Industrial Art. Barber was no stranger to McFadden, who as a museum trustee had been a sitting duck for the director's entreaties for money and support. (Barber died suddenly in 1916.)

Both men were forthright in their professional relationship; neither was a shrinking violet. Barber would sometimes ask for outrageous sums, occasionally to facilitate museum purchases that he cared about. However, McFadden might not always be interested. Just as frequently as the heat-seeking barrage of appeals came in, McFadden was quick to bat them back. From "yes," to "maybe," McFadden finally learned "no."

But one of Barber's requests particularly grabbed McFadden's attention. The request was related to Barber's role as a founder of the Walpole Society, an élite men's society dedicated to the appreciation of American decorative art, architecture, and history. Barber had written in November 1913 to McFadden, then in Liverpool, asking if he could visit 19th and Walnut with "about a dozen" Walpole members participating in a national meeting in Philadelphia. Coming six months after the *American Art News* published its stellar review of his collection, the appeal seemed to McFadden an opportunity for further momentum.

Writing from Worsley House in Liverpool, the budding art promoter wrote, "I shall be only too pleased if you take them to the house, and I will write my son[13] to forward you a card for your friends and yourself."

McFadden's extra-artistic indulgence was a more private matter. His library was not mentioned in his will. Nor was his book collection mentioned in the few biographical sketches published on McFadden's life, let alone McFadden's specialty in an offbeat sub-genre, as a die-hard collector of Napoleania. Indeed, the library itself—the actual room, that is—was described only for the first time in a newspaper review in 1912.[14]

McFadden's passion for all things Napoleonic was fanned by a strange geographical intersection. In 1817, the recently deposed king of Spain, José I, had moved to Philadelphia. He was otherwise known as Joseph Bonaparte, Emperor Napoleon Bonaparte's older brother, who had ruled as King of Naples and Sicily before his unfortunate reign in Spain. In choosing his exile, Joseph deemed it prudent to distance himself from those who might want to do him harm. A sizeable French community clustered around Philadelphia, and Joseph decided to bide his time there. Among his possessions were jewels appropriated to finance his Philadelphia sojourn, and seventy volumes of the full works of Voltaire. The first-printing texts were rare, expensive, and a gift to Joseph by Napoleon himself. This meant they were known as "association" copies, vastly increasing their value.

Almost 100 years later, the cache of books, by way of a circuitous provenance, fell into the hands of John McFadden. Held in high regard as one of Philadelphia's premier art collectors, McFadden also entertained a lesser-known sideline as a collector of high-priced antiquarian books. The Voltaire compilation, known as the Beaumarchais Edition after the French polymath and publisher Pierre Beaumarchais, had been previously owned by two of Philadelphia's most prominent medical men. The first was Dr. Nathaniel Chapman, the founding president of the American Medical Association, who himself had received the tomes from the former king, then known as the Comte de Survilliers. Chapman's son, Dr. Henry Chapman, later acquired the texts, and it was his widow who sold the books to McFadden.

No purchase price was mentioned. But cost was a small matter.

The physical library was in fact unusual, having eight walls, something the newspaper called "a modified octagon." McFadden had cleverly modified a once-rectangular room with partitions, removing corners to create "five wall spaces." The library was McFadden's personal space, or what we would call a den. To reach the inner sanctum, a visitor would veer right in the entrance hall through what the homeowner called an antechamber, or reception room. His jewel in the crown, Thomas Gainsborough's *Lady Rodney*, claimed pride of place "in the center of the library, opposite the elaborate mantel." Lesser-cut jewels, near the Gainsborough, came in the form of pictures by Romney, Constable, and Crome. "The room is so handsomely proportioned and so well adapted to the canvases here displayed, that it might well have been designed for their reception."[15]

The interior décor was pure McFadden, dark and somewhat forbidding. Reporter Helen W. Henderson provided the following: "The walls are terra cotta, or Pompeiian red, in color, the lower parts lined with book cases in Flemish oak, with doors of leaded glass. There are rich rugs upon the floor and Chinese cushions in oriental colorings, restful and at the same time satisfying to the eye."[16]

As for the books lining the walls, many newer texts had uncut pages. McFadden was not a reader. He was a bookman first. He looked on his bibliographic gems much as he did his pictures, for their pleasing, visual appeal. Content was only a runner-up. So was appreciated value.

By the standards of the age, his book collection was not large. Only one bookcase, under the portrait of Lady Rodney, was depicted in a family photograph, maybe with enough room for some two hundred volumes. Given recorded evidence, other texts—as many as up to four hundred—must have been stored elsewhere. Despite its size, the collection was memorable for a studied quirkiness that spoke volumes about its owner. His books were pristine, and most had Morocco leather bindings. Some boasted full-levant bindings, book spines in rich colors gleaming behind the glass doors of book cabinets. Other volumes were printed on handmade paper, creating an intrinsic value not readily visible to the casual observer.

McFadden's books fell into several categories: many, by authors such as Mark Twain, Charles Dickens, Francis Parkman, and Lord Byron, were part of the canon in almost any well-stocked Victorian-era library. The collection differed in its emphasis on militaria, an unlikely genre for someone more attuned to admiring, in pictorial form, the genteel sensibilities of the British bourgeoisie. Besides accumulating dozens of memoirs by Napoleon and biographies about him, he also collected a stash of volumes by Bonaparte's battlefield nemesis, the First Duke of Wellington.

One specialty, important books with fine colored prints, appealed to his interest in eighteenth- and nineteenth-century British artists. McFadden's 1817 first edition of *The Vicar of Wakefield* by Oliver Goldsmith featured "delightful"[17] colored plates by Thomas Rowlandson, the late-eighteenth-century English illustrator and satirist. English caricaturist George Cruikshank contributed illustrations to more than a dozen other volumes. McFadden's sixty-volume edition of *The Works of Charles Dickens*, illustrated by this nineteenth-century artist, was nonpareil. "A handsomer set of Dickens cannot be had," declared Stanislaus Vincent Henkels, a bookseller, collector, and auctioneer who produced, in 1923, a McFadden book catalogue, the only known record of the Philadelphian's collection.

McFadden's interest in yachting showed up in a three-volume set, *Yacht Register, Lloyd's Register of British and Foreign Shipping,* with colored plates of flags for 1900, 1902, and 1904.

We have no way to know what prompted McFadden to add a certain four-volume set to his collection: *The Bibliomania; or, Book-Madness; Containing Some Account of the History, Symptoms, and Cure of This Fatal Disease,* an 1809 treatise by the Reverend Thomas Frognall Dibdin, an English bibliographer. Dibdin sounded a cautionary note, believing readers of his tome could "either suppress or soften the ravages of so destructive a malady." McFadden's set, one of 583 copies printed in Boston in 1903, was a full-levant edition in slipcases. McFadden apparently evaded "book-madness" himself, as the pages were uncut.

What was missing, as the Henkels catalogue made plain, was any reference to McFadden's other enthusiasms in medical science, exploration, and art history. The cotton industry was also pointedly ignored.

McFadden sought books of quality and of high value. First editions, privately printed editions, and limited editions ranked high. The Beaumarchais edition of Voltaire's works, according to Henkels, was "the most complete and beautiful edition of the works of the great Frenchman and best arranged of all."

No evidence suggested that McFadden ever parted with any book once it entered his collection. The entire assembly was believed to be intact at his death, and when it was sold at auction by Henkels in 1923. Henkels was given to notoriously florid descriptions, some drafted in a convoluted, broken English, which also characterized his auction catalogues. Henkels titled the McFadden catalogue "Magnificent Books from the Library of the Late John H. McFadden, of Phila." "Sumptuous bindings" were on offer. Books were "extra-illustrated."

Other than McFadden's purchase of the Voltaire Beaumarchais edition from Dr. Henry Chapman's widow, there is little information to shed light on how McFadden had assembled his collection. Henkels likely figured in the mix. McFadden had an account at a bookseller named Champion & Co. in Philadelphia. A paper trail has also led to A.S.W. Rosenbach, who operated the legendary Rosenbach Company at 2008 Delancey Street, not far from Rittenhouse Square. Son Jack was a Rosenbach patron.

FROM THE SECOND floor of 19th and Walnut, the McFaddens had a bountiful south-facing view of Rittenhouse Square. The square was still configured in its original form, with a parade running on a north-south axis, an interior oval path, and a circular outer walkway. If McFadden looked right from his window, he would see the neo-Romanesque-styled Church of the Holy Trinity, the square's spiritual anchor. Otherwise, mammon and its acolytes were spread before him.

His neighbors bore such stellar names as Drexel, Wanamaker, Cassatt, Lippincott, Pepper, and Van Rensselaer.[18] McFadden would tip his silk top hat to his neighbor across 19th Street, one Algernon Sydney Roberts, Jr. These Rittenhouse stalwarts formed a tableau of mercantile princes and captains of industry. At work, they networked in a web of crony capitalism. At home on Rittenhouse Square, they enjoyed the luxuries of Proper Philadelphia.

Out of a city population in 1900 of about 1.3 million, fewer than 60,000, or about one-half percent, lived within the confines of Center City, river to river, Vine to Pine. Even fewer lived, of course, within the immediate Rittenhouse Square quarter,[19] the city's redoubt of wealth and power.

Historian E. Digby Baltzell remarked on this axis: "At no other time in the city's history, before or since, have so many wealthy and fashionable families lived so near one another."[20] Proper Philadelphian William C. Bullitt, who served as ambassador to France during the administration of Franklin D. Roosevelt, elevated the square to even more exalted status. In his novel about an early-twentieth-century Rittenhouse Square family, *It's Not Done*, published in 1926, Bullitt mused, "Is there any other city of a million in the world in which everyone who counts lives in an area three streets by eight surrounding a Sacred Square?"[21]

JOHN'S BROTHER GEORGE Henry also moved to Rittenhouse Square, with his wife, Emily, and their three children: George; Ella L., the middle child; and Barclay, the youngest. For several years before, they had been living west of Broad Street at 1428 Walnut Street, after moving from 2044 Chestnut Street. Many years later, Ella recollected this period, in the early years of 1900, in an unpublished memoir. By the time she transcribed her remembrances, Ella, who went by the family nickname Ellie, was Mrs. Edward "Ned" Browning. Ellie summed up her days at 1428 Walnut Street as a time of idyllic innocence, a variant of the *Life with Father* domestic tale.

"The house was the center of all the gaiety of George's friends and mine. We had friends there day and night. 'Pink Teas' we called them, in the front parlor, as we sat in window seats looking out the window. Next door was Mrs. Wm. Thomson's older daughter who had been divorced. As children we would point to her out the window and say, 'There goes Mrs. Roberts. She's divorced.' At the time it was something unique to be divorced."

Ellie's recollection of her family's frequent trips to Europe, more like extravagant cavalcades including friends and her father's associates, added context and texture to her memories of wealth and privilege. Even though she was in her late teens, and certainly aware of her special circumstances, Ellie's breathless description of her family's lifestyle never suggests that she perceived a less advantaged world outside her Proper Philadelphia cocoon.

Approaching her twenty-seventh year during one European summer trip in 1904, Ellie was perilously close to spinsterhood. Everyone, she admitted, called her "Plain Jane."

"We went to England, as usual, and crossed by Channel steamer to France. On the steamer were Ned Browning, my future husband, and his friend Sam Bell, who were going to Paris after a coaching trip through England and Scotland. [Ned] had invited seven guests to go over to England to take this trip with him. These two older men [Ned and Sam] talked to me during the crossing, and I was very much flattered by their attention."

Flattered? Actually, Ned had met his match. Despite an air of bewitching naïveté, Ellie was no fresh-faced gamine. By journey's end, no one would have been surprised if Ellie was already secretively planning nuptials.

How rich were the George H. McFaddens, their Rittenhouse circle, and by extension John McFadden, was laid bare in a memoir by R. Sturgis Ingersoll, who was a contemporary of the younger McFaddens. Like Ellie, he, too, appeared blissfully unaware of his privilege, blithely categorizing the costs of the Philadelphia good life. A modest one at that, he claimed.

Ingersoll used his mother-in-law, one Mrs. Fowle, as a model of sensible frugality. Though she was described by newspapers as the "fabulously rich" Mrs. Fowle, she was "always amused" by this reference, according to Ingersoll. Actually, she was budget-minded, and had to make do with only the $20,000 annually ($556,000 today) she inherited from her father. That meant, no yachts, no polo ponies, and no substantive art collecting, Ingersoll opined. But it did mean that his mother-in-law was able to maintain her principal house on Clinton Street, near the Pennsylvania Hospital; a country place near West Chester, in the Philadelphia environs; three servants; a Pierce-Arrow and chauffeur; a European vacation each summer; and French haute couturier fashions. (Her favorite was the House of Worth in Paris.)[22] Such was the hardship.

Servants were plentiful. They were almost always female, Irish, and Catholic. The most recent immigrants from Donegal and Cork, dewy-eyed and reverentially hopeful, would line up at local employment offices awaiting placement. The going rate was between $4 ($111 today) and $6 ($167) per week, depending on experience. Ingersoll's father always recommended large kitchens "so the servants won't fall over each other."

A fully operational household, such as John McFadden's at 19th and Walnut, would require, at a minimum, a cook; a "waitress," or server; and several parlor maids and chambermaids. Their uniforms matched the formality of their employers' dress. They were all required to wear the same outfit: a long black dress trimmed with a white Peter Pan collar; a white apron; and a white, bell-shaped cap. If the servant was well received in a household, the lady of the house would grant them her greatest compliment, "a delightful Irish girl." (Ellie McFadden could be equally patronizing. She called the family nurse, who cared for her young brother Barclay, "old Annie.")

John McFadden put Mrs. Fowle's income to shame. In a good year, each of the McFadden brothers/partners would draw about $220,000 ($6.1 million today). Florence could have her pick in household help. For his part, John was served by his valet, Potts, and he kept a yacht. Of course, a sizable fraction of his income also went to maintaining his multi-million-dollar art collection.

CHAPTER NINE

Pater Familias

1909–1917

OTHER FAMILY MATTERS CONSUMED the newly transplanted Philadelphian's time and attention. The transition from Liverpudlian to Philadelphian went more quickly than McFadden had anticipated. There was no accounting for love: budding romances of two of his children, Alice and Philip, turned serious. Engagements soon followed, and McFadden's attention turned to fatherly duties.

Alice and Philip married their spouses three years apart, and they remained close in subsequent years.

Alice, in 1909, was twenty-six years old, six years younger than her cousin Ellie McFadden, who had already married Ned Browning. As her own spinsterhood approached, Alice wanted to follow her female cousin up the aisle. Alice's fiancé was Jasper Yeates Brinton, a thirty-one-year-old scion of another prominent Rittenhouse household. He was also an "attorney-at-law," as he listed himself on his marriage license application. In less formal circles, Brinton was also known as "a prominent clubman."[1] Alice left her own "occupation" line blank. But in the press, she was styled as "prominent in society and amateur theatricals."

The bride's mother, Florence McFadden, undoubtedly had her hands full in wedding planning. Especially since the prospective bride and groom set a wedding date in the midst of the Christmas season, scheduling their nuptials for December 28, 1909. Lightening the planning angst, the marriage site, the Church of the Holy Trinity, stood just a stone's-throw away. The staid *eminence grise*, the square's religious cornerstone, was just catty-corner to the McFadden house at the "N.E. Cor." of 19th and Walnut Streets. The wedding's officiant, the church's fifth rector, the Reverend Floyd W. Tomkins, was also well known to the bride-to-be and her family. Jasper's elder brother, Dr. Ward Brinton, a physician, was best man.

There was no indication that John's aged mother, Charlotte, attended, and she probably remained at the McFaddens' Jersey Shore "cottage," where she lived. (She died on March 12, 1910, at the age of ninety-seven.)

To everyone's delight—and, no doubt, relief—the event was proclaimed "one of the smartest weddings that society has witnessed for some time...."[2] It was also one of the shortest, from 4 to 4:30 p.m. (Presumably, no time-consuming sacramental Mass was performed.) When the ceremony wrapped up, the bride and groom returned to the McFadden house across the street. Guests could not help but admire the floral décor of "beautiful" white lilies and American Beauty roses scattered "here and there" in high silver vases.

Alice adopted Jasper's brownstone at 1423 Spruce Street, settling in as lady of the house in their shared home. The first order of business: Servants needed to be vetted and hired. The up-and-coming lawyer became a successful one, soon becoming a trusted legal counsel to his father-in-law John. Alice followed up with customary social affiliations, joining the Acorn Club and the Colonial Dames of America, the two most blue-blooded of Philadelphia's women's societies. Other family routines were upended. According to *Town & Country's* reporting on such matters, soon after their marriage, Alice started spending summers away from London and Kent, where the senior McFaddens usually summered *en famille*. As proof, the society magazine's investigative reporter breathlessly revealed sighting the Brintons lolling beachside in Cape May, New Jersey, during the summer of 1911.

Five years later, Alice gave birth to Florence's and John's first grandchild, John Brinton. The newborn's parents were still summering at the beach—this time in and around Newport, Rhode Island. The infant was born in Providence. Alice's and Jasper's subsequent child, Florence Pamela Brinton, was born during the winter of 1918, in Philadelphia.

PHILIP'S COURTSHIP OF New York debutante Annette Buckley was swift. Philip had spent his bachelorhood in New York, having been assigned, at twenty-three, to Geo. H. McFadden & Bro.'s Wall Street office at 56 Beaver Street. As an Oxford University graduate, a poloist, and a rich merchant, he fell in easily with New York's somewhat louche élite, who were then populating Fifth Avenue and the Upper East Side. Annette's father, architect Richard W. Buckley, had been responsible for the design of much of the upper crust's new residences as they resettled from their former digs around Washington Square. Popular with the Vanderbilts and others in New York's 400 orbit, Buckley also lived within the new fiefdom, then forming as a larger version of Rittenhouse Square. Its green space was Central Park. The Buckley family, including Annette, lived in a five-floor townhouse at 18 East 82nd Street.

Philip, then thirty-four, married Annette on April 11, 1912 at her divorced mother's house on East 73rd Street. Annette never

gave up living in New York, and Philip never gave up ties to Philadelphia. He listed his Pembroke College, Oxford, affiliation on
an application as a non-resident member to the University Club
in Philadelphia. He also maintained a non-resident pied-à-terre
at 1510 Walnut Street, a block away from his Uncle George's
house at No. 1428.

That proximity between uncle and nephew only lasted
until the fall of 1912, when the George McFaddens moved to
a fifty-five-year-old Italianate villa at the northeast corner
of 18th and Spruce Streets. The place was distinctive, noted
Charles Joseph Cohen, writing in *Rittenhouse Square: Past and
Present*, for its wood-framed construction, in contrast to the
Rittenhouse Square vernacular of brick or stone. McFadden
"made extensive improvements, resulting in an attractive mansion," Cohen reported.[3]

WITH THE MARRIAGES of two of his children behind him, Mc-
Fadden's attention turned to his youngest, John Junior, or, as he
was better known, Jack. Attention became concern. What he
had been reading about Jack in *The Philadelphia Inquirer*[4] drew
his displeasure. A year after graduation from the University of
Pennsylvania in 1913, the twenty-four-year-old had taken up
with a Miss Fachierl of London, and they had both spent a good
part of the early summer of 1914 in Jamestown, Rhode Island.
The couple had now returned to Philadelphia, where, instead of
taking separate suites, the lovers scandalously shared a suite at
the Bellevue-Stratford Hotel.

The pair had intended to sail to Europe on August 11, but,
following the outbreak of the war, the trip was postponed, *The
Inquirer* told its gossip-hungry readers. Uncle George provided
a temporary solution to the young lovers' residential plight. He
offered them his country seat, Barclay Farm in Villanova, if

they wanted it. They did. Two months later, Miss Fachierl was no longer in the picture.

Officially, at this time, Jack had already joined the firm. But in October, three months after France became embroiled in World War I, Jack took another rebellious turn: he enlisted in the American Field Service (A.F.S.), a front-line volunteer organization that served with French forces. Many young Ivy Leaguers were doing the same. Their enlistment was considered selfless and idealistic, and the A.F.S.'s recruiting materials were somewhat maudlin. An institutional history published in 1920, to which Jack contributed, was dedicated "To Our Mothers."

Once in France, Jack helped found the A.F.S.'s Ambulance Corps, later made famous by Ernest Hemingway in *A Farewell to Arms*. Although the American volunteers were officially non-combatants, ambulance driving was dangerous, especially at night. The hazards were made worse, Jack stated, by "the difficulties of starting from the top of that hill with a car full of wounded and driving down a narrow hillside road in a blackness impenetrable for more than a yard."

In early 1916, he returned to Philadelphia to raise funds, and he was steered to the Huntington Valley Country Club, one of his father's many watering holes, to address a dinner meeting there. Before he could complete his talk, a club member interrupted, "I will give an ambulance."⁵ By the end of the night, he walked away with money for four more. Earlier in the week he had similar success at the Philadelphia Cricket Club. In all, during his six weeks at home, he raised funds for nineteen ambulances. Unrestricted cash also flowed in from a day of fundraising on Wall Street.

To the *Evening Ledger*, Jack was a self-effacing hero. "It's remarkable how a young man…has stuck to his work, and what splendid work it is," the newspaper reported. A Penn alumni magazine gushed, "Personally, we think the University ought to be, and is, quite proud of this young man, and sends with him its best wishes for his personal safety in the war zone."[6]

When the United States entered the war in 1917, John and Florence could only be marginally relieved. With the rank of an Army captain, Jack found relative safety as a military attaché posted to the American Embassy in Paris. For his overall service, he was awarded the French Legion of Honor.

JACK DEFERRED ENTERING the family firm, even after the war ended in 1918. His was going to be a military life, at least for the time being. He was following in the "boot-steps" of his uncle J. Franklin.

Frank was nominally a senior partner in Geo. McFadden & Bro., though he was the brother unrecognized in the company's title. Everyone knew that the "Bro." referred to John. Frank returned the favor. Well before the turn of the century, he was spending as little time on company affairs as he could. Instead he burnished his credentials as a regular at the Philadelphia Club and by dedicating himself to racquetball and polo.

As a member of the Philadelphia and the Bryn Mawr polo clubs, he brandished a respectable, internationally recognized 3 handicap. Brother George Henry merited a 5-goal ranking from the United States Polo Association, placing him as one of the top players nationally. From time to time, George and Frank played together, or against each other, at home and at away matches, often at Narragansett, Rhode Island, and on Long Island.

Frank and brother John were Radnor Hunt members. Frank fox hunted; John partook of the club's other, less horsey amenities. Frank also belonged (oddly enough, as the least cerebral of the three brothers) to the Athenaeum (established 1814), a private library on Washington Square. No record indicates that he ever showed up.

One honor that came Frank's way was ironically associated with the family firm: he was appointed Japan's honorary consul in Philadelphia. Later, the Emperor of Japan conferred upon him the Order of the Rising Sun of the Fifth, or Officers', Class.

Frank married Mary Adèle Lewis, daughter of a local lawyer, Silas Weir Lewis, on April 18, 1888. Frank and Adèle, as she preferred to be called, had been next-door neighbors on Spruce Street: Frank at No. 1932; Adèle at No. 1928. Their wedding in Philadelphia, according to city records, was officiated by a Louis K. Lewis, an Episcopal priest who had been serving at the time at St. Peter's Church in Medford, North Dakota. (His relationship with them is unknown.) The couple moved to 321 South 17th Street. In 1894, according to the *Blue Book*, Philadelphia's society manual, the couple resided at 1836 Delancey Street, once the house that the City of Philadelphia granted as a grace-and-favor residence to the Civil War general George Meade.

Like George, Frank was dashing and handsome, and he got better looking as he aged. He had an athletic build, which he had maintained since his undergraduate years at Penn. He had excelled at sports there, prominently on the football team. His Big-Man-On-Campus popularity was such that in his senior year, in 1882, he was elected treasurer of the University Athletic Association. Loyal to Penn's Quakers, he retained annual box seats at Penn's football stadium, Franklin Field.

Of the three brothers, Frank was the most beholden to the rituals that shaped and upheld Proper Philadelphia's vision of High Society. *The New York Times* recorded that Frank's daughter, Katherine, was the only one among the three McFadden daughters (the others being George's Ellie and John's Alice) to be presented as a debutante. Frank's and Adèle's only child was just about two weeks short of her nineteenth birthday at her coming-out ball in January 1908, held at the city's most fashionable Bellevue-Stratford Hotel. (George Widener's Ritz-Carlton Hotel had not yet been built.) Rittenhouse Square strutted.

"Miss McFadden, who wore a gown of white satin made in empire style and trimmed with lace, received the guests with her mother, who wore a gown of pale yellow satin trimmed with point lace. The guests comprised all the season's debutantes and the younger men," the *Times* reported.

Frank's greatest interest was in soldiering. Even in the late 1890s as Geo. H. McFadden & Bro. reached its greatest success, with George managing the Philadelphia office and John in Liverpool, Frank was conspicuously elsewhere: specifically, in Puerto Rico where he served during the Spanish-American War. He was mustered into Army service in 1898, and, after the war's first year, never looked back. His commission as a second lieutenant in a mounted unit, the First Troop Philadelphia City Cavalry, was well suited. His experience as a horseman came in handy. Equally important, the First Troop, Proper Philadelphia's military alter ego, allowed Frank to cut the Society rug while even in uniform. (Many of the Troop's uniforms were bespoke numbers from Brooks Brothers' Philadelphia branch.)

The First Troop seemed particularly well tasked in putting down civil unrest. Frank joined a swath of other prominent Philadelphians, among them Cadwaladers, Madeiras, Ingersolls, Markoes, and Whartons, in confronting workers and unionists in what the University of Pennsylvania's alumni magazine, *Old Penn*, gingerly called "disturbances." They were, of course, riots. From 1892 to 1902, as part of the Pennsylvania National Guard, the First Troop saw action in a series of violent encounters with organized labor in Homestead, Hazleton, Tamaqua, and in Panther Creek Valley, northwest of Philadelphia.

Frank hung up his spurs and McClellan saddle after a tour on the U.S.-Mexican border, resigning from the troop in 1917. Even after thirty years of service, capping his troop membership as captain, the group's highest rank, Frank's military mission was not done. At the ripe age of fifty-five, Frank, now an Army major, quickly segued to the war front in France. A year later, he was mustered out as a lieutenant colonel.

Frank was a Philadelphia paragon of the era's gentleman sportsman-soldier. This WASP virtue was widely popularized nationally by the exploits of Yale man and poloist Tommy Hitchcock, who had made a name for himself in the volunteer Escadrille Lafayette, a French flying squadron during World War I. Later Hitchcock went on to play high-goal polo on Long Island, in a Gatsby-like social swirl.

When winding down his military career, Frank found time to sever his ties with the family firm. Shortly thereafter, he and his son-in-law, Harold Aymar Sands, Katherine's husband, established a competing cotton trading firm, McFadden, Sands & Co. According to *Old Penn*,[7] the once unrecognized partner at Geo. H. McFadden & Bro. was now the new company's "senior member." Frank finally had his name on the door.

CHAPTER TEN

Hero

I N 1903, THE ANTARCTIC explorer Ernest H. Shackleton made his way safely to London after a harrowing, unsuccessful mission to reach the South Pole. He was alone. He had returned a year earlier than expected; he was weary and debilitated. Other Discovery Expedition members landed in England on time in 1904; their effort, too, a failure.

Shackleton's premature arrival home did not bode well for his reputation. Almost immediately, charges of personal weakness befell him; the public ridiculed him as a slacker.

In ironic contrast, six years later in 1909, after completing another arduous—and this time successful—voyage to the South Pole region, Shackleton was received with spirited fanfare in Britain and around the world. Admirers hailed his courage, fortitude, and the honor he brought to king and country. All was forgiven. He was knighted by King Edward VII, dubbed "Sir Ernest." He had become a flesh-and-blood marvel. In the ensuing years, his exploits played out on the world stage, including in fundraising and publicity tours in the United States and Canada.

Wherever he went, his celebrity would be equivalent, in a contemporary sense, to that of a moon-landing astronaut.

Among the heartiest celebrants of Shackleton's success in 1909 was John McFadden. Early in Shackleton's preparations for the 1907–1909 Antarctic journey, McFadden had gambled a sizeable sum on the adventurer's second effort. The Philadelphian's faith in Shackleton had been borne out. The explorer had just predicted that "honor and recognition" might come his way. What he had not expected was glory.

———— ✕ ————

A LARGE, STANDING globe in a conspicuous corner of McFadden's book-lined library was suggestive of the Philadelphian's modern worldview. It was a world, geographically speaking, of adventure. It was a world claimed by the hearty, brave, and few. It was one, as enjoined by the family motto his grandfather Samuel McFadden brought among his immigration papers, governed by "A Strong Hand Uppermost."

For McFadden, there was no better personification of the hero-explorer than Shackleton. That he also embodied English virtue and perseverance just made a stronger case. Lord Curzon, president of the Royal Geographical Society, framed Shackleton's commitment, in a letter to the adventurer, in jingoistic terms. "…[T]hat it is the work worthy to be taken in hand cannot be doubted; that it ought to be undertaken by an Englishman is to me quite clear, and that of living Englishmen you are the best fitted by training, knowledge, experience and prestige to carry it to a successful issue…."[1] Animated by an Anglophilia that shared those prejudices, McFadden might well have echoed Curzon's ode to English *invictus*.

As markings on the globe made clear, Sir Ernest was not alone among McFadden's dare-devil heroes. Other polar explorers infatuated him. Sites of Vilhjalmur Stefansson's encounters in the Arctic were pinpointed. McFadden also followed Admiral Robert Peary Sr.'s North Pole expedition in 1909, tracing the journey every step of the way. At the South Pole, in 1911, Captain Roald Amundsen became the first to reach that mythic site. The Norwegian was recognized by another pin. Finally, Sir Ernest, an Amundsen rival, was given his due for being the first to set foot at the Antarctic Magnetic Pole. Like any fan, McFadden was also interested in autographs—at least to the extent of applying facsimile signatures of the four explorers at appropriately corresponding spots on the globe.

ON APRIL 12, 1917, McFadden was working from the family firm's office at 56 Beaver Street in New York.

A telegram addressed to him arrived from San Francisco.

"ONE NIGHT IN PHILADELPHIA AM WELL BUT TIRED"[2]

The signature read, "SHACKLETON."

Back in Philadelphia, McFadden prepared a return missive, a Western Union Night Letter dated April 19, to the St. Francis Hotel, where the explorer was staying. He confirmed, "my plans seeing you care Geographical Society."

Shackleton had not forgotten McFadden's support and largesse on his successful 1909 mission. He visited Philadelphia on at least five occasions from 1910 to 1918. His current mission involved fundraising to defray debts and, since Britain's entry in World War I in 1914, to "fan the rising war-spirit"[3] on behalf of the British military effort. To McFadden's delight, Shackleton was also always ready to present him with trinkets memorializing his polar achievements.

In 1910, on February 5, a year after his return from the South Pole, the Philadelphia Geographical Society had provided Shackleton with a "great and hearty audience." The evening was "illustrated" by "moving pictures" and slides, according to the society's *Bulletin*.

The Briton later continued his tour west and north, as far as Montreal. Lady Emily Shackleton remained in Philadelphia, the guest of Mr. and Mrs. Craige Lippincott, president of publishing firm J.B. Lippincott Company. "He left her there in all the luxury that wealth and taste enable cultured Americans to provide," according to a Shackleton biographer.[4] On his return to Philadelphia, Shackleton joined his wife for several more days of luxury and culture at the Lippincotts' Rittenhouse Square mansion. (About a year later, their 64-year-old host shot and killed himself at the same premises, at 218 West Rittenhouse Square.)[5]

The Geographical Society singled out McFadden as one of Shackleton's "many friends" in the city—maybe even the Briton's local favorite. During the 1910 tour, McFadden might have found time to entertain Emily Shackleton. He certainly had the opportunity to wade into a heavy tome, a picture book of the 1909 expedition, titled *Aurora Australis*, that the explorer had given him. The inscription, written in Shackleton's careful, schoolboy-like script, filled a full page.[6]

> To John Howard McFadden
> with kindest wishes from
> its Editor Ernest Shackleton.

He also inked a formal signature: "Ernest H. Shackleton," followed by his rank, "Commander, B.A.E. [British Antarctic Expedition] 1907–09." The volume was authenticated as "the only book of its kind."

> As stated the following pages
> Every bit of this book was
> made, written, and produced
> in the Antarctic during the
> long months and this
> is the only book of its kind
> ever produced in the Polar Region.

Sometime later, McFadden received some more weighty, late-night reading: Shackleton's two-volume memoir of the 1907–1909 expedition, *The Heart of the Antarctic*.[7] The pair had just shared an Atlantic crossing from Liverpool to New York, in first-class accommodations on the *Mauretania*. The journey took five days, three hours, and twenty-seven minutes, docking at New York on March 28, 1913. The first volume was inscribed somewhat coolly, "To John Howard McFadden with kindest wishes from the author, Ernest Shackleton. March 1913." The second volume inscription showed more warmth: "To my friend John Howard McFadden whose interest in Science and sympathy towards Exploration has prompted me to inflict these heavy volumes on him. Ernest Shackleton. March 1913."

This gift followed a formidable coup by the Philadelphia Geographical Society. The group had arranged for the "Three Polar Stars"—"Captain Roald Amundsen, Rear Admiral Robert E. Peary, and Sir Ernest H. Shackleton," as they were referred to formally in publicity materials—to appear jointly at the Academy of Music. The white-tie affair, on January 16, 1913, was the trio's first-ever joint public meeting. A standing globe, behind which they had lectured, later served as a backdrop in a series of photographs.

The "intrepid and modest"[8] Amundsen was the keynote speaker. Henry G. Bryant, the society's president, presided over the "historic" occasion that brought together "the only living men who had been at the opposite ends of the world." It was a fortuitous, *carpe-diem* moment for McFadden to acquire the authentic autographs he always sought.

Amundsen had arrived earlier in the day, on January 16, to address an afternoon gathering at the Art Club of Philadelphia. McFadden, the club's president, was eager for Shackleton to attend, and had arranged for the thirty-nine-year-old explorer, fourteen years his junior, to settle in at 19th and Walnut. Six days before, Shackleton had arrived at Broad Street Station from New York. He was pronounced by a *Philadelphia Inquirer* reporter as "pleasant-faced... youthful-looking," and with "the poise of naval training...."[9] McFadden's favorite adventurer, who was indeed a Royal Navy commander, then dashed the short distance to the Philadelphian's "palatial" Rittenhouse townhouse.[10]

Accompanied by his patron, Shackleton visited Amundsen at the Bellevue-Stratford Hotel, at 200 South Broad Street. His Norwegian rival had already announced in a press interview his intention to lead another expedition. This time, to the North Pole. Shackleton was already formulating plans to head south again, but he remained mum. After this less-than-candid hotel encounter, Shackleton and McFadden stopped briefly at the nearby Art Club to ensure that all was ready for the upcoming Amundsen lecture.

That evening, after the Geographical Society's presentation, McFadden and Sir Ernest returned to 19th and Walnut. Shackleton was still coy, telling the persistent *Inquirer* reporter, who remained in tow through the day, that he had "something of importance to announce," and would only do so when he returned to Philadelphia in about two weeks.

Shackleton extended his stay in Philadelphia for several additional days,[11] and surely McFadden showed the Briton his festooned library globe. Like his art collection, it was also always on the house tour.

True to his word, Shackleton was back in Philadelphia in less than a month, on February 5, 1913. This time, the Geographical

Society arranged for a smaller venue. Its choice was Wither-
spoon Hall, a chamber often used for graduation ceremonies
in a building of the same name at 1319 Walnut Street. Shackleton's talk included "moving pictures as well as lantern slides
and charts of the region traversed." It did not include any reve-
lations of the mysterious "something of importance."

That came in a *Public Ledger* scoop later in February. The report was unwelcome by McFadden, and he let it be known.

In a letter dated January 19, McFadden had confided in Edwin AtLee Barber,[12] the Pennsylvania Museum's director, that
he had planned a "surprise" loan. McFadden was an influential
museum trustee; formalities were dispensed with. He wrote
(with fuzzy spelling), "I have the greatest surprise for you and
I think a pleasant one: Sir Earnest Shackleton, the An-Artic
explorer has given me the finest collection in the world of geo-
logical specimens gathered during search for the South Pole.
They are too numerous to mention here, but I propose to give
them to the Museum...."[13]

In March, writing from Liverpool,[14] McFadden detailed the
trove. He began affably, "We have a magnificent specimen of a
White Seal, Penguins and other birds, and a young Emperor Penguin, and any amount of eggs and sponges of various growth,
bombs which have been thrown up a distance of 18 miles out of
Mount Erebus,[15] any amount of rocks and this is going to make
one of the most attractive [exhibits] ever sent to America and [it
is] going to be a great advertisement...."

He then went on to scold Barber for the *Public Ledger* leak.
"[B]ut," he continued, "do not do anything whatever in the way of
advertising until I see you, as it was very unfortunate that this
ever got into the newspaper, so do not let it get there again."

By return mail, Barber defended himself forthrightly. He
could have backed away from confronting the powerful trustee, one he also counted on for financial support. He did not. "I
had nothing to do with the matter," he declared. "On the con-

trary, I strongly advised that it should not appear until after you had been consulted, and I [understood] that the matter would be referred to you, and supposed that it had been." He added a zinger: "I strongly doubted the advisability of making a premature announcement, but when I found the notice had appeared, I supposed it was [with] your sanction."

The dustup ended there.

In April 1913, the *S.S. Mackinaw* sailed into the Port of Philadelphia with the first of several shipments. The crates included everything that McFadden had previously cited, and more exotica: moss, grass, and shrubs; insect specimens; flowers; minerals; forty-six "magnificent" photographs, including several of "a big glacier that blocks the way to the South Pole"; "numerous jars of alcoholic specimens"; "twenty-eight species of invertebrates from South Victoria Land and New Zealand," and one of Shackleton's overland sleds. For customs purposes, a "nominal value" of £100 ($11,200 today) was placed on the lot.

A local writer, Charles Franklin Warwick, who turned to journalism after a stint as Philadelphia's mayor from 1895 to 1899, had high praise for the "very valuable," one-off collection, which would appeal especially to "naturalists and mineralogists." The journalist J. St. George Joyce weighed in. Of the "magnificent" photographs in the "superb collection," he opined, many were of "the giant glaciers and wide expanses of ice that mark the frozen deep around the southern extremity of the world."[16]

As McFadden traveled across the Atlantic, Barber arranged that the items be sorted, categorized, and readied for display before "we throw it up to the public." Everything was "now spread on tables in a locked room," he told McFadden. A May 1913 opening was scheduled. For his part, McFadden seemed pleased with the progress, but reminded Barber, somewhat sternly, that according to Shackleton's "conditions," the exhibit be labeled, "Shackleton Collection Loaned by John H. McFadden." As if Barber would forget.

On June 23, in a letter to Barber written while at sea, Mc-
Fadden showed growing anxiety about the exhibit's public
reception. The cause for his concern is uncertain. But he likely wanted to provide, indeed to *impress* Shackleton with a
successful turnout and expression of acclaim in Philadelphia.
In a sharp turnabout from his previous command that Barber
stay mum, McFadden was eager for widespread promotion. "I
am rather anxious to read the account of the same [publicity]
that you had published in the newspapers and hear from you
personally the interest that it has created in the city." McFadden
expected a blockbuster. Barber, in a letter on June 28, let him
down gently. "While a great many people have been interested in the collection, it does not appear to have drawn unusual
crowds," Barber related.

As the exhibit was winding down, Barber found McFadden
surprisingly amenable, in October 1914, to loaning a key piece,
the explorer's sled, to the Oakland Public Museum in California. The loan was open-ended. The sled would return when the
museum was through with it. McFadden had, moreover, placed
only two conditions on the loan, that the California museum
pay all expenses and "protect it [the sled] in every way possible."

What had been a loan to the Pennsylvania Museum became,
in February 1915, a gift to the Academy of Natural Sciences. The
academy, to its surprise, received everything.[17]

IN MAY 1913, in the early months of the Shackleton collection's
display in Philadelphia, Sir Ernest and McFadden and their
wives met in New York. John and Florence planned to spend
June and July in London and at their house in Kent, as was their
custom. The Shackletons were also returning to England, and
the two families had decided to share the sea voyage. As part

The Adelphi Hotel, Liverpool's finest, was the John McFadden family's first residence when they moved from Philadelphia to England's premier port and cotton trading city. This view, above, dates from 1881, the same year McFadden ventured to Liverpool to establish the first overseas branch of Geo. H. McFadden & Bro.

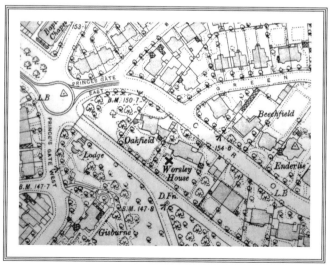

From the Adelphi Hotel, the McFaddens moved to a residence in the posh Prince's Park district of Liverpool. The estate was titled Worsley House (seen here marked by an X). The place suited Florence McFadden. It was big enough for her growing family and a contingent of live-in servants.

No. 57.—Mr. JOHN H. McFADDEN.

Cartoon image of John McFadden, in his sartorial finery, depicts him as an eminent Liverpool cotton trader. It was said that McFadden was one of the most fashionably attired traders. His cigar was usually unlighted. Liverpool artist J. Wallace Coop drew this cartoon as part of a series. Because of its alphabetical listing, McFadden wound up as No. 57.

John McFadden's house was located on the north side of Rittenhouse Square, not far from the Church of the Holy Trinity. McFadden simply called the place "19th and Walnut" after the intersection where it was located.

McFadden razed "19th and Walnut" and built The Wellington in its place. It was only the second high-rise building on Rittenhouse Square and as such was a controversial addition to the square's residential environment. The building housed a hotel, as well as residential apartments. McFadden lived on the top floors, surrounded by his art treasures.
CONTEMPORARY VIEW COURTESY OF WRITERS-CLEARINGHOUSE

Billy Goat, *a sculpture by the local artist Albert Laessle, was donated by Eli Kirk Price II, an eminent Proper Philadelphian. It wound up in the southwest corner of Rittenhouse Square, where it has entertained children over many generations.*
CONTEMPORARY VIEW COURTESY OF WRITERS-CLEARINGHOUSE

Left: George H. McFadden was John's elder brother and the senior partner of Geo. H. McFadden & Bro. He presided over the family business from its head office in Philadelphia. REPRODUCTION OF PORTRAIT BY HUGH H. BRECKENRIDGE COURTESY OF JOHN H. MCFADDEN

Right: The youngest of the McFadden brothers was J. Franklin McFadden. Though a partner in Geo. H. McFadden & Bro. and a beneficiary of its financial rewards, Frank had little interest otherwise in the family firm. Polo and his career as a cavalryman came first.

The influential gallery owner Lockett Agnew was John McFadden's art whisperer in London. McFadden bought almost all of the paintings in his collection from the Bond Street art house. This portrait of Agnew was by Luke Fildes.

The Bellevue-Stratford Hotel, at 200 South Broad Street, was Proper Philadelphia's entertainment center. In particular, it was a favored venue for débutante balls. Holding to Proper Philadelphia's outward values, women were not allowed to smoke publicly on the hotel's premises.
CONTEMPORARY VIEW COURTESY OF WRITERSCLEARINGHOUSE

The Art Club of Philadelphia at 220 South Broad Street, founded in 1887, was not far from the Bellevue-Stratford Hotel. For many years, John McFadden was its enthusiastic president. Women were banned from membership.

Memorial Hall on the grounds of the Centennial Exhibition of 1876 became the first home of the Pennsylvania Museum of Art, later the Philadelphia Museum of Art. This is a contemporary picture. Note the modern automobiles. Otherwise the exterior has not changed.

*The Toff: Portrait
(1917) of John H.
McFadden in his
splendor by Philip
Alexius de László.*

*McFadden bust, occasionally
displayed with the McFadden
Collection at the Philadelphia
Museum of Art. It was
donated by his daughter Alice.*

*Left: Eli Kirk Price II, a premier Proper Philadelphian, was his period's
"foremost civic and cultural leader." He and John D. McIlhenny were
responsible for overseeing the construction of the modern museum on
Fairmount Hill. He was a lawyer. But he never bothered practicing.*
REPRODUCTION COURTESY OF THE PHILADELPHIA MUSEUM OF ART

*Right: John D. McIlhenny (1866–1925) rose to become the Pennsylvania
Museum's influential president. Despite that status and his great wealth,
McIlhenny never was a fully-blooded Proper Philadelphian.* REPRODUCTION
COURTESY OF THE PHILADELPHIA MUSEUM OF ART

*Fiske Kimball was the irascible director and artistic lord of the Pennsylvania
Museum of Art, later the Philadelphia Museum of Art. He had impeccable
professional credentials. Dressed to the nines in Brooks Brothers-tailored
suits, Kimball looked as if he were a Proper Philadelphian. Nevertheless, he
was blackballed by the Philadelphia Club.* REPRODUCTION COURTESY OF THE
PHILADELPHIA MUSEUM OF ART

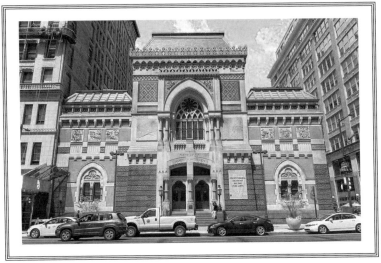

John McFadden was a director of the Pennsylvania Academy of the Fine Arts. Its façade on North Broad Street is seen here. McFadden held the first public exhibition of his collection there in 1916. CONTEMPORARY VIEW COURTESY OF WRITERSCLEARINGHOUSE

Despite the boldness of its engraved tile, John McFadden also found room in this mausoleum in Philadelphia's Laurel Hill Cemetery for his wife Florence. CONTEMPORARY VIEW COURTESY OF WRITERSCLEARINGHOUSE

of their holiday, the McFaddens had also arranged a "motor trip on the Continent."[18]

At summer's end, McFadden returned to Philadelphia. Though separated by two continents, McFadden and Shackleton continued to make news. With McFadden back in the city, on January 25, 1914, Philadelphians awoke to the following attention-grabbing headline in *The Philadelphia Inquirer*:

M'FADDEN WILL NOT
FINANCE SHACKLETON

McFadden was rarely quoted in the press. He offered few, or at least infrequent public utterances. This time, he was emphatic. "I have no interest financially in the [upcoming 1914–1917] expedition," McFadden declared.[19]

> Sir Ernest Shackleton is getting his money on the other side, and it is entirely a British expedition. I am interested to the extent that I hope to see him successful, but I have no money in it.
>
> Simply because I entertained Sir Ernest Shackleton as my guest for several days a year ago is no reason why I should finance or help to finance the expedition.

Not everyone was so sure.

The London press had previously reported that the Philadelphian had pledged a staggering amount, $250,000 ($6.2 million today), for an upcoming Shackleton Antarctic venture in 1915, and the Philadelphia newspapers had sensed good copy—combining an eccentric local millionaire, an international superstar, and financial intrigue. Had an on-board agreement come about during their trip together the previous summer?

By September 1914, several months after his public reversal
of support, McFadden had returned to London. "I have just seen
Sir Ernest Shackleton last week prior to his leaving for South
America to join his ship there to attempt the crossing of the
Antarctic from the South," he wrote home.[20] "He seemed to be
full of courage and I trust he will be successful in his perilous
undertaking."

McFadden's own spirits were not equally buoyant. The war
with Germany, which had just started the month before, in
August, weighed on him. Moodiness set in. At his lowest point,
writing in September, he told his correspondents in Philadelphia that he planned to spend all the war years in England. "I
shall probably remain in England till after the war, as I cannot
leave my business." By December, he was still claiming that "the
exigencies of my business require me to remain here...." His
plan, finally, was revised again, to return in Spring 1915. His
Black Dog had lifted.

In the event, by May 1, 1915, McFadden had made his way
back to Philadelphia, and wound up in the Hospital of the University of Pennsylvania for treatment of a broken ankle. On May
11, released from HUP, he traveled to Atlantic City for a few days
of rest at his summer home there.

THE SHACKLETON LECTURE mentioned in the telegram from San
Francisco was held at the Academy of Music on April 24, 1917.
The lecture would include an appeal on behalf of the British
Red Cross as one of the principal orders of business. His visit to
Philadelphia followed a swing through New York, with a joint
conference there before the American Geographical Society
and the American Museum of Natural History. The announced
topic for Philadelphia was the Briton's "thrilling experiences"
during his 1915 return journey to Antarctica.[21] Tickets went

on sale at C.J. Heppe and Son's, a popular piano dealer at 1119 Chestnut Street, from 50 cents ($10 today) to $2 ($40).[22]

The lecture covered Shackleton's now-familiar themes of polar daring. He also praised America's recent entry in the Great War. Adding a dash of cockiness, Shackleton wore his British sea captain's visored cap jauntily tilted to the left. (McFadden had taken to doing the same during sea cruises aboard his yacht.)

Shackleton's last visit to the city was in 1918, when he received the Philadelphia Geographical Society's highest honor, the Elisha Kent Kane award. The gold medal memorialized its namesake, himself a former Arctic explorer and a Philadelphian.[23]

SHACKLETON HAD AN unusual way of honoring his Philadelphia friend, especially considering the friend's primary passion was for art. The 1917 telegram announced, "NAMED GLACIER IN REMEMBRANCE OF YOU." There was no way of knowing where the million-year-old glacier, of the Pleistocene era, was located. Shackleton provided no coordinates. McFadden, in Philadelphia, was ebullient at the news. He wired in return, "I am unable to express to you my great appreciation at your wonderful and kind thought in the midst of all your suffering to name a glacier after me as a token of friendship, which is heartily reciprocated. John H. McFadden."[24]

CHAPTER ELEVEN

Builder

1913–1920

T HE WINDS OF CHANGE had blown gently over Rittenhouse Square, until 1913, that is. That year, a gale struck, shocking Proper Philadelphia from its languid rhythms. It came in the unlikely form of new-fangled entity: a high-rise apartment house, the square's first. Almost as unnerving, the new building, at 1830 Rittenhouse Square, meant the demolition of one of the area's iconic mansions, that of the late Colonel Thomas Alexander Scott, a former president of the Pennsylvania Railroad.

The *Philadelphia Telegraph* reported how merciless the destruction was: contractors were ordered "to wipe the old house off the map in a hurry."[1]

Proper Philadelphia saw this incursion for what it was: a rending of the residential fabric of Rittenhouse Square. The seventeen-floor building was an omen. The square's storied lifestyle, an enclave of single-family houses built around a singular preserve, was being threatened. An apartment building meant greater numbers populating the square. If the barbarians were not exactly at the gate, it would seem that way to many old-timers. Surely riffraff would seep in. Even, *quelle horreur,* an anonymous nouveau-riche horde.

Worse, the building represented a stab in the back by one of their own. The building's owner was Samuel Price Wetherill—a colonial descendant and himself an area resident. Even the building's financing scheme, a joint-venture "syndicate," underwent scrutiny, as it introduced a vaguely foreign-sounding real estate term. For a milieu in which most residents had built their mansions with family wealth, the notion that a new dwelling needed a cadre of investors seemed alien—even déclassé.

Neighborhood comity was rattled. Some new residents of the Wetherill, as the building was named, had an unobstructed view of the square, one never before seen. To their horror, they could now plainly see through windows below; some were scandalized by what they saw. The distinguished diplomat, Rittenhouse Square-bred William C. Bullitt, Jr., once described the tension in his 1926 roman à clef, *It's Not Done.* One contretemps involved a Proper Philadelphian being rebuked by a Wetherill upstart for shaving in the buff.

The building did make concessions to Rittenhouse sensibilities. Designed by Frederick Webber, Philadelphia's go-to apartment house architect at the time, it exuded a comforting Beaux-Arts style. The building could have fit in nicely on Fifth Avenue, somewhere in the Seventies. Its doorman, or footman, stood snug under an entrance canopy, fancifully fabricated in wrought iron and glass. Servants were closeted in their own quarters, on the top two stories. Did anyone notice that they had the best view in town?

AS IF THE Wetherill's construction were not enough of an upheaval, its début coincided with the almost unspeakable: a renovation of Rittenhouse Square itself. Sponsors of the landscaping redesign, in 1913, came again from within the inner sanctum. The Rittenhouse Square Improvement Association was a socially connected, well-heeled, and powerful civic group. One of the group's officers was related to Eli Kirk Price II, arguably the city's most influential lawyer. Conveniently, Price was a member of the Fairmount Park Art Association, the panel that would eventually rule on the plan. Acceptance of the proposed redesign was a forgone conclusion.

The Improvement Association's membership largely comprised wealthy matrons with Francophile leanings—an affectation common to that era. (The city's Alliance Française de Philadelphie, organized in 1903, had its first meeting in the Acorn Club, Alice McFadden's social haunt.) Elizabeth Martin, Price's sister, even floated the absurdity that Rittenhouse Square could be remodeled after the Parc Monceau in Paris. Among the differing plans, à la française won out. Paul P. Cret, a young, Lyon-born professor of architecture at the University of Pennsylvania, was designated to undertake the renovation. The handsome wunderkind, himself a Rittenhouse insider, could be counted on if needed to exhibit the European charm particularly ingratiating to the ladies.

Cret's exact brief was open to interpretation. That, in itself, struck the horror of the unknown in the hearts of some Old Philadelphians, who still remembered the square in the previous century when a chest-high iron fence dissuaded undesirables from entering. The park's planned renovation took shape against a background of urban disquietude, even a sense of siege, as other neighborhoods began to advocate for demolition of the "Chinese Wall" along Market Street. Though no one thought that Cret's background in Continental architecture would lead to any mini-grand scheme in the mold of Paris's modern designer, Baron Georges-Eugène Haussmann, an edgy uncertainty lingered. Cret mollified dread by borrowing from another fellow countryman, Pierre L'Enfant, who had laid out

Washington in 1791. The result was nothing short of brilliant. Cret unveiled an intersecting, maze-like design that actually invigorated the square, despite its minimal seven acres, with enduring wonder and vitality.

THREE YEARS LATER, another gust of change swirled through the square. It emanated from the north side of Rittenhouse Square, at the corner of 19th and Walnut. As the Wetherill had been an unlikely force for upheaval in 1913, another unlikely game-changer stepped forward. Though approaching sixty with an almost impeccable reputation for *not* attracting public attention, John McFadden suddenly did exactly that. In early 1916, he delivered the final blow to Rittenhouse Square as a nineteenth-century enclave.

That coffin nail was the Wellington, the square's second high-rise. The building, imagined and overseen to completion by McFadden, involved a form of residential self-immolation: the destruction of his own dwelling at 19th and Walnut. McFadden was flush with cash, and his building scheme offered a quick way to make more. Even if it meant brushing aside sentimentality and the residential traditions of Rittenhouse Square. Although only a real estate amateur until now (his ownership of a garage on Locust Street had been his boldest venture to date), he approached construction transactions for the Wellington with professional acuity. As an experienced hotel dweller, in Philadelphia, New York, Liverpool, and London, McFadden knew a thing or two about big buildings and what made them tick. (In London, he also had an equity interest in his hotel haunt, the five-star Carlton.)

What really galled Proper Philadelphia was that the Wellington was not, like the Wetherill, strictly an apartment house. McFadden branded the property as a residential hotel,

combining luxury flats and hotel suites. As such, McFadden
must have seen an upmarket Walnut Street address as contributing added value.

The building's main entrance was re-sited accordingly. The Wellington's multi-use format further damned the
building. Not only did Rittenhouse Square gentry frown on
apartment-house interlopers, they also took a dim view of
transients, whatever their social stratum or affluence. They
were all arrivistes.

A hotel was not a new concept to the area—that is, in *this*
area. The Aldine had been in its midst since 1887, and, in fact,
McFadden and his family had lived there for a year before his departure to Liverpool in 1881. Dampening consternation over the
staid Aldine was its location, in the 19th Street block of Chestnut
Street and sufficiently removed from the sacred square itself. If
publisher J.B. Lippincott, who had developed the Aldine, could
be forgiven his folly, McFadden soon learned he would not be
so fortunate. The Aldine had been a pin-prick. To many rock-
ribbed Proper Philadelphians, the Wellington was a violation
of the square's virtue. One might have thought that McFadden
would have had a sympathetic ear for his critics, given his own
hapless experience, in 1902, as a neighbor to St. Regis Hotel in
New York. He did not.

Like Samuel Wetherill before him, McFadden understood
that a syndicate would be needed to finance his venture. That
involved, according to real estate records, twelve months during
which McFadden consolidated his financial team. The 19th
and Walnut house itself exchanged hands no less than three
times, until it was "flipped" finally to the Rittenhouse Square
Realty Co., the consortium McFadden had finally put together.
Rittenhouse Square Realty's mortgage, held by Fidelity Co., was
a sizeable $1 million ($19.3 million today).[2] Again, Rittenhouse
back-benchers tut-tutted.

If architect Frederick Webber had injected a soothing Beaux-Arts style to Wetherill, the Wellington's architect, the Philadelphia-trained Ralph Bowden Bencker, erected a fifteen-floor, 173-feet tall stone slab of unremitting gray blandness. (Architectural catalogs all agree on one point: none can come up with a description of the Wellington's architectural style.) Given its lack of character and imagination, one wonders if the Wellington was financed on a cut-rate budget despite the $1 million involved. Bencker went on to do better—much better. His art-deco Ayer building, located directly on Washington Square, is an accomplished example.

McFadden gave his building a tongue-in-cheek moniker, one surely puzzling to anyone not privy to his library's holdings. The *Wellington* McFadden had in mind was the First Duke of Wellington, the military nemesis of his bibliographic favorite, Napoleon Bonaparte. (If history had been perverse, and the French emperor had won at Waterloo in 1815, McFadden might well have christened the building the "Napoleon.")

The Wellington featured several novelties. Among them was McFadden's household space itself. He had set aside the building's top two floors for personal use.

Though McFadden had clear-cut the site at 19th and Walnut, the destruction was not the scorched-earth demolition—"to wipe the house off the map"—that was visited upon the Scott house four years earlier. In fact, McFadden *preserved* his house, at least a key part of it. McFadden wanted to remain faithful to his collection's presentation in the razed house. To do so, he created a duplex penthouse to retain the interiors of the old house. The new living quarters, according to *The Philadelphia Inquirer*, approximated "the same size and proportion" and followed "the old [picture] arrangement and decoration."[3] Richard Dorment, the collection's most recent cataloguer, also noted that the new installation, high above Rittenhouse Square, was spared street-level "dust" and the "possibility of light being cut off by buildings."[4]

While construction was underway, McFadden had arranged for the artwork to be loaned to the Pennsylvania Academy of the Fine Arts.[5]

Despite his major equity interest in the property, McFadden's tenancy was ruled by the same stipulations that applied to other building residents. His annual lease was $16,500 ($318,000 today).[6]

Why would John McFadden—a man who was ostensibly devoted to family life, and who had spent years personalizing his home to suit his refined aesthetic tastes—have decided to demolish that historic structure, and replace it with a stylistically neutral high-rise building? As with so many aspects of his life, he left little record of the thinking behind this decision. But, looked at through another lens, clues to his motivations do emerge.

By 1913, McFadden had been building his art collection for over two decades. He was in his sixties, at that time an age nearing the end of life. As we shall see in later chapters, his thoughts focused more and more on the ultimate disposition of his collection. By the time he signed his will four years later, his ideas had evolved.

Up to this point, however, it appears that he had envisioned preserving his home as a "house museum," with his beloved paintings on view exactly as he had arranged them to be seen. McFadden was probably aware of existing examples such as the Wallace Collection in London, a collection built by the marquesses of Hertford and Sir Richard Wallace, and housed in the magnificent Hertford House, opened to the public in 1897. Isabella Stewart Gardner had opened her purpose-built museum and residence, inspired by the Venetian Palazzo Barbaro, in Boston, also in 1897. In Philadelphia, John G. Johnson had long planned to leave his own residence to house his incomparable collection after his death. (He died in 1917.)

Supporting this idea is McFadden's frequent welcoming of art-world luminaries to his home. More to the point, for a number of years, he also opened his home to the public every Wednesday. He pressed his daughter Alice into service as do-cent. Though occupied with her own household chores, she would nevertheless rush over from her Spruce Street house to serve tea to visitors, many of whom were surely fellow Acorn Club members.

In a way, his plan to build the Wellington could be seen as a more pragmatic version of Gardner's swan of a museum building. Gardner designed her museum to include her liv-ing quarters on the fourth and highest floor. McFadden, too, planned to live on the top floors of the Wellington. In his case, his new home would duplicate his old one down to the exact ar-rangement of his collection; later, future generations could visit his art aerie high above Rittenhouse Square, while the lower floors produced income.

As we will see, other developments would cause him to aban-don this plan for his collection. But by then, construction on the Wellington was well underway.

WITH THE CONSTRUCTION of the Wellington, McFadden turned Rittenhouse Square on its tail. Some of the stodgiest Proper Philadelphians were whispering *sotto voce* that McFadden was nothing less than "a traitor to his class"—a phrase that would later be thrown at the future president, Franklin D. Roosevelt. In the end, the Wellington propelled the square's transition to modern, integrated cosmopolitanism. The neighborhood, no longer marooned by its insularity, could not turn back the clock. Other tall buildings would soon materialize. As these giants rose, some Proper Philadelphians wondered whether they could live side by side with the transformations.

Ironically, John's brother George Henry was spared any immediate impact from high-rise construction. George had been among the first to embrace a country lifestyle, spending each summer far from the city's heat starting in 1892, at his suburban Villanova estate, "Barclay Farms," named after his youngest son.

In 1913, George became a year-round resident at Barclay Farms. His new living arrangements coincided with the death, in April 1913, of his wife Emily. Her death was not sudden. She had always been frail, and had once been hospitalized for exhaustion after, it was said, socializing too vigorously.[7] Apart from the party circuit, Emily had burnished her socialite credentials as the president of the board of managers of the Saunders House, a home for indigent men in West Philadelphia. The institution reeked of Victorian Gothic—residents were called "inmates" and the facility, located at 39th Street and Powelton Avenue, was better known as the "Old Man's House." Following Emily's death, the inmates adopted a resolution honoring her, stating "We have lost a friend."[8]

George's daughter Ellie remembered her family's bucolic life in Villanova, distant from the routines of urban Rittenhouse Square. "The farm was about six or seven miles from [the town of] Bryn Mawr....As our only means of conveyance in those days were horses and carriages, it seemed quite far away," she recalled.

The Wellington's completion in November 1916 catapulted Rittenhouse Square into an uneasy twentieth-century version of itself. For many of the Old Guard, that also meant a loss of the square's serenity and allure. Worse, its nobility. McFadden's Wellington, it might be said, was Rittenhouse Square's "Waterloo." More and more Rittenhouse residents began to consider the "far away" country life as less an idyll than a necessity. Declining enrollments at Episcopal Academy and at the Delancey School, the two most socially sacred secondary schools, confirmed a westward population shift to the Main Line was well underway.

To stem bleeding enrollments and red ink, the Delancey merged with Episcopal Academy in 1915. A few years later, the academy itself moved to the Main Line.

The square was no longer a multi-generational space. In one stroke, a chronicler of the square observed, "The Episcopal boys who had played, skated, and taunted each other were now gone from the Square."[9] R. Sturgis Ingersoll's favorite juvenile pastime had been spinning tops. That was gone too.

Ten years on, the square's deconstruction was complete. By 1927, *The New York Times* summed up, the square's "ancestral quietness," "low-roofed homes," and "social exclusiveness" had been replaced by "cubistic apartment hotels,[10] all planes, angles and undecorated faces."[11]

PART II

I will not cease from Mental Fight,
Nor shall my sword sleep in my hand:
Till we have built Jerusalem,
In England's green & pleasant Land.

—WILLIAM BLAKE, "JERUSALEM"

ABOVE: Lady Rodney *by Thomas*
Gainsborough.

CHAPTER TWELVE

Trustee

1910–1921

JOHN MCFADDEN'S STEWARDSHIP OF Philadelphia's arts community combined the usual trinity of time, talent, and treasure. His leadership included governance of the Art Club of Philadelphia, as president; the Pennsylvania Museum and School of Industrial Art, as a trustee; and the Pennsylvania Academy of the Fine Arts as a director. For good measure, McFadden was also an honorary vice president of the Philadelphia Art Alliance, an advocacy group founded in 1915. This work was never tedious, sometimes interesting, and almost always diverting. More important, it afforded him the power to shape the city's arts patrimony—and to advance the public stature of his art collection. His was a snug harbor, Philadelphia's Old Boys' Club, where nary a woman trod.

Compared with the Metropolitan Museum of Art, overseen for the most part by powerful corporate lawyers (Philadelphian John G. Johnson was an example; J.P. Morgan was an exception), the makeup of the city's prominent arts leadership was slightly more egalitarian. You need not be an attorney, so long as you were white, male, Protestant, and rich.

And willing. Other Philadelphia tycoons were richer; their collections far more vast. But by near the end of the decade of the teens, John McFadden had set himself apart. Not only was he at the top of the heap, he was the heap's most enthusiastic member. No other Philadelphian wielded such pervasive influence over *all* the city's arts institutions. Armed with the Excalibur of being a leading arts patron, McFadden might fairly consider himself Philadelphia's unofficial arts czar.

AT THE HIGHEST level of institutional Philadelphia, a closed, cozy circle of interlocking boards spun. At any given time, McFadden was serving with Joseph E. Widener (Pennsylvania Museum and PAFA); Edward T. Stotesbury (Pennsylvania Museum and PAFA); Charlemagne Tower (PAFA and the Art Club); and other busily networking colleagues. He served on the Pennsylvania Museum board with his son-in-law, Jasper Yeates Brinton, newly elected in 1916. Until he died in 1917, John G. Johnson was PAFA's lawyer, a Fairmount Park Commissioner, and the Wilstach Collection's trustee. Brother George figured as a PAFA director and treasurer from time to time.

Unlike the Art Club and PAFA (both firmly all-male administrative bastions), the Pennsylvania Museum established a second-tier advisory board exclusively for women. As early as 1906, Florence and Alice, both normally shy of public engagement, were serving on the museum's Associate Committee of Women to the Board of Trustees. John joined the governing trustee board later that same year. From 1906 to 1920, the period of McFadden's tenure, the all-male rule was broken three times—once, notably, for a wealthy lady from Indiana who styled herself as a Portuguese countess. (More on her later.)

The Art Club's founders were Philadelphia aristocracy, dripping with blueblood names like Biddle, Shippen, and Wister. Merchants (Strawbridge), manufacturers (Lippincott), and industrialists (Widener) also had a hand in establishing the organization. Modeled after the Salmagundi (founded 1871) in New York and the Arts Club (founded 1863) in London, its doors opened in 1874. Its focus mixed the socially soothing aspects of arts appreciation with an equally fine appreciation of *une vie raffinée*. In other words, it was a suitable playground for Proper Philadelphia. This was done in a large, four-story clubhouse at 220 South Broad Street that, in its quasi-European architectural style, fostered the look of a glamorous Italian *palazzo*.[1]

The club's charter was sweeping and to the point: art blended with sedate entertainment. The mission was "to advance the knowledge and love of the Fine Arts, through the exhibition of the works of Art, the acquisition of books and papers for the purpose of forming an Art library, lectures upon subjects pertaining to Art, reception given to men or women distinguished in Art, Literature, Science or Politics, and other kindred means, and to promote social intercourse among its members."

The charter restricted the status and movements of female visitors. A Ladies' Reception Room and a Ladies' Restaurant would only accommodate a woman if she were accompanied by a member. A male, of course. "Ladies will not be admitted to any other parts of the house except to exhibitions and receptions."

McFadden joined the club in 1887, while still living in Liverpool. From 1910, when he became president, he reigned over an organization that in its number counted, besides Biddles, Shippens, and Wisters, a Clothier, a Wanamaker, and no less than six Lippincotts. He was friendly with members Edward T. Stotesbury, John Story Jenks, and John D. McIlhenny (all Pennsylvania Museum trustees as well). Though they fell short as duly inducted Proper Philadelphians, Peter A.B. Widener was a member until his death in 1915, as was his son, George D. Widener, a victim of the *R.M.S. Titanic* sinking in 1912. George H. McFadden was a member, getting the jump on his brother by a year.

In his first annual report to members, in 1911, McFadden was reassuring. He provided the requisite boilerplate. "[It] is a source of pleasure to me that I can present such a satisfactory account of the progress of the Art Club in the development of its aims and the fulfillment of the purpose of the Club as set forth in the Constitution." McFadden congratulated various committeemen for satisfactorily tending to the club's "enjoyable" "social life." "Financial affairs" were in good stead, he said. And he lamented the deaths over the year of some "valuable" members, "a constant source of keen regret."[2]

John McFadden's role was predominately social, and of a chummy nature. He introduced Sir Ernest H. Shackleton to the club's confines. Sarah Bernhardt also dropped by. The famed French stage actress attended one of Philadelphia's most celebrated galas as its honored guest, on February 1, 1911, soon after McFadden took office. The partying began at midnight, and Philadelphia Orchestra-goers at the nearby Academy of Music could not but fail to hear the commotion. Dress was white-tie, and more than nine hundred of Bernhardt's fans packed the premises. It was a mesmerizing, if kitschy, event.

"Madame Bernhardt," as a fawning press styled her, had just completed her evening's performance in Alexandre Bisson's tearjerker *Madame X* at the Walnut Street Theatre. Albert G. Hetherington and other kindred swells, Charlemagne Tower (a PAFA director), Thomas Skelton Harrison (a Pennsylvania Museum stalwart), and William Henry Newbold (a happy party-goer), escorted the aging thespian, who was then sixty-seven. Another Reception Committee member, Pennsylvania Museum trustee Edward T. Stotesbury, the mega-rich Drexel Bank impresario and a well-known Society Jack-in-the-box, tagged along.

"John Howard McFadden…welcomed Madame Bernhardt at the club entrance…. The guest, with the hostesses [Florence and Alice were among them], had dinner about a big walnut table in the Red Room....Madame Bernhardt expressed delight at the reception and in a short speech thanked the members of the club and the guests for honoring her. She paid tribute also to Philadelphia theater goers and said that audiences of this city were unusually sincere," *The Philadelphia Inquirer* reported.[3] McFadden was equally upbeat, seeing Bernhardt's visit, "the only one she accepted while in America," as a model for "similar affairs" by "distinguished figures."[4]

McFadden had a particular fondness for the Art Club; he ran it as his fiefdom. And it attracted John's largesse. Less than a month after Bernhardt graced the club, its curators mounted a show of works by Augustus B. Koopman, a French-trained American artist and a PAFA graduate. The exhibit's "place of honor" went to Koopman's *The Old Troubador*, a picture McFadden had donated to the club two years before.[5]

The club had a serious side as an important venue for individual and group shows. Its annual artist's award, a gold medal, was sought after nationally. Even Alice, contrary to the club's forbiddingly misogynistic rules, was able to advance the group's stated art ethic, serving as the patron of an exhibition of etchings in April 1916. More than seventy works were sold, and the event, according to *The Philadelphia Inquirer*, was "a great success."[6]

Fact-finding was another undertaking. McFadden and his Sarah Bernhardt partner, Albert G. Hetherington, while on a club-sponsored field trip to the Walker Gallery in Minneapolis in 1912, caught the attention of the *New York Sun*. (The gallery was a precursor to Walker Art Center.) Even as a consummate cosmopolitan, the newspaper reported, McFadden was not deterred from having a favorable impression of the hinterland museum and its permanent collection, numbering more than three hundred pictures. "[T]o the amazement of the two Philadelphians, instead of the usual local gallery filled with copies

or indifferent specimens bearing great names, they found the
gallery literally crammed with distinguished pictures and fine
old Chinese porcelains."[7]

The Art Club never courted controversy. But in the summer
of 1918, in the final months of World War I, McFadden had to
face an embarrassing club-related incident that spoke volumes
about America's adherence to free speech, and, in particular,
how Proper Philadelphia reacted to its exercise by one of its
own. At first blush, the event seemed like a minor, local brou-
haha. Except that the dust-up's principals were two well-known
Philadelphians, the internationally respected artist and Art
Club member Joseph Pennell and his wife, Elizabeth Robins
Pennell, a prominent art critic, food writer, and bicycling enthusiast. The pair had just returned to Philadelphia after many
years in London.

The controversy ignited during a hot-tempered visit to
the club earlier in the year by Pennell, a former instructor at
the Slade School of Art in London and a close friend of James
McNeill Whistler. On that occasion Pennell encountered several English army officers, and promptly started to disparage
them with "bitter anti-English and claimed [on Pennell's part]
pro-German attitude."[8] Given that Pennell had been a long-time
London resident, his caustic attack on the soldiers was ironic.

Mrs. Pennell added fuel to the fire with supportive remarks
in the June edition of the *North American Review*. Without
meaning to, the Pennells kickstarted a more far-ranging national dispute over First Amendment rights. That dispute arose in
an atmosphere already fired up by the controversial Espionage
Act of 1917, a repressive anti-free speech law enthusiastically
promoted by President Woodrow Wilson.

The ensuing scandal divided Philadelphia's arts and civic
community. Pennell was suspended from the Art Club. Fearing
expulsion, he later resigned. For its part, the University of Pennsylvania also withdrew an honorary degree it had planned to

give the artist. Conversely, and just as controversially, the Philadelphia Sketch Club "eulogized" Pennell, and invited him to join Sketch Club members "socially." The *American Art News*, in an editorial titled "Is Phila. Truly Patriotic?" expressed outrage, wondering how "Philadelphians who considered themselves loyal Americans" could support the disgraced artist.[9] A letter writer cried, "Halt! and Shame!"

Making matters worse, Mrs. Pennell was then serving on the high-profile hostess committee of the Pennsylvania Academy of the Fine Arts. The *American Art News* would have none of it:

> We have the greatest respect for the old Academy, and we have always thought Philadelphia the most loyal and patriotic of American cities....Why, of all the women in Phila., should Mrs. Joseph Pennell, the wife of a man who openly abused our Ally—England..., and who was publicly discredited in consequence by the action by the Phila. Art Club and the University of Penna., and who herself publicly, and over her own name, condemned her own city and countrymen and women, [have] been honored by such an institution as the old Pa. Academy passes our comprehension, as we believe it will that of all loyal Americans.[10]

McFadden was caught in the middle. With son Jack serving in the armed forces in France, it would have been understandable if he had aligned himself with the anti-Pennell detractors. But his public position was more Solomon-like. As Art Club president, he went along with Pennell's rebuke. As an academy director, he acquiesced to Mrs. Pennell as a hostess committeewoman. As for the Pennells, they escaped the wrath of Wilson's draconian law by simply moving to a freer "nation"—New York.

McFADDEN'S LONGEST ARTS-RELATED tenure, from 1906 until his death in 1921, was at the Pennsylvania Museum. He was a committed trustee. If not away, his attendance at monthly meetings was spotless. If he could not attend—whether because of illness, travel to England, or, as was the case in April 1913 when he attended the funeral of brother George's wife, Emily—he was mindful to inform colleagues. Most frequently, he was in touch with museum director Edwin AtLee Barber. When he could not forward his regrets on his own, Florence would.

McFadden never warmed to the Fairmount Park institution. He considered it, at best, as its name indicated, a hybrid. (The School of Industrial Arts, the second part of its name, was located in an early nineteenth-century building, once the site of the Pennsylvania Institution for the Deaf and Dumb, on South Broad Street in Center City.) He was all too familiar with the Victoria and Albert, and he saw no point in expanding that more eclectic institutional model to the Pennsylvania Museum, its inchoate kissing-cousin. McFadden much preferred the strictly fine-art mission of a museum such as London's National Gallery.

The board, socially inbred and somewhat disengaged, offered little to no resistance to transformation. Over the years, through McFadden's time as a trustee, members included a like-minded array of McFadden intimates, colleagues, and business associates: a son-in-law, Jasper Yeates Brinton; a friend, financier Edward T. Stotesbury; a Republican mayor who supported the new museum, John E. Reyburn; a museum director, Edwin AtLee Barber (1907–1916), who was also supportive; a former director, William Platt Pepper (1877–1879 and 1899–1907); power lawyer Eli Kirk Price II, a behind-the-scenes force in advancing an enlarged museum; a department store scion, Rodman Wanamaker (McFadden's neighbor in Atlantic City); a progressive collector, John D. McIlhenny; Langdon Warner (1917–1923), an Indiana Jones-like director-adventurer who spent more time in Asia than in

Philadelphia; and Joseph E. Widener, the younger son of the late mega-collector P. A. B. Widener.

Two trustees owed their prestige to the Stetson Company, the famous Philadelphia-based hat manufacturers. One was the prominent businessman Theodore C. Search, the Stetson Company's managing director. The other was a sort of gilded window dressing on the otherwise all-male décor: the sixty-three-year-old Countess Santa Eulalia, the former Elizabeth Shindler of Indiana. As a pretty, quick-witted ingénue, she had married rich, to John Batterson Stetson of Philadelphia. When he died in 1906, she tactically traded up to nobility, marrying Count Alexio de Queiroz Ribeiro, the former Portuguese consul in Chicago. He died in 1917, leaving the fifty-nine-year-old widow to kick up her heels in Philadelphia. She giddily fancied herself as a museum maven.

The board's most arresting figure was long-term trustee John Story Jenks, also a Philadelphia-based cotton merchant. In his seventies, in his later years on the board, the hirsute Jenks could have passed as a body double for Moses. He was rich, imposing, and accomplished. Like John McFadden, Jenks was also a fervent Anglophile, and was prominent in an international association that formed to celebrate the hundred years of peace (from 1814 to 1914) between the United States and Britain. He was also a prime mover in the restoration and furnishing of Sulgrave Manor, George Washington's ancestral home in England. Fifty-five years earlier, the same John Story Jenks was a young member of the family firm Randolph & Jenks, the same cotton-trading firm that the McFadden brothers' father, George M. McFadden, had joined in a preliminary partnership when he returned to Philadelphia from Memphis during the Civil War. Jenks was, in this sense, almost like family.

Even before McFadden joined the Pennsylvania Museum board, more and more Proper Philadelphians had begun to embrace the idea of a Louvre-sized museum, with a Louvre-sized capacity for holding and exhibiting fine art. In the 1890s, a tentative initiative in that direction was led by Dalton Dorr, after he was elevated from chief curator to a joint, outsized post as curator, secretary, *and* director (the museum's third). Empowered by the trustees, Dorr fostered an expansion effort, and by 1895, in the third year of his seven-year-long administration, the wheels began to turn. Slowly.

With the museum's blessing, the Philadelphia City Council undertook a first step, seeking designs for a new building. A competition, jointly sponsored by the Museum and the city, prompted dozens of proposals for sites in Center City and in Fairmount Park. The plan stalled. Adequate funding lagged, and the project seemed all but dead.

In 1907, during William Platt Pepper's second term as museum director, the inimitable P.A.B. Widener took Mayor Reyburn aside and "made the mayor an irresistible offer."

> He said that if the city would provide a site on the flat top of a hill at the edge of Fairmount Park. where a reservoir had recently been closed, and realign a planned boulevard radiating northwest from city hall on the Fairmount axis, he would pay for a museum building and fill it with his pictures.[11]

Nothing was put to paper, and Widener's daring proposal, if the legendary tale was true, never bore fruit. The putative plan evaporated forever when Philadelphia's most voracious art collector died eight years later, in 1915.

The press was shunted aside from the process.

Expansion efforts remained on life support until 1911. Edwin AtLee Barber, an archeologist,[12] began quietly spearheading new construction after taking over as museum director. In a letter dated January 14, 1911, Barber invited McFadden and other executive committeemen to an "informal" meeting "for the purpose of listening to proposals which involve the raising of money for a new building."

The meeting was held on January 16 in the Arcade Building, in Center City, in the office of museum trustee and Stetson managing director Theodore Search. Rather than meet at City Hall, as they usually did, the trustees met in executive session—in other words, closed to the press, and away from the glare of public scrutiny.

Five years later, in May 1916, the irrepressible Eugène Castello, *The American Magazine of Art*'s Philadelphia correspondent and an accomplished artist in his own right, was still pining for what would be "a veritable Temple of Art…if we ever see it finished." At that point, the only thing finished was "a very beautiful and imposing" 25-feet-to-1-inch relief model of the proposed museum. It was displayed in the courtyard at City Hall, just more than a mile away from where the real thing was supposed to be.

MCFADDEN HAD NEVER subscribed to the museum, donating regular amounts each year. There was no need—he contributed generously upon request. In 1913, its trustees' executive committee elected him as "a Patron member of the Corporation." It was a lifetime sinecure. Others of three dozen or so "patron members in perpetuity" had a membership fee to pay, $5,000 ($125,000 today). Theirs was an exclusive club: the usual suspects, a smattering of Drexels, a Lea, a Wister, and a Lippincott, were some of the hands on deck. Stalwarts such as Jenks, Search, and McIlhenny were also life members. So was chemical king William Weightman, the squire of one of Rittenhouse Square's largest mansions at 18th Street and Walnut. McFadden *did* pay for Alice's lifetime "fellowship" membership, a lesser category.

Despite its flaws and undulating purpose, the Memorial Hall museum attracted widespread public support—especially on

Sundays. (The museum was free and open seven days a week.) In typical years, between a quarter-million to a half-million visitors would manage to find their way to Fairmount Park. This in spite of the fact that the trek from Center City to West Philadelphia was never easy. For most Philadelphians, walking was not an option. A 1910 edition of *Bulletin of the Pennsylvania Museum* reported dispiritedly, "[T]he public is dependent on the street car service for reaching Memorial Hall."

During the McFadden years, the museum also inaugurated the nation's third specialized children's museum in 1918, after Boston (1913) and Detroit (1917). Joseph E. Widener was in charge of details. The opening, according to the 1919 edition of the museum *Bulletin*, "went off with much éclat...." McFadden was in the audience, surrounded by ship models, toy vehicles, maps, photographs, war medals loaned by Bailey, Banks and Biddle, a totem pole, a model of the Centennial grounds, and "other objects calculated to entertainingly instruct children...."

McFadden was generous when called upon. Actually, he was generally a soft touch. Even when bombarded with entreaties from museum director Barber.

Over the preceding decade, the requests had come in a torrent. On April 4, 1906, at Barber's request, McFadden contributed $100 ($2,600 today) to purchase display cases for the textile department. Almost exactly a year later, on April 3, 1907, he supplied $100 for the "lining" of the cases. On September 11, he subscribed $250 ($6,000 today) to help underwrite a study trip by Barber to Mexico. In March 1909, he provided for another display case with a $53 ($1,400) donation. And so on.

McFadden faithfully paid a continuing subscription of $100 ($2,600 today) to help fund the salary of Mrs. Cornelius Stevenson as an assistant curator (she was also the wife of the museum's longtime curator of arms and armor). There was no reason to believe Mrs. Stevenson's qualifications were not commensurate with her job, especially after 1920 when she received a doctorate. Her entanglement with her husband was also not quite nepotism: Stevenson was an "honorary" curator of arms and armor, and presumably served without pay. Nor, seemingly, did Mrs. Stevenson's position suggest any conflict of interest with her membership, in a volunteer capacity, on the Associate Committee of Women to the Board of Trustees.

As for Barber, hectoring for funds did not embarrass him.

On December 21, 1907, he asked McFadden for $150 ($3,800 today) to purchase a "so-called" Martha Washington china cup; and $300 ($7,600 today) for a china plate formerly owned by the Cincinnati Society, a group of descendants of soldiers who had served with George Washington.

With that, McFadden had enough. "I am very much obliged to you for calling my attention to the old plate that was made in China for the Cincinnati Society, after the Revolutionary War, but I am not in the market at the present moment for anything of this character, as I have no collection of this description and do not care to commence one."

Six months later, on June 23, 1908, Barber again approached McFadden. This time, he proposed that McFadden buy a vase, made by "Josiah Wedgwood himself," for $2,000 ($51,000 today).

McFadden again brushed him off. "I do not presume that we would care to go into anything as this, but as you know more about those matters of this nature than I do, if you have any information to give me I shall be very pleased to hear from you."

Barber was persistent. In a return letter from Liverpool, on August 13, 1908, McFadden slammed the door. "I regret exceedingly there is no one here to purchase the vase you refer to. I have not seen it, but if I have a chance I will do it."

McFadden was willing to adopt a promotional role, if his personal interests needed to be served, as his midwifing of the Shackleton Collection in 1913 had shown. A year earlier, in 1912, McFadden informed the director to expect the arrival of a hansom cab. Horse-drawn hansom cabs were once as popular in London as black cab taxis are today. But they were on the way out, replaced by motorized taxis, and McFadden discerned the time was right to memorialize the old-age transport—in Philadelphia. McFadden apparently got the idea for the installation from the Victoria and Albert, which had previously added a cab to its own collection.[13] "As in time to come such vehicles will be regarded with great curiosity," McFadden wrote from London, "I have succeeded in getting a fine specimen, by an eminent London maker and perfectly equipped and very little used." As in the case of the Shackleton exhibit, McFadden did not stand on ceremony. The cab exhibit was a *fait accompli*. It arrived in November 1912. Disassembled, and in a crate. Barber had to figure out how to reassemble it.

The Pennsylvania Museum was a fine depository for such bits and bobs, McFadden seemed to say. But his art collection did not harmonize with it.

McFadden's fitful back-and-forth with Barber came to an end in late 1916 when the museum director died suddenly.

Barber's successor, Langdon Warner, was a peripatetic adventurer, and someone more inclined to traverse the Silk Road in China than take quill to parchment. Once he got the appointment in October 1917, eleven months after his predecessor's death, Warner dashed off to Japan. He was in search, he declared, of artworks that "were thought too good to lose."

THE PENNELL PUBLIC scandal in 1918 was an aberration. For the most part, McFadden's remit as a director at the Pennsylvania Academy of the Fine Arts, which began in 1916, the year McFadden joined the board, ranged from the routine, ridiculous, and mysterious, to the sublime—in the few weeks while his art collection was displayed at the academy.

Those nuances were not covered in Curtis Wager-Smith's yearly PAFA review for 1916, the year McFadden joined the board. Writing in the *American Art Annual*, published in 1917, he set out a uniformly upbeat appraisal. "A brilliant year," he asserted.[14] Wager-Smith attributed the academy's strong showing to the past year's Water Color and Spring Annuals, a presentation of "Swedish pictures," and a Shakespearean Exhibition. Membership stood at a healthy 3,547. Income was $40,000 ($905,000 today). No doubt, treasurer George McFadden thought that figure could be better.

More important, the instinctively conservative board was even then feeling the aftershock of the 1913 Armory Show in New York, which introduced then-daring new forms of modernism to the country. Nevertheless, brother George selected Hugh H. Breckenridge, one of about a half dozen "avant-garde stalwarts"[15] on PAFA's faculty, as his portraitist. The picture was completed when George was seventy. His appearance was beefy; he no longer cut the figure of the polo-playing swain of his younger years.

Breckenridge's portrait still managed to depict George as a contemporary figure, attired in a three-piece suit, a soft-collared dress shirt, and a necktie tied fashionably in the four-in-hand manner. The picture was strictly representational, showing no evidence of Breckenridge's modernist experiments following the Armory Show. Breckenridge was also a steadfast member of the conservative Art Club and a longtime member of the PAFA faculty. Thanks to "George H. McFadden, Esq." (as the painting was titled), Breckenridge was the recipient of the 1917 Edward T. Stotesbury Prize, named for Drexel Bank's Edward "Ned" Stotesbury, one of America's richest capitalists and John's fast friend.

George cut a similar figure in a photo portrait taken by Henry C. Phillips, a Society photographer and "a pillar of photography in Philadelphia."[16] He maintained a studio at 1206 Chestnut Street.

PAFA directors managed such mundane minutiae as staff hires. In February 1916, shortly after McFadden joined the Board, McFadden and his fellow directors approved the exemplary Miss Anna M. Davis as stenographer for $30 ($680 today) per month. There were no nay votes. At the same meeting, Mrs. H. S. Prentice Nichols petitioned the directors for permission to use the galleries for an evening reception of the Biennial Assembly of the Women's Foreign Missions. The board came down hard. "Refused." No comments were recorded in the board's minutes.

On another occasion, the board learned that a lamppost in front of the Furness building had mysteriously toppled. Academy secretary John Andrew Myers revealed:

> I wish to report the condition of the curb lamp-post on the Academy's property on the corner of Broad and Cherry streets. According to the officer who witnessed the destruction of the post, it was the case of an accident; it had to be a choice on the part of the driver of the truck of running down an automobile or running into the lamp-post. The driver of the truck has deposited $50 [$700 today] with the Academy against the repairs of the post.

That summer McFadden undertook another field trip. As he had done for the Art Club of Philadelphia four years before, McFadden again set out—this time, on behalf of the academy—to less-known territory. Instead of Minneapolis, his exploration took him to West Chester County, a rural area west of Philadelphia. Instead of his Art Club colleague Albert G. Hetherington, McFadden recruited his friend and fellow director Ned Stotesbury. (Like McFadden, Stotesbury never seemed to put in much time at the office.) The idea was to inspect thirty-seven acres and a "number" of buildings in Chester Springs as a possible summer school site.

The rural walkabout was an unusual event for the two urbanites. (McFadden likely exchanged his typical city look, including top hat and cane, for more appropriate country attire, his shooting-box tweeds.) After traipsing through the wooded thicket, the PAFA directors were evidently pleased with the site. It was purchased for $16,000 ($360,000 today).

The next year, in May 1917, the board was presented with the highly irregular case of a Thomas Eakins picture gone missing. The portrait, of Eakins's friend and fellow artist Charles Fussell, had hung in the academy's 100th Anniversary Exhibition in 1905. Was the picture lost?

In 1908, three years after the show, it was assured, the academy had still had the portrait in inventory. Until, that is, it was sent on Eakins's "order" to his New York agent, Charles F. Hazeltine. Eakins had died in 1916, and his widow, Susan Macdowell Eakins, now wanted an update on the picture's whereabouts. "We have been unable to find [a] record of its return to the Academy," PAFA secretary John Andrew Myers informed the board. After a quickly mounted, worrisome search, the painting was finally found—squirreled in some undocumented corner of the cavernous Frank Furness building—and returned to Mrs. Eakins.

———————✕———————

IT IS NOT uncommon for a high-profile figure to be appointed to a community board in a *quid-pro-quo* arrangement—somewhere between a reward for a quietly proffered tangible (usually a sizable monetary donation) and a less-than-becoming overt payoff.

Thus, it should not have been a surprise when, soon after McFadden joined the board, the academy announced a plan for an exhibition of his art collection. In early February 1916, the academy made it official:

The John McFadden collection of paintings of the
English school is probably the finest and most notable of its kind in this country. A long residence in
England has given Mr. McFadden unusual facilities
for obtaining the choicest and most representative
examples of the artists included and the selection
has been made with the utmost care and knowledge....

It is an unusual piece of good fortune that en-
ables the Academy to give the public the opportunity
to view this collection which has been loaned to it
for this year.

RESOLVED that the thanks of the Board of Directors of the Pennsylvania Academy of the Fine Arts be
and are hereby extended to John H. McFadden, Esq.,
for his loan to the Academy, for public exhibition, of
his incomparable collection of pictures representing
the eighteenth century and early nineteenth century English school of painting, and for bearing the
expenses incidental to such exhibition, representing
the most important collection ever publicly shown
in Philadelphia.

McFadden must have been longing for public recognition
of his art collection, although notably, he had never offered to
exhibit it at the Pennsylvania Museum. His acknowledgment
as a leading collector was overdue. Now, as a director at PAFA,
he was eager to facilitate such an exhibition. Indeed, he was so
eager, he was willing to pay for the exhibit out of pocket—an unusual funding scheme for an institution of PAFA's stature.

There was also the practical matter of having his collection
in safe hands, as McFadden was at that moment "homeless"
while the Wellington rose on the site of his demolished home at
19th and Walnut. Of course, he could have put it in storage—but

this solution offered a stellar side benefit. Now for the first time, thanks to the academy, the collection was going public in a premier gateway show.

McFadden was heady with anticipation. He left nothing to chance. With the exhibition slated to open in April, less than two months away, he arranged and executed every detail—none was too small. The layout and hanging of the pictures even came under his purview.

Eugène Castello shared McFadden's enthusiasm. Writing in *The American Magazine of Art*, the Philadelphia critic spun the exhibit as baring "the altruistic spirit of the owner, free from any ostentation or commercialism" and exemplifying McFadden's desire "to give the art-loving world an opportunity to share his enjoyment of these priceless treasures."[17]

But six months later, Castello had second thoughts as to how selfless McFadden's motives were. Usually an encyclopedic chronicler of the academy's affairs, he failed to mention the McFadden show in a late-year round-up for *American Art News*. But he underscored the collector's election as a PAFA director at the beginning of the year. More sharply, he speculated whether this "personal honor" was somehow tied to a veiled campaign to secure "a permanent home in America for his remarkable collection."[18]

CHAPTER THIRTEEN

Exhibitor

1916

THROUGH 1916, JOHN MCFADDEN edged closer to determining his collection's fate.

An unexpected near-disaster lent urgency to his decision. On February 15, 1916, a devastating electrical fire swept through the first-floor dining room at 19th and Walnut. Firefighters contained the blaze, barely saving the entire picture collection from a fiery, catastrophic end. The loss of McFadden's true life's work was narrowly averted.

In the end, only one painting, Thomas Lawrence's 1810 portrait of *Miss Nelthorpe,* which he had purchased on December 3, 1895, was lost.[1] As was the £1,200 ($217,900 today) McFadden paid for it.[2] By the time of the fire, it had appreciated to £6,630 ($1.2 million today). Despite some insurance, McFadden's monetary loss was still significant, almost a half-million in today's dollars.[3]

Thomas Gainsborough's mid-sized oil, *A Pastoral Landscape,* bought on November 7, 1904, was minimally damaged, hurt by smoke and firefighting chemicals. McFadden immediately dispatched the painting to conservators in New York for repair.[4]

Lawrence's *Miss Harriot West* (bought December 12, 1907) barely escaped. William Roberts, the collection's cataloguer, looked on the bright side. "[T]he beautiful *Miss West* is still present with us in all the loveliness of youth," he observed.[5] Unscathed was the collector's dining room's centerpiece, J.M.W. Turner's *The Burning of the Houses of Lords and Commons*.[6]

McFadden took heart that Gainsborough's *Lady Rodney* was spared. Purchased on June 5, 1893 for £2,677 ($469,425 today), *Lady Rodney* was McFadden's first major acquisition, and he showered it with the nostalgic affection usually reserved for a first love.

McFADDEN HAD THOUGHT his Wellington aerie might serve as the collection's high-rise permanent home. McFadden soon realized that any attempt to create his own private house museum—in the mold of Lord Iveagh's in London or Mrs. Gardner's in Boston—would be problematic at best. The Wellington could only be its temporary home. The collection was too narrowly curated, he concluded, to attract the large-scale audience he desired.

McFadden finally decided to seek an institutional safe harbor for his collection. And the Wellington ironically helped provide the answer: while the high-rise was under construction in 1916, McFadden had to find a temporary home for his art. That was easily arranged; McFadden was an influential insider as a director at the Pennsylvania Academy of the Fine Arts.

The academy installation was scheduled to open in April and run through the summer of 1916. Initially, in the aftermath of the February dining-room fire, McFadden saw the six-month exhibit as a temporary refuge for his life's patrimony. He was also beginning to appreciate the nuances of public relations, a field in its infancy. Unlike some collectors who saw the amassing of art in bulk as a high road to personal immortality, McFadden sought glory for the collection itself; any ensuing recognition and fame would only affirm his impeccable taste. Promoting his paintings so publicly for the first time, McFadden believed, would put the John H. McFadden Collection in the national spotlight. It did.

National attention would be only a step away. Actually, just more than two hours away. By train. In New York.

THE PAINTINGS OCCUPIED all the wall space of Gallery F, a north, second-floor location. To ensure no mistakes were made, Mc-Fadden himself "handsomely arranged" the setting.[7]

The exhibit's début was preceded, on the afternoon of April 27, 1916, by a music and tea vernissage. Overseeing the preview were fifteen "society women of Philadelphia," including Florence; Alice; Mrs. Eli Kirk Price, wife of the PAFA trustee and prominent local lawyer; and Mrs. George Wharton Pepper, wife of the future United States senator. Mrs. Edward T. Stotesbury and Mrs. Cornelius Stevenson and other matronly doyennes rounded out the volunteer roster. A $2 fee was charged, with proceeds benefiting the Fraternité des Artistes. (During World War I, the charity fundraised on behalf of French soldier-artists and their families.) The exhibition opened the following morning. No music. No tea. But free admission.[8]

The Philadelphia Inquirer called McFadden's first love, Gainsborough's *Lady Rodney*, the "clou," or nub of the collection. The painting was set off on its own, "placed in what [was] known as the place of honor in the gallery."[9] Eugène Castello pulled out the stops: the painting, he declared, "radiates aristocratic elegance, the high bred dignity of the pose and the effective draping of the figure in the artist's favorite blue making it, in the opinion of connoisseurs, one of the best of his works in portraiture."[10]

Gainsborough's *A Pastoral Landscape* was still in New York for repair. When the picture was added later, *The Inquirer* reported that it had "gained greatly in beauty by the process."

The presentation was a sensation. While the Three R's, Reynolds, Romney, and Raeburn, were becoming better known in the United States, many visitors got acquainted for the first time, thanks to the show, to lesser lights such as David Cox, Watson Gordon, and George Morland. Philadelphians were also savoring a new taste for Turner. Other depictions of *The Burning of the Houses of Lords and Commons* existed. But local enthusiasts were now seeing the "Philadelphia version," their own hometown *succès d'acclaim*.

McFadden's selections of Gainsborough and Hogarth stretched conventional notions of those artists. In his *A Pastoral Landscape*, Gainsborough detoured to a less well-crossed countryside setting. McFadden's two Hogarths, *The Assembly at Wanstead* and *Conversation Piece with Sir Andrew Fountaine* (both purchased on September 5, 1910), depicted anodyne social groupings with none of the biting societal commentary for which Hogarth was best known.

Most memorably, McFadden introduced the great horse painter George Stubbs (1724–1806) to Philadelphia. His mid-sized canvas, *Laborers Loading a Brick Cart* (purchased October 10, 1913), painted in 1778, was a visionary purchase. For the sum of £693 ($109,125 today), McFadden picked up what was arguably the first work by the now much-revered equestrian artist to be acquired and displayed in the United States by an American collector. Whether visitors realized that the Stubbs McFadden took home from London was less than typical of the artist's horsey *oeuvre* was not certain. For McFadden, Stubbs was a home-town favorite—for Liverpool, that is, McFadden's home away from home, and Stubbs's birthplace, rather than Philadelphia.

A friend of Stubbs noted that the oil version of *Laborers* that eventually wound up in Philadelphia was Stubbs's favorite rendition. The friend, Ozias Humphry, a fellow Liverpudlian, had recorded Stubbs's life in a brief, contemporaneous biography that was re-edited in the late nineteenth century by "art patron" John Mayer, also of Liverpool. "Stubbs tells us that he was a long time in catching the idea, making the men load and unload their cart, which they did in a style that scarcely lent itself to painting," Humphry reported. "At length they fell into a quarrel about the manner of fixing the tail-piece in a cart, and gave the watching artist his opportunity."[11]

Philadelphians visiting PAFA's Gallery F believed they were marveling at *the* John H. McFadden Collection, full stop. Publicity had said as much. In its resolution to accept the McFadden loan, PAFA's trustees pulled no punches, declaring the works as "representing the most important collection ever publicly shown in Philadelphia." In truth, in 1916, the assemblage was still in some respects a work in progress.

On view were actually thirty-six of the forty-three pictures that would eventually reside in the fully formed collection. Still, visitors never felt shortchanged; the exhibit was supplemented by nineteen prints, six of *Letitia* (purchased January 18, 1909) by George Morland, and thirteen of *The Cries of London* (purchased June 1, 1907) by Francis Wheatly. Also included were *Tivoli* by William Shayer and the David Cox-attributed *Crossing a Rustic Bridge*, which had been in McFadden's possession for at least three years when the prints were first reported seen at his Rittenhouse Square house.[12] Another displayed work, a watercolor sketch of the fan-friendly *The Horse Fair* by Rosa Bonheur, was "not part of the [McFadden] collection proper."[13]

The exhibit also solved a mystery, though almost immediately creating another. Though never mentioned in any list of paintings in the show, two full-length pictures by 17th-century English portraitist William Dobson made an unexpected and welcome appearance. The pictures were the "tall" Dobson paintings that had been hanging in McFadden's former house at 19th and Walnut, and were seen there only on private tours.[14] Otherwise, they were not widely known to be part of McFadden's holdings. The pictures of King Charles I and of Lady Frances Howard (purchased June 7, 1907) were painted by Dobson when he was the King's Sergeant-Painter, a position he held after the death of the previous office holder, Sir Anthony Van Dyck.[15]

On May 7, McFadden happily learned there was another way to showcase his collection—via publicity in New York. Thanks to an almost unprecedented full-page review in *The New York Times*, New York came to Philadelphia to recognize the McFadden group as a national treasure. And a public one, no longer closeted within the confines of 19th and Walnut. *The Times* report gushed—along with some New York-centric bellyaching about the anguish of rail travel to Philadelphia. The newspaper's anonymous critic also took a gratuitous backhanded swipe at PAFA's Frank Furness-designed building. "[T]hose who love Reynolds and Gainsborough, Turner and Constable, and the others of the English group," the critic sniffed, "will make their little pilgrimage to that dour shrine without counting the time lost in transit."[16] The critic, probably unknowingly, validated the same opinion proffered by Harrison S. Morris, a former academy director, who twenty-five years before had labeled the Furness-designed building as "a heavy tomb."

PERHAPS WITH A view to rounding out his collection, and feeling the urgency of advancing age (he was sixty-six at the time), McFadden embarked on a buying frenzy. In London, in October 1916, he expanded his palette by seven pictures. Included were works by Constable, Romney, Raeburn, Morland, Crome, and Wilson. Reporting on this harvest in a dispatch from London, *The New York Times* declared that the group purchase was "considered the most important art transaction of the year...All seven are regarded as pictures of the first rank...."[17] The spurt had been a challenge; never before had he bought as many paintings in a single month. (His purchase of six pictures in September 1910 held the previous record.)

Among the October purchases were such notables as George Romney's *The Shepherd Girl,* better known as *Little Bo-Peep,* purchased on October 18 for £4,000 ($475,000 today); and a third Morland, *The Happy Cottagers,* purchased on October 12. Perhaps it was over-eagerness, or the pressure to consummate deals, but the October buying surge also resulted in two of McFadden's greatest follies, the purchase of the misattributed *Woody Landscape at Colney* and *The Dell at Helmingham Park.*

The Times was relentless in chronicling McFadden's latest round of buying. The following month, in November, the Philadelphian was back in New York, alighting from the Holland-American liner *Nieuw Amsterdam* in the company of such notables as Mrs. Henry van Dyke, wife of the American ambassador to the Netherlands; Commander P. Symington, U.S. naval attaché at the London embassy; and Mrs. R. St. Farnam, recently decorated by the King of Serbia for her Red Cross work. Also traveling with McFadden were some of his newly acquired artistic gems. Their estimated worth, according to *The Times,* was $300,000 ($6.8 million today). The paintings also represented more than 15 percent of the eventual total of pictures in the McFadden Collection.

The Times also floated a tantalizing tidbit: was the Philadelphian traveling with another Gainsborough?[18] By 1916, McFadden had owned four works by the artist. Two, *Lady Rodney* and *A Pastoral Landscape,* he famously kept. The others, *View near Ipswich* (December 2, 1900) and *Captain Thomas Cornewall* (September 2, 1907), were sold. Despite *The Times's* report, there was no record of another Gainsborough purchase. At least, not yet.

CHAPTER FOURTEEN

Curator

1917–1920

T HE FOURTEENTH OF MAY 1917 could have been another shopping day at Thos. Agnew & Sons. It was not. On this day, John McFadden set out to add the "missing" piece in his now almost fully realized collection. His choice was to be controversial.

The mid-sized oil, *A Coast Scene* by early nineteenth-century landscapist Richard Parkes Bonington, highlights a girl gathering shells as part of a seaside family scene. For years, McFadden had wanted a representative nature setting by Bonington, something like that in *A Coast Scene*. He "promptly secured" it.[1] Already holding some of the best of British landscape portraiture, McFadden was convinced the picture would slide comfortably into his assembly of pictures.

Why McFadden finalized his collection with this picture, at this time, is unknown—especially in that Agnew's remained for years to come a shiny lure for the Philadelphian. So much so that he crossed the Atlantic at least ten more times through 1920—even as his health was declining—to buy almost twenty more paintings. Meaningfully, some of those additional acquisitions—another by David Cox, another by John Hoppner, another by George Romney, *two* more by Joshua Reynolds, and an additional *two* by Thomas Gainsborough—could have also easily found their way into the collection itself.

As could have even a "conversation piece" by the obscure Dutch painter Louis François Gerard van der Puyl. McFadden took a chance on van der Puyl's *Thomas Payne, His Family, and Friends* in a purchase from Agnew's on December 2, 1918. Though Dutch, van der Puyl met two other McFadden criteria: he was a nineteenth-century painter and his subject was an English bookseller (not the American Revolution's Thomas Paine). It was an expensive roll of the dice for a work by a little-known painter. Its retail price was £3,520 ($193,970 today).

Many of the pictures in this slew of post-1917 purchases were never included in the official collection. Notable among these were four paintings: Paul Sandby's *The North Terrace at Windsor Castle, Looking East* (purchased January 12, 1920); Romney's *David Hartley, M.P.* (purchased March 18, 1920); van der Puyl's *Thomas Payne, His Family, and Friends;* and Gainsborough's portrait of his nephew, Gainsborough Dupont (purchased February 4, 1920). The Sandby, the Romney, and the van der Puyl wound up with McFadden's son Jack. Daughter Alice took possession of the Gainsborough. (Her father paid Agnew's £7,000 [$427,000 today] for the picture.)[2]

IN BUYING THE Bonington, McFadden was no doubt tugged by nostalgia, remembering his first acquisition from Agnew's twenty-four years before, Thomas Gainsborough's study in serenity, *Lady Rodney*. McFadden could well have felt that purchase of a masterpiece by a marquee painter elevated him, in midlife (he was then forty-two), to the first rank of serious art collectors. The notion that *A Coast Scene* would close a remarkable career, placing him at sixty-seven years old in the forefront of great American art connoisseurs, was something to be similarly savored. The only hitch: unbeknownst to McFadden, *A Coast Scene* was *not* a Bonington. Only years later would scholarship prove the point.[3] The transaction cost McFadden £5,000 (today $473,350).

IN PREPARING TO leave London in May 1917, McFadden was nearing the end of his more than two-decade-long odyssey through British art.[4] After a desultory business trip to Liverpool, again staying at the Adelphi, McFadden wrapped up one of his last long-term visits to England. There is no way of knowing whether he had planned to cap his artistic romance with England on this occasion, marked by the Bonington purchase. Nor do we know whether he weighed his impending five-day sea voyage to New York with trepidation. World War I was raging.

The British had been at war with Germany for three years, and the Great War was expanding. In the previous month, on April 6, the U.S. Congress had declared America's entry into the conflagration. What had been principally land warfare in France had escalated to include ferocious naval combat. Under nebulous rules of engagement, German U-boats were unleashing their might against commercial vessels, and even passenger ocean liners were not spared. Memories of the sinking of the *R.M.S. Lusitania* by German torpedoes, just two years before, were still fresh. Almost 2,000 passengers and crew, including 128 Americans, had lost their lives.

Understandably, these war years took their toll on business. A McFadden company history, meant for internal consumption, mentioned some of the significant upticks in costs experienced by the firm, the consequence of potentially perilous crossings. "Due to submarine war, steamship freight from the United States to ports in Europe advanced to 8 or 10 cents a pound, and one time, freight to France and Italy was quoted at 18 cents a pound." Insurance costs also jumped to about "20 percent of the value of the cargo, and on sailing ships, which were still used quite extensively at that time, insurance was about 30 percent."

These increased charges severely dented cotton exports. In the prewar years, annual exports from the United States had averaged about 8 million bales, with up to half of this amount to Liverpool.

DESPITE THE POOR business climate, 1917 amounted to a watershed year for McFadden's art collection. The Philadelphian also carried home from London an up-to-date collection catalogue, an essential step in formalizing the group's provenance, authority, and value. (The bogus Bonington was included in the record.) For drafting the catalogue, McFadden had turned to William Roberts, a fifty-five-year-old art historian who had acted as art critic for *The Times*. Roberts was a leading expert on Britain's native art and artists and a particular expert on George Romney, a McFadden favorite. In addition, Roberts held down a sideline as a certifier of authenticity, always an awkward job that required a delicate balance of advocacy between buyer and seller.

Roberts's selection involved an apparent conflict of interest: he was recommended by their mutual friend Lockett Agnew. Roberts was the closest McFadden ever got to a Berenson-like picture-whisperer. But the Bonington, as some other pictures in the final collection, failed to live up to expectations.

Roberts produced a 10- by 12-inch, blue cloth-covered book, titled the *Catalogue of the Collection of Pictures formed by John H. McFadden, Esq., of Philadelphia, Pa.* The book was privately published in 1917 by the Chiswick Press in London, in a limited edition of 100. Included in the ninety-four-page volume were monochrome images of the forty-three-picture assembly. Unfortunately, some of the black-and-white reproductions blurred in a muddy wash.

In a preface, Roberts lauded the works as "remarkable," "imposing," and *"sui generis."*[5]

Roberts was a well-respected art historian. He had less competence as an arts watchdog, accepting the ersatz Bonington as genuine. *A Coast Scene*, he declared, was "a fine example of [the artist's] work."[6] Elsewhere he upped the ante, calling it "a splendid example" of the artist's *oeuvre.*[7]

In all, he was susceptible to Lockett Agnew's attribution and provenance claims. None of McFadden's pictures was a forgery. That is, barring the questionable creation of *The Dell at Helmingham Park* (purchased October 12, 1916), attributed to John Constable, but later found to have been executed by an unidentified "imitator." *A Coast Scene* was found to be an "independent" picture in the "style" of Bonington, who had died in 1828, at twenty-six.

Eventually four other paintings were found to be victims of misattribution. *Branch Hill Pond, Hampstead Heath* (purchased February 6, 1900) was partly painted by John Constable, but finishing touches were contributed by a "studio" artist, that is, an assistant artist working alongside the artist. *Wood Landscape at Colney* (purchased October 18, 1916), an oil attributed to John Crome, was determined to be "after an etching" by the artist. *Mrs. Hoppner* (purchased September 9, 1910), a portrait of the wife of the painter John Hoppner, was done in the manner of the artist. And *Rt. Hon. Edmund Burke* (purchased September 5, 1910), misattributed to Sir Joshua Reynolds, probably misnamed the sitter, as well.

A Philadelphia *Public Ledger* writer was willing to accept prevailing wisdom. With boundless ardor, he asserted there was "absolutely no deadwood" in the collection. "Each picture represents in itself a fine thing made all the finer by its association with other works that represent the collector's mature knowledge and practically amounted to a genius in appreciation."[8]

All in all, the number of duds and near-misses in a collection of the size and scope of McFadden's, less than 15 percent of the total, demonstrated a remarkably good average. Such putative eagle-eyed experts as Lord Joseph Duveen, Bernard Berenson, and Wilhelm Reinhold Valentiner did no better, and arguably a lot worse, in curating individual pictures and groups for their Philadelphia clients, P. A. B. Widener, William L. Elkins, Edward T. Stotesbury, Henry P. McIlhenny, and John G. Johnson.

Johnson was very much a case in point. For all his efforts against being duped, his selections were not always skillfully acquired. Johnson liked to consider himself a smart, self-guided buyer, and had established his credentials as a knowledgeable and astute player. He presented himself as no easy mark for suave, unscrupulous European sellers, and he claimed that he disregarded "names" and provenance. Quality purportedly came first. On yearly buying trips to Europe, he scooped up the best works of Flemish, Spanish, French, Italian, and Dutch Old Masters of the fifteenth and sixteenth centuries.

Yet despite his well-honed self-regard in terms of knowing the finer points of connoisseurship, Johnson still counted on Berenson, exalted as an expert in Italian Renaissance painting; and the German-born Valentiner, a former textile curator at the Metropolitan Museum of Art, who had become a New York-based dealer and consultant. Their track records were spotty. Regardless, Johnson charged Berenson with cataloguing his Italian pictures, and gave Valentiner the brief for his northern European collection. The pair tackled their assignments with unmitigated hubris. Recent research has shown they were too often wrong.

McFadden got more mixed results when he went without Agnew's guidance. In 1889, before he had established himself as an Agnew's acolyte, McFadden was an inveterate Mayfair *flâneur*. In his peregrinations, he fell within the orbit of the Grosvenor Gallery, a short-lived, avant-garde establishment that represented Edward Burne-Jones, Lawrence Alma-Tadema, James McNeill Whistler, and other then less-than-mainstream artists.

McFadden saw two pictures he needed to have. The oils were part of the obscure S.S. Joseph Collection, and as McFadden went about cherry-picking the canvasses he came to covet two by John Crome: *The Blacksmith's Shop near Hingham, Norfolk*, and *Woody Landscape at Colney*. Whether because of inexperience, or lack of fortitude—he only began seriously collecting three years later—McFadden passed up the paintings. The Grosvenor Gallery abruptly closed its Mayfair location the following year. He had lost his chance.

For the moment. Even later, when he was well on his way as an established collector with Agnew's as his dependable consultant and dealer, his purchasing habits were still somewhat tentative. Within a few years, however, his commitment stiffened—especially when one Crome oil from the former Grosvenor Gallery, out of sight in private hands, popped up at Agnew's. This time, sensing a major purchase in the offing, McFadden moved without hesitation. He purchased *The Blacksmith's Shop* on May 9, 1896. He also displayed a buyer's gold-standard negotiating card—patience. Twenty years later, he bought *Woody Landscape at Colney*. Alas, warts and all.

In one instance when he navigated *without* Agnew's rudder, he was happy with his success. In 1913 McFadden met Richard Luttrell Pilkington Bethell, better known as Lord Westbury, Third Baron Westbury. The nobleman was a collector on an eminent scale. The Philadelphian, by then a seasoned collector, was confident enough to enter into direct negotiations. McFadden came away with two fabulous pictures by George Henry Harlow, the *Portrait of the Misses Leader* and *The Leader Children*. The cheery family scenes depicted in the paintings were tailor-made for McFadden.

Westbury explained in a letter who was who, the two fetch-
ing elder Leader girls and the playful younger ones, two boys and
two girls. In the letter, dated September 21, 1913, Westbury wrote:

> My dear McFadden: —
> The portraits in the two pictures by Harlow are
> those of my great uncle John Temple Leader, who
> was a contemporary at Oxford of Mr. Gladstone, and
> sometime Member of Parliament for Westminster,
> and his Brother and four Sisters.
> He ([Mr.] John Temple Leader) is the baby held on
> the donkey by his sister Ann (afterwards Mrs. Dash-
> wood); the donkey is being led by his elder brother
> who died before his father, and the other figure is
> that of my sister Jane (my godmother, who became
> Fownes-Luttrel).
> The other picture represents his sister Fanny
> (who became Lady Peregrine Acland) and his sister
> Mary who married 1) Captain Edward Lowtear Crof-
> ton R.N. and 2) Captain Woodley Losack.

TWO WORKS THAT might have been in the McFadden collection
have gone missing. Nine months before McFadden purchased
his sentimental favorite, Gainsborough's *Lady Rodney*, his first
important stabs at buying occurred on June 15, 1892. In this,
McFadden tested his still untried relationship with Agnew's, at
the firm's 1 Castle Street branch in Liverpool. He moved gingerly, buying an oil, *An Alexandria School* by John Callcott Horsley,
a Victorian contemporary best known as the illustrator of the
first English Christmas card. McFadden also picked up a watercolor, *Reaping on Yorkshire Coast*, by the Scottish artist Robert
Anderson. These works are untraced.[9]

Thus initiated, McFadden was heady with anticipation. The following day, the 16th, he bought five more drawings, including J.M.W. Turner's *London from the South*. Six days later, on June 22, returning to 1 Castle Street, he expanded his nascent collection by three more drawings, including the popular favorite, *The Horse Fair* by French artist Rosa Bonheur.

DESPITE ITS FLAWS (most, to be sure, were less than grievous), the Roberts catalogue was pivotal in establishing what was to become the *official* record of McFadden's collection. As the PAFA exhibit in 1916 showed, along with the unaccounted whereabouts of the Horsley and Anderson pictures, the *unofficial* McFadden collection was a fluid thing. Some pictures never made the final cut. Others served up perplexing, contradictory provenances.

As early as 1913, McFadden displayed two "tall" pictures by William Dobson in his Rittenhouse Square house. Dobson was English, to be sure. But his works were well outside the eighteenth- and nineteenth-century time frame to which McFadden adhered. Dobson died in 1646. The collection, at that time, also included *two* pictures by David Cox. Ultimately only one, *Going to the Hayfield* (purchased February 19, 1900), found its way to the final collection. (The other, *Girl Crossing a Rustic Bridge* [purchased January 30, 1893], was probably misattributed.)[10]

McFadden also broke in this period from his largely unwavering commitment to British practitioners. In one hallway at 19th and Walnut hung a work by Boston native John Singleton Copley, *Portrait of George Beaumont, Esq.* Copley, however, established his British bona fides by moving to London and dying there, a Tory, in 1815.[11]

The question of the collection's completeness is somewhat mysterious. Even near the decade's end, any resolution of what was to be the official compilation of McFadden's art treasury was a puzzling and, seemingly, a private matter. Since he started forming the corpus of his works, it was largely assumed the collection was created by consecutive purchases, painting after painting. Little noticed was the collection's evolution by *deaccession*. Several works in exhibitions in 1917 were hardly keepsakes. Pictures by Dobson, Cox, Copley, and Bonheur—and even earlier examples and, as noted previously in this chapter, purchases *after* 1917—have been lost to the vagaries of time, theft, destruction, and the dubious sale practices of High Street galleries.

Even such a professional insider as William Roberts was bewildered as to what did—and *would*—constitute the formal McFadden collection. In 1918, writing in *Art in America*, Roberts praised McFadden for resisting "all temptations to extend the scope of his activities as a picture collector." "Mr. McFadden," he declared, "remains loyal to the British school, and his recent additions strengthen and consolidate a collection already without rival."

At the time, the collection was believed to be fixed; Roberts memorably catalogued the works the year before. Two years later, however, again writing in *Art in America*, the Englishman cited van der Puyl's *Thomas Payne, His Family, and Friends* as a new addition. Roberts, of course, had no knowledge of McFadden's 1917 will, which excluded all paintings acquired after the Bonington purchase in May of that year.

Son Jack *did* know the will's details, and he suggested privately that the Philadelphia probate listing (known as a "schedule") of his father's collection could be expanded.

After his father's death, Jack claimed "4 or 5 of his father's paintings" as his own, according to museum records.[12] Most startling, the younger McFadden revealed he "bought [the paintings] from the estate under the terms of the will,"[13] and that paintings "could be hung with father's collection...."

The museum records[14] note that Jack referred, specifically, to Romney's *David Hartley, M.P.* The younger McFadden admitted that it had become his sentimental favorite since "it was last one bought by my father...." Of the other "4 or 5" pictures Jack cited, these presumably included the aforementioned paintings by van der Puyl and Paul Sandby.

In the event, the Sandby joined the museum's British Painting department, but was set apart from the official McFadden artworks. Its label cited it as a "Gift of John H. McFadden, Jr." The van der Puyl went to the Northern European Paintings department. The Romney was not so lucky. After Jack donated the painting in 1949, it was sold at auction in 1956, despite its pedigree and the younger McFadden's fondness for the piece. It now resides at the Avery Architecture and Fine Art Library at Columbia University in New York.

═══ ✄ ═══

YET MORE DRAMA ensued. In 1916, McFadden recruited the Hungarian-born portraitist Philip Alexius de László to execute his likeness, and directed that a reproduction of the portrait wind up as the catalogue's frontispiece. The forty-seven-year-old de László, whose career was accelerating in Society circles, was stamped with Lockett Agnew's approval—in fact, Agnew's represented the artist. His works were not cheap.[15]

Despite his success and Agnew's imprimatur, de László was stigmatized as a "society artist." Nevertheless his image was burnished by his frequent mention, almost always in the same breath, as being akin to John Singer Sargent. Though wags might add, akin as a lesser, second-rank Sargent. The venom was unwarranted, and disregarded the artist's demonstrated skill, popularity, and success. De László accumulated a stellar client list, including nobles and notables. And at least three kings, Spain's Alfonso XIII, and Britain's Edward VII and George

VI. Any sitter for a de László portrait would know that the painter would render more than a simply sympathetic appearance. In McFadden's case, de László endowed the Philadelphian with a countenance of self-satisfaction and congenial benevolence. In other words, a charitable millionaire.

For all his talent and connections, de László was still a controversial selection, and his picture almost did not arrive in time for publication in the William Roberts catalogue. Though de László was a naturalized Briton, he was still suspected by authorities as retaining an allegiance to his Hungarian homeland, a German ally. As the war dragged into its third year, de László was arrested in September 1917 as an enemy alien, and was interned for twelve months.

Before de László's unfortunate internment, and before the Philadelphian's own May 1917 departure for his hometown, McFadden had commissioned another portrait by the artist. He instructed de László to work on a larger canvas. Both ego and size were amplified in what became a three-quarter length depiction of a Mayfair boulevardier, kitted with cane and top hat.[16]

De László was among a cadre of modern realists who swirled in and out of Mayfair Society. McFadden had just picked one. But if he had set his mind to it, McFadden could have formed another version of his English collection, in nineteenth- and twentieth-century garb. Pictures by Augustus John, John St. Helier Lander, Walter Sickert, Alfred Munnings, and John Lavery were also available for cash and carry. For a lot more cash, there was the Anglo-American Sargent. Interestingly enough, these modern English artists were doing the same thing that McFadden's favorite Three Rs—Romney, Reynolds, and Raeburn—were doing in their time: chronicling the lives of the rich and famous in pictorial form.

McFadden sought out other pictorial self-images. As summer approached, he moved to his New Jersey shore house in

Atlantic City. There he sat for Wayman Elbridge Adams, best known for his portrait of the author Booth Tarkington, a fellow Indianan. The Tarkington and McFadden pictures and other Adams portraits were later displayed at the Art Club of Philadelphia.

McFadden also turned to sculpture to immortalize himself. In 1919, he commissioned a near-two-feet high bronze bust by the English sculptor Frank Lynn Jenkins, a frequent visitor to Philadelphia. (A marble version has also made its way into a museum photograph.) The bronze, like the de László, became part of the "unofficial" McFadden collection, figuring in later-day exhibitions.[17]

McFADDEN'S DIRECT DEALING with Lord Westbury in 1913 followed what appeared to be a seamless tutorial in solo buying a year before, in Philadelphia. This earlier 1912 purchase of two portraits had a distinct one-off quality that distinguished it from McFadden's other non-English acquisitions—even those he had bought by the Anglo-American Copley and the American expatriate Augustus B. Koopman.

First, McFadden's eye came to rest on a thoroughly American artist, the New Englander Gilbert Stuart, active in the late eighteenth and early nineteenth century. In addition, the pair of Stuart works in question depicted two non-English subjects, the German Baron and Baroness von Seeger. The typical grace and nobility that McFadden sought in his English portraits were missing in the Stuart portrayals. The sitters glower. Like the Dobson, Cox, and Copley works, the Stuart oils were never destined to join the permanent McFadden collection. Nor were they ever hung at 19th and Walnut.

Instead, he donated them to the Pennsylvania Academy of the Fine Arts, on May 8, 1912. Their destination was a toss-up:

McFadden was a Pennsylvania Museum trustee, as well as an academy director. The real mystery was why he acquired the paintings in the first place, straying as he did from his affinity to the English *oeuvre*.[18] McFadden was nevertheless pleased enough about the anomalous additions that he inserted an announcement about the donation in the 1913 edition of the *Pennsylvania Society Yearbook*.[19]

McFadden must have felt pleased to have these paintings by the iconic Stuart find a home in PAFA's permanent collection. The only snag came long after his death: after several years of back and forth, in 1979, PAFA downgraded the paintings to "Unidentified Artist (formerly attributed to Gilbert Stuart)."

THE ACADEMY SHOW's success the year before had launched, unknowingly at the time, what had become the first leg of what the Philadelphia press had come to refer to as the McFadden collection "tour."[20] More stops and recognition were in store.

The tour also paralleled a growing awareness among Philadelphia arts cognoscenti that John G. Johnson's posthumous directive for the future display of his art was unachievable. Johnson, who had died on April 13, 1917, had hoped to preserve his massive collection in two adjacent townhouses, at 506 and 510 South Broad Street in South Philadelphia. The properties groaned with his immense assembly of about 1,200 objects,[21] including masterworks by Botticelli, Titian, Rembrandt, El Greco, and other artistic Olympians. In the end, no endowment was available to make the plan sustainable. The properties could not be adequately maintained. The unattended houses, once showcases, were devolving into little more than art-storage spaces. And firetraps.

For McFadden, this development spelled out a vivid lesson. If the long-term provisions for Johnson's vast, stellar collection faltered, McFadden could infer there was little hope that his could succeed in a similarly independent setting. This knowledge, coupled with the near life-altering dining room fire in early 1916, virtually shut down any notions he had held of establishing a private museum. McFadden began to fixate on how best to safeguard the now fully formed collection within an existing art institution. Which museum would get the prize? Masking his intention was no longer an option. The collection was no longer "homeless." McFadden and family had moved into the Wellington after it was completed during the previous Thanksgiving season.

McFadden decided, in effect, to audition two museums, by lending the collection for special exhibitions. (The "bastard" child, the Pennsylvania Museum and School of Industrial Art, was not in the running.) The first show was sponsored by the Department of Fine Arts of the Carnegie Institute in Pittsburgh, and ran from April 26 to June 15, 1917 as part of the institute's Founder's Day Exhibition. Like the PAFA show, the Carnegie rollout garnered national attention, another credit that pleased the collection's owner. The influential *American Magazine of Art* weighed in with praise. The *International Studio*, a New York-based quarterly, ballyhooed, "Mr. McFadden's collection is the most representative in America of the richest period of English art...."[22]

The Carnegie presentation also showed evidence of the kind of curatorial due diligence so lacking in the previous Philadelphia exhibit. Still, the exhibition organizers allowed in the painting *Girl Crossing a Rustic Bridge*, the bad penny attributed to David Cox. And in a surprise turn, two pictures by the eighteenth-century Welsh-English artist William Williams, *Courtship* and *Matrimony* (purchased October 30, 1916), debuted as part of the holdings.[23] The works addressed themes atypical of McFadden's interests. Though its two-part narrative was deemed "amusingly clever,"[24] the romantic subject did not ring true to McFadden's proclivities. The pictures were subsequently dropped from the tour.[25]

One picture *not* in the show was the putative Bonington; Mc-Fadden would purchase it later that year.

Publicity was building a head of steam, and the next show, at the Metropolitan Museum of Art in New York, took McFadden's art to the country's premier showcase and bully pulpit for connoisseurship. Less than a week was allotted to transfer the trove from Pittsburgh to New York for the show there, scheduled for "as soon as possible" after June 18, to extend to its conclusion in October. An ample second-floor display space had been arranged in Gallery 6.

The Met's June 1917 *Bulletin* suggested that the McFadden show was just one brick short of a blockbuster:

> The trustees announce an event of very considerable interest, the exhibition during the summer months and into the autumn of the important collection of pictures belonging to John H. McFadden of Philadelphia. The paintings are by the most famous British artists of the eighteenth and early nineteenth centuries. During the building of the owner's new house these pictures have been publicly shown, first in the Pennsylvania Academy of the Fine Arts in Philadelphia and lately in the Carnegie Institute in Pittsburgh. The collection has been forming for the last thirty[26] years and is regarded by certain authorities as the greatest in private hands consisting solely of works of this school.[27]

From the Pittsburgh show to the New York event, some prestidigitation occurred. Within a matter of days, the spurious *Girl Crossing a Rustic Bridge* had vanished. *Courtship* and *Matrimony* also parted company. By the time of the exhibit's opening, the misattributed Bonington had also arrived from London. Still more curatorial magic was in the making. An unnamed oil, *A Sketch* by George Romney, suddenly became the ninth work in the artist's lineup. The Met offered no detail, other than that the work was painted between 1782 and 1783. The picture was never incorporated in the final collection. Its fate is unknown.

These changes surely reflect the judgments of the Metropolitan's curator, Bryson Burroughs. Burroughs, a painter (when he felt like it) and the author of the ponderously titled *Catalogue of Portraits and Landscapes of the British School Lent by John H. McFadden*, sidestepped any mention of Romney's *Sketch*. Actually, Burroughs never got around to mentioning very much in his somewhat discursive catalogue—really just a collection of potted thumbnail biographies of the eighteen English masters represented in the exhibit.[28]

Despite the perfunctory language in his exhibit catalogue, Burroughs's support was an important indication of establishment acceptance. That knowledge was heady enough for McFadden. He donated a copy of the catalogue to the Pennsylvania Museum, as a kind of consolation prize.

As everyone knew, the Met wrote the first draft of the nation's arts agenda. In addition, Bryson Burroughs was an increasingly powerful administrator. It was a time that reflected, if nothing else, a symbolic benchmark for the Metropolitan. Following the deaths of founding trustee Joseph H. Choate, once the museum's guiding light, and of trustee John G. Johnson, the Philadelphia collector, both in 1917, the Met was transitioning into the new century with new leadership. In 1913, Robert W. T. de Forest was elected the institution's fifth president. Edward Robinson became its third director in 1910. Burroughs, who seemingly had the run of the place, was part of the new century's lineup.

The curator and the Met exuberantly embraced the McFadden Collection. So did the public. The catalogue's first run of 1,000 copies sold out at 10 cents each ($21 today); in August, the museum ordered another thousand. Though admission was free, the Met's "box office" did well with McFadden, with catalogue sales alone at $200 ($4,200 today). McFadden must have felt paroxysms of joy. In a brief eighteen months, from Philadelphia, to Pittsburgh, to New York, the erstwhile cotton magnate had been transformed into a fully vetted, recognized art baron. There was no better feeling. In his gratitude, following in Johnson's footsteps, McFadden became an enthusiastic acolyte of New York's forward-looking fine arts museum. What was more, no one had asked him for a donation. Yet.

Less than two months later, in Philadelphia, at the offices of Ballard, Spahr, Andrews & Madeira, McFadden made it clear that he saw his collection's true place as being on the world stage. In the will he and his lawyers drafted, he also gave it a new name. The nomenclature reflected what would be a posthumous self-regard, uncharacteristic in life. Going forward, the newly minted art baron decided, the collection would be known as "The John Howard McFadden *Memorial* Collection."[29] For the time being, he savored "public appreciation." "Frankly yet modestly," it was said.[30]

McFADDEN TURNED QUIXOTIC. The war over, following the signing of the Armistice on November 11, 1918, and with son Jack safe, serving as a military attaché at the American Embassy in Paris, it was a time of jubilation. And, in McFadden's mind, reckoning. Not surprisingly, what was on his mind had to do with art.

A month later, speaking on December 8 to the 1918 annual meeting of the Pennsylvania Society in New York, McFadden floated a proposal that stolen art by the German military, principally in France and Italy, be accounted for in a new museum. Although his idea was never fully fleshed out, McFadden's con-

cept called for a "Museum of Restitution" to be founded by the
Allies in Reims, France, the home of that country's famous thir-
teenth-century Nôtre-Dame de Reims (not to mention a high-end
Champagne). Despite pledges that the cathedral would be pro-
tected, the Germans had nevertheless wreaked heavy damage
on the church. In short, McFadden told the society gathering,
the museum would "assemble" and display "all works stolen by
the Germans."

The museum's creation never came to pass. Still, McFadden's
proposal was not as farfetched as it might be supposed. In fact,
the Armistice's peace terms included clauses that mandated
the restitution and restoration of looted works of art. A museum? Reims? The plan got nowhere. Yet it revealed an instance
of McFadden's passion for art extending beyond what he owned
or might buy, and a rare intersection of his love of art and his
philanthropic impulses.

———————✕———————

THERE WAS NO restraining him. Though his John Howard Mc-
Fadden Memorial Collection was complete, and inventoried in
his will, McFadden went to Agnew's one last time in 1919. His
purchase might have been nostalgic. For whatever reason, it
took his adventure in art full circle, closing the loop tidily in
a symmetrical arc. What began in 1893 with the acquisition of
Thomas Gainsborough's *Lady Rodney*, ended twenty-six years
later with his penultimate purchase, a Gainsborough portrait
the artist had worked on between 1775 and 1776 of his nephew
Gainsborough Dupont.

As already noted, Alice wound up getting the picture, which
was never inventoried, nor bequeathed in his will. Through
twists and turns of provenance, the portrait of the dashing
Gainsborough Dupont, Esq., has now come to rest at the Memphis Brooks Museum of Art, fittingly in the same Tennessee city

where John's father, George McFadden, created the financial un-
derpinnings for his art trove.

McFadden's final purchase was Romney's *David Hartley,
M.P.*, bought five weeks after *Gainsborough Dupont*, on March
18, 1920. As we have observed, son Jack took an especially keen
liking to this painting, representing his father's last hurrah as a
collector. "It is a Romney in good style and the historical interest
is considerable," Jack told a colleague.[31]

CHAPTER FIFTEEN

Founder

1920–1921

W ELL INTO HIS LATE sixties, McFadden adhered to a gruel-
ing travel schedule. Frequent commuting to his New York
office from Philadelphia by train was in itself tedious. Crossing
the Atlantic, for a voyage of more than 3,000 miles each way, to
London and Liverpool up to six times annually (twelve trips
of at least five days each at sea) constituted, despite luxurious
amenities, an exhausting schedule. His routines in Philadelphia
were equally demanding, with rounds of meetings, consulta-
tions, and, in later years, vexing personal concerns calculating
the best interests of his art trove.

There were mishaps. In 1915, he slipped, broke his ankle, and
was admitted to the University of Pennsylvania Hospital.

In between, McFadden suffered from what he generically referred to as "colds." Bed rest was often recommended.

In 1912, while in Liverpool, he wrote to his frequent spar-
ring partner, Edwin AtLee Barber, the Pennsylvania Museum's
director, that he was ailing from a "very bad cold, only getting
out of bed for a short time today."[1] On the same day, January 10,

he wrote to fellow museum trustee Theodore C. Search that he had "been ill for the past four or five days and unable to attend to anything. I am still confined to the house since last Saturday."[2] On another occasion, in a letter to Barber, he apologized for missing a trustees meeting. "I am still confined to the house since last Saturday, with a very bad cold…."

Colds are one thing. But in a time before lifesaving antibiotics, particularly penicillin, a greater threat to health, especially in the elderly, was pneumonia. McFadden contracted the lung infection a year later, in 1913, while still in Liverpool. He was sixty-three. At the time, hospital wards were full of patients battling the infection. McFadden was spared a hospital stay. Writing from his sickbed at home in Prince's Park, just before Christmas, he told Barber, "I am just recovering…."[3] Early in January, Barber responded, offering his best wishes for a speedy return to good health. "I am exceedingly sorry to hear of your illness, and I sincerely hope you will soon be entirely recovered."[4]

Meantime, he was losing weight. By 1920, photographs depicted the formerly rotund McFadden as almost gaunt. He was no longer the robust, jaunty figure of just a few years before. For most of 1920, if not months earlier, he had been in "poor health," according to *Commerce and Finance*, a trade publication that tracked the cotton industry. The *American Wool and Cotton Reporter* said "he had not been well" since 1917.[5]

In the same year, 1917, McFadden had completed his "official" art collection with the Bonington purchase. Later, in December, he drafted his will, and fatalism set in. He purchased Lot 188 in Laurel Hill Cemetery, in northwest Philadelphia, and arranged for John M. Gesslers Sons, of 39 Baltimore Avenue, to build a four-pillared, stone mausoleum to house his remains. That his immediate family was also to find a permanent resting place in the crypt was not made clear from the engraved block letters just below the vault's triangular-topped pediment: JOHN HOWARD McFADDEN. (His fiduciary agent, the Girard Trust Company, paid $2,000 [$25,000 today] to Laurel Hill for the mausoleum's perpetual care.)

McFadden was hospitalized at Penn in January 1921. *The Philadelphia Inquirer* attributed the cause to a "nervous condition" that subsequently resulted in a "nervous breakdown."[6] After a few days of supervised care, he left the hospital on January 21 when "physicians pronounced him greatly improved." Chief among them were Dr. John G. Clark and Dr. Francis R. Packard. Almost immediately, he departed for further recovery to his Atlantic City cottage. Just more than three weeks later, McFadden confronted his final illness. On Sunday, February 13, he contracted a "chill, which quickly developed in pneumonia."[7] A newspaper report called the initial condition a "cold."[8] On Wednesday, February 16, John McFadden died, at seventy. Dr. Edward J. Porteous, McFadden's local physician, attended.

By his side, according to *The Inquirer*, were Florence, Jack, and Alice. Frank got to Atlantic City later in the day. George, the newspaper reported, was on his way from Georgia. His eldest son, Philip, remained in New York City, and, according to newspaper reports, did not seem to bother with travel plans.

McFadden's funeral was held two days later, on Friday, February 18, in his backyard church, the Church of the Holy Trinity, Rittenhouse Square. The 11:30 a.m. Eucharistic service, introduced by a funereal organ fugue, was officiated by rector Floyd W. Tompkins, the same cleric who had married Alice and Jasper Yeates Brinton. A delegation from the New York Cotton Exchange attended. McFadden's remains, in a casket "banked" in a bower of red roses, were later returned to the family's Wellington apartment.[9] The following day, at noon, the casket was placed in the family mausoleum. Center City undertakers R. R. Bringhurst & Co., at 1924 Arch Street, handled the details. Internment, scheduled for noon, was private.

McFadden's obituaries were predictably officious—up to a point. Neither of the city's two biggest dailies, *The Inquirer,* nor the *Public Ledger*, positioned its obituary on page 1. The *American Art News* also broke with its usual fawning coverage of McFadden's art career. At death, he was downgraded to a one-paragraph death notice. In the same issue, on February 19, James Gibbons Huneker, an art critic and friend of McFadden, who died on February 9 and who had once dedicated a book to McFadden in honor of his connoisseurship, received eight paragraphs.[10] Dr. H. C. Ross, the English cancer researcher, contributed a "tribute" in a letter to the editor to *The Lancet*, the British medical journal. Ross wrote, "By medical men he will be remembered for, among his many activities, his practical interest in medical research."[11]

Two years earlier, as McFadden's health was declining, the Irish-born Philadelphia writer, J. St. George Joyce, claimed a stake in limning McFadden's personality. The Philadelphian embodied "an inherent urbanity, a rare personal magnetism, a wide and a varied knowledge of men and things, a cultured mind, a charming manner and an almost inexhaustible fund of humor...."[12]

The local press, understandably, emphasized the stature of McFadden's art collection, most relevant to a city where McFadden defined its evolving cultural patrimony.

In *The Philadelphia Inquirer*, McFadden was an art patron. In the *Public Ledger*, the "dead collector" was described as "a genius in [art] appreciation." From there, it was full speed ahead. The McFadden collection was

> ...overwhelming in its general effect, while the individual merit of certain of the larger canvases easily surpassed any works by the same artists in either American collections, and were more comparable to the best in foreign galleries, public and private. The McFadden Collection is notable largely because the dead collector knew what he wanted and let noth-

ing stand in the way of his getting the very best that
came before him for selection and purchase. There is,
therefore, absolutely no dead wood in the collection.
Each picture represents in itself a fine thing made all
the more finer by its association with the other works
that represent the collector's mature knowledge and
what practically amounted to a genius in appreciation. Both in this country and in Europe, where he
frequently traveled, Mr. McFadden was known in-
timately by virtually all the great artists, sculptors,
actors and medical men.[13]

McFadden's death had no effect on the company's name. The
now-vestige "Bro." remained, even as the firm expanded with
additional family members joining as partners. Since their majority, John's sons, John Jr. and Philip; and George's sons, George
H. McFadden, Jr., and Barclay, had inherited positions in the
company's hierarchy. Though still anchored at 121 Chestnut
Street, the company had modernized, as it had done in the previous era by expanding to Liverpool. The local office had a new
telephone number, Lombard 515, and cable address, "Macfadden, Philadelphia."[14]

John's death did have a temporary debilitating impact: capital depletion. McFadden's life share in the partnership was
worth $918,127 ($12.7 million today). In addition, his estate was
owed $128,333 ($1.8 million today), John's share in profits ac-
crued from the beginning of the company's fiscal year, August 31,
1920, to the time of his death. The estate cashed out his remaining shares of the Liverpool Cotton Association, $2,730 ($37,000
today); and of the New York Cotton Exchange, $16,250 ($224,000
today). No reference was made to his investment in, nor the fate
of the District Messenger Service and News Company, Ltd. In
1890, McFadden had had high hopes for the London-based travel
information startup.

Nowhere in the obituaries was there any mention of McFadden's will. Or the fate of his artwork.

In that regard, McFadden's wishes were straightforward. Ballard, Spahr, Andrews & Madeira had drafted his will three years before, and it was signed December 2, 1917, on the heels of the collection's successful show at the Metropolitan Museum of Art. McFadden appointed sons Jack and Philip as two of the estate's three executors. As an out-of-state resident (New York), Philip needed to post a surety bond of $750,000 ($10.3 million today). The third executor was Alice's husband, Jasper. By 1921, Jasper had established himself as a prominent local lawyer, and had become a trusted advisor and friend to "J. H.," his newly fashioned nickname for his father-in-law.[15] R. Sturgis Ingersoll represented Ballard.

McFadden had divided his estate into two parts, a cash and an asset-based life-interest bequest to Florence and the children; and made a separate designation for his art collection. In all, the estate was valued at about $5.2 million ($73 million today). Of that, his art collection accounted for at least $2 million ($29 million today).[16] That amount set aside, Florence received a one-third share of the balance, about $1.7 million ($24 million today). The three siblings divided the remaining two-thirds in equal amounts, about $500,000 ($7 million today) each.[17]

The will was the clearest window into McFadden's quotidian spending in both great and small measures, apart from the funding of his art collection. His photographer was a local studio known as Marceau. He kept important documents in a safety deposit bank at the Girard Trust Co. His supplier of spring water was the Great Bear Spring Co. Flowers came from the London Flower Shop. He liked butter and eggs from W. M. Moyer. Poultry came from brother George's suburban Villanova homestead, Barclay Farms. He paid retail.

THE FUTURE OF his art collection had also been settled privately, almost furtively. In 1917, when he drafted his will, McFadden
gathered three of Philadelphia's most prominent lawyers to act
as the collection's trustees. Each was a luminary in his own right.
Robert von Moschzisker, son of a Polish immigrant father, rose
to become Chief Justice of the Pennsylvania Supreme Court.
Proper Philadelphian lawyer George Wharton Pepper followed
a career driven by a sense of civic duty. His public life included
a term as a U.S. senator from Pennsylvania.

The third trustee was Jasper Yeates Brinton, McFadden's son-
in-law. His selection suitably kept McFadden's interests within
the family. Brinton's pick was also a shrewd choice, inspired by
Brinton's legal acumen and an affection and respect McFadden
and Brinton had discovered for each other. Brinton had become
a confidant, and he shared his father-in-law's bullish advocacy
for his art treasures. Like his brother-in-law Jack, Brinton had
served in France during the war. His legal skill led to an appointment as a judge advocate in Bordeaux with the suitable rank of
colonel. Later, he was an assistant U.S. attorney in Philadelphia,
Some years after that, he served as a justice of the Court of Appeals of the Mixed Courts of Egypt.[18]

McFadden's will created a challenge. In the aftermath of the
collection's stellar turns at the Pennsylvania Academy of the
Fine Arts, the Carnegie Institute, and the Metropolitan Museum
of Art, McFadden realized that his artworks had the power to
influence—whether on behalf of, in its loftiest form, connoisseurship or, in its lowest, commercialism. If the collection could
not move mountains, it might at least precipitate the Philadelphia Museum and School of Industrial Art to move to a familiar
hill in Fairmount.

Unlike John D. McIlhenny, McFadden had never promised
that the collection would wind up in the local museum. He
was not being coy. He was just reserving judgment. Undoubtedly, if anyone asked—and assuredly no one did (even the pushy

director Edwin AtLee Barber lacked such hubris)—the interlocutor would have received stone silence. His lack of esteem for the existing Pennsylvania Museum—a counterpoint to his regard for the Metropolitan's "dignity and responsibility"[19]—had been tacitly made plain when he sidestepped the local institution for exhibits at PAFA, the Carnegie, and the Met.

McFadden's most powerful extension of cultural clout would come after death. In his will, he proposed a deal with the city's arts leaders, urging the end of shillyshallying about the museum's future. Either build the new museum forthwith, or forever lose the John Howard McFadden Memorial Collection. He then rubbed it in: and lose it to the Metropolitan Museum of Art.

McFadden gave Pennsylvania Museum trustees and other "proper representatives of the City of Philadelphia" seven years from "the date of my death" to erect a new museum and "a gallery suitable as a permanent home for the collection." Otherwise, "at the expiration of seven years...then and in such case I desire and direct that my Trustees shall forthwith tender the collection to the Metropolitan Museum of Art...."[20] Bryson Burroughs, who had curated the collection's 1917 exhibit, must have crowed when he learned of this provision.

McFadden was cautious. The fate of the John G. Johnson collection had been a warning. Despite Johnson's brilliance as a corporate lawyer, he was less astute in probate law. In the mistaken belief that his collection would continue to be housed in his premises on South Broad Street and overseen by city officials, Johnson had imprudently donated his artwork to the City of Philadelphia. Technically, that meant that its fate would wind up in the Philadelphia Court of Common Pleas Orphans' Court, the probate agency that protects and manages the personal and property rights of incapacitated persons, or their estates. With oversight transferred to Orphans' Court, Johnson's testamentary control was effectively lost. In addition, the Johnson bequest was mired in unforeseen Pennsylvania and federal estate tax claims.

McFadden was careful to dodge that bullet. He ordered that von Moschzisker, Pepper, and Brinton withhold any negotiations with city officials until the seven-year deadline was met, if indeed it was. McFadden cited "delays which have existed in the building of the said museum and of the uncertainties as to the completion thereof...." Therefore, "I direct that the collection shall not in any event be transferred under the powers herein, to the City of Philadelphia or such other body or corporation as is above specified, until such gallery is completed and the pictures are received therein...." Only then would the Orphans' Court get involved.

McFadden wanted the collection to remain in the public eye. He stipulated that his trustees should consider moving the artwork from the Wellington to a temporary home such as the Met, "or some other museum or gallery of equal dignity and responsibility."

The will turned the screws even tighter. Not only did the Pennsylvania Museum need to reinvent itself in Fairmount; the new museum would forever have to display the collection "in its entirety, in a single gallery," guaranteeing its "dignified, fitting and permanent maintenance...." Given McFadden's proclivities, "dignified" and "fitting" probably meant a formal setting. Maintenance costs would come from an annual stipend of up to $7,500 ($103,353 today).[21]

THE YEAR 1921 not only triggered the seven-year stopwatch. It also marked the beginning of an otherwise unrelated five-year run of internal McFadden family turmoil, shame, and front-page scandal. In death, John was shielded. But trustees George Pepper and Jasper Brinton, in separate cases, were drawn in.

Pepper was a bit player in what became the year's tawdriest opéra bouffe, involving a French-born governess, $500,000

($7 million today) worth of pilfered jewels, a reputed Parisian "grand duke," and George H. McFadden, Jr., John McFadden's hapless nephew, an 1893 Penn graduate and nominal member of the family firm. (Twenty-five years before, George and his sister Ellie were frequent summer guests of John's family in Liverpool.) Regardless of its risible nature, the ensuing tale of theft and marital deceit was serious enough that it wound up in court.

The accused was Jeanne Auberlet, the live-in governess and French tutor to George McFadden Jr.'s fourteen-year-old daughter Caroline. Auberlet's job at Bloomfield, the family Villanova estate, did not include bribery, specifically $50,000 ($689,000 today) in hush money that Auberlet was demanding, as George charged in the proceedings. In itself, the Frenchwoman's tale sounded preposterous. Nevertheless she alleged that the jewels, including a $150,000 ($2.1 million today) pearl necklace, were stolen from McFadden's Bloomfield mansion by none other than his wife, Josephine, a doe-eyed beauty—and *her* grande-dame mother, Mrs. Benjamin Franklin Clyde of Bryn Mawr. Mother and daughter, according to Auberlet, planned to dump the cache to fund a getaway to Paris, where they hoped to cuckold George with a "grand duke." George Pepper had the thankless task of acting as Mrs. Clyde's lawyer.[22]

In late March, the case against Auberlet fizzled out as mysteriously as it had emerged. All charges were dropped. Mrs. McFadden and Mrs. Clyde returned to their social swirl in Philadelphia. The jewels, just as incomprehensibly, were never found.

To the family's chagrin, George provided much material to feed an insatiable press, always hungry for salacious news about the rich and mighty. In January of the same year, Josephine—just months away from being accused of feathering a Parisian love-nest—made her début on page 1. She and several other Philadelphia Society matrons had been threatened with physical harm unless they each paid blackmailers up to $2,000 ($27,560 today). Fortunately, the culprits, a "gang" from Pittsburgh, were quickly apprehended before any injury was inflicted.[23]

Then, in April, George's valet was stricken and died on McFadden's private railway carriage during a trip with his employer.[24] *George H. McFadden, Jr. Valet. Private rail car.* Another press splash.

Unlike Pepper, a peripheral figure in the jewel-heist sideshow, Brinton was a principal in the scandal that swept him up—his divorce from Alice. Their marriage had been fragile for many years before their official separation in 1924. In the year of McFadden's death, Brinton had moved to Egypt to take up his judgeship. Alice and the children, John, eight, and Florence Pamela, six, remained in Philadelphia. The grass widow pursued her interests in local amateur theater as a member of the Plays and Players Club and as chairman of the Drama Committee of the Art Alliance.

The Brintons' falling out was rancorous. Their divorce was also sensitive enough, and fraught with the attendant social implications in Philadelphia, that legal proceedings took place "discreetly" in Paris.[25] Alice had a tenuous connection to the French capital. Her parents were married there; her maternal grandparents, the Bateses, had lived there.

The divorce was hard on the children, involving a long-term, divisive separation from each other and any mutual relationship with their parents. Soon after, John Brinton moved to Alexandria. Pamela Brinton started to divide time between Philadelphia and New York, her mother's new, part-time home. In 1925, Alice married Laurence Eyre, a popular Broadway playwright. (Alice had originally gotten to know Eyre, a native of Chester, Pennsylvania, from the Philadelphia theater scene.)

Despite the awkward, strained circumstances, Jasper Brinton remained faithful to "J.H." Even from a great distance, he was a fierce defender, out of loyalty and respect, of his late father-in-law's artworks.

PART III

If there is any truth in the saying that every people has the government it deserves, it is even truer that every civilization, every race, ever epoch finds itself reflected as in a mirror in its architecture.

—PAUL P. CRET

ABOVE: *The Philadelphia Museum of Art on Fairmount Hill*

CHAPTER SIXTEEN

Aftermath

1921–1928

FOLLOWING HER HUSBAND'S DEATH in February, Florence sought a place for mourning and solace away from Philadelphia. A few months after John's burial, she closed the Wellington apartment and made her way to son Philip's summer cottage—he called the rustic getaway "Green Bay Camp"—in Upper Saranac Lake, New York. The town, nestled in the remote, upstate Adirondack Mountains, surrounded by numerous lakes, was a posh summer retreat for equally posh New Yorkers and Proper Philadelphians who wanted to avoid Newport glitz. (Nearby was the somewhat flashier Saranac Lake, which attracted the likes of the more modish Vanderbilts.) By train and car, it was just more than six hours and almost 400 miles away from Rittenhouse Square.

Florence, two years older than John, was suffering from heart disease,[1] and had planned to spend the summer idly recuperating with Philip and his wife, Annette. Florence had many "warm friends"[2] she had made during frequent summer visits to Green Bay Camp.

Florence died on August 14, seven days after her seventy-third birthday. Death was attributed to heart failure. After a funeral two days later in the Church of the Holy Trinity (the Rev. Floyd W. Tompkins was again pressed into service), Florence's casket was placed near her husband's in the family crypt, in Laurel Hill Cemetery.

Philip and Annette remained in Philadelphia for the remainder of August, missing the annual midsummer ball, held August 20 in the Casino at the New York campgrounds.[3] Members of the Upper Saranac Lake "colony," who did attend the ball, told a visiting reporter from the *New York Tribune* they felt a "personal loss."[4]

Florence was the last resident of the two-floor penthouse in the landmark Wellington. Her death stirred consternation that her husband's folly, as the apartment-hotel was uncharitably viewed by some crusty Philadelphians, might go on the selling block. Or worse, be demolished, setting the stage for an even cruder replacement. By autumn the rumors were rampant, even getting an airing in newspaper reports. Horace H. Fritz, McFadden's associate in the Rittenhouse Square Realty Co., the Wellington's development company and owner, attempted to quash the idle talk in a series of advertisements in *The Philadelphia Inquirer.*

> The Wellington
> 19th and Walnut Streets
> Philadelphia
>
> Because of unfounded statements recently appearing in the public press indicating that negotiations were pending for the sale of the Wellington Apartment Hotel, the ownership management, in fairness to itself and to its patrons, desires to make this public announcement of the fact that no negotiations for

the sale of the property are pending or are even being considered.

THE RITTENHOUSE SQUARE REALTY CO.
By Horace H. Fritz, President[5]

The newspaper notices were for public consumption. Knowledgeable Philadelphians knew the Wellington's fate was secure. At least, for as long as John McFadden's pictures were still housed there. For the time being, trustees Robert von Moschzisker, George Pepper, and Jasper Brinton could assure those in their Rittenhouse circle that the paintings were not going anywhere.

———— ✕ ————

FOR ALMOST TWO weeks following John McFadden's death, no word about the will's contents, nor the disposition of the art collection, had been leaked to the press. Pennsylvania Museum trustees and city officials held their breath. On February 28, R. Sturgis Ingersoll, on behalf of Ballard, provided the information they had awaited, by filing McFadden's will for probate with the Philadelphia Register of Wills. On March 1, readers of the *Philadelphia Inquirer* could exhale with relief: "Art Works Valued at Millions Given City by M'Fadden." Philadelphia readers of the same day's *New York Times* gasped. The *Times*'s headline: "McFadden Art Collection to Philadelphia if Home is Provided; If Not, Will Come Here."

The *Inquirer* was reluctant to report McFadden's challenge. That revelation came in its story's tenth paragraph. And, then, with further trepidation, on page 13: "In the event that the proposed gallery shall not have been completed within seven years or the terms and conditions shall not have been agreed on for the transfer of the collection to the city, the will directs that it shall be tendered to the Metropolitan Museum of Art in New York...."[6]

The Times got to the point in the *second* paragraph: "...the
only stipulation being that the Municipal Art Museum to house
the paintings be completed within seven years after Mr. McFadden's death. Should the city fail to meet this requirement, the
pictures go to the Metropolitan Museum of Art in New York."[7]

Left murky was the question of how the collection would
be transferred to the city or the Met. McFadden's will mandated that his paintings be transmitted to the City of Philadelphia,
and that a fiduciary "trust" be established to "transfer and con-
vey" the collection to any institution that would house it. While
the *new* Pennsylvania Museum would be understood to be the
qualifying entity to display the paintings, the museum would
never actually own the collection, only maintain and present
the works. In the end, Philadelphia Orphans' Court, a division
of the Court of Common Pleas, would oversee the proper administration of the trust. Over time, these details would seep
out for public consumption.[8]

In the short term, enthusiasm reigned. In staking a claim for
the city's receipt of McFadden's bounty, *The Inquirer* subsequently made amends: the philanthropist's February 16 obituary had
been buried deep in the newspaper's back pages. Two weeks
later, with the realization that Philadelphia could be enriched
by McFadden's fabulous art collection, *Inquirer* editors reconsidered their original judgment: by March 1, McFadden's legacy had
risen to a page 1, above-the-fold status.

Even city officials who had not been heard from before, in
the immediate aftermath of McFadden's death, were now lining up to praise their newly remembered native son. Mayor J.
Hampton Moore's comments in the article reached hundreds
of thousands of *Inquirer* readers, but they were largely directed to an audience of three: trustees von Moschzisker, Pepper,
and Brinton. "This gift crowns a distinguished life," Moore
said. "It is a fitting climax to a career largely devoted to public
service." And,

> Mr. McFadden was one of Philadelphia's leading citi-
> zens, a commanding figure in the world of commerce,
> a life-long benefactor of scientific research, and one
> of America's connoisseurs of art. He was a far-seeing
> man. Contact with work gave him a broad view of life.
> He was constantly looking ahead, encouraging others
> in work by which future generations would benefit.

He went on to say:

> His contributions to the investigation and cure of such
> scourges of mankind as cancer, the hookworm, mea-
> sles and scarlet fever will make the world of tomorrow
> his debtor. He was a native Philadelphian, and well
> before he was of age, one of the founders of the great
> business house which bears his family name. His fig-
> ure was as familiar in the capitals of Europe as at home.
> His coolness and courage were proverbial and he was a
> citizen of which any city would have been proud.

Moore's paean came across as self-serving and unctuous.[9]
  City officials went on to dangle tax incentives, quickly dis-
pelling any suggestion that the McFadden bequest would result
in the "immense" federal tax burden that the donation of the
John G. Johnson Collection, just four years before, had imposed
upon the city. The McFadden Collection, city officials told the
trustees, would fall under a new 1918 "special exemption," al-
lowing art bequests to public bodies to be free of federal tax. In
addition, state inheritance taxes would be waived.[10]

MAYOR MOORE WAS no novice at political arm twisting. He had
cut his teeth as a reporter for the *Public Ledger*. After serving

seven terms as a U.S. congressman, he resigned in 1920 to run
successfully for Philadelphia mayor. (That ostensibly downward
transition was not unheard of at the time.) Moore was known as
an "old-fashioned Republican,"[11] meaning he placed the interests
of Philadelphia's business élite—and the ruling Proper Philadelphia hierarchy—as a top priority. But the mayor soon found that
influencing decision-making in the disposition of the McFadden
bequest was even beyond his oleaginous skill-set.

Just before McFadden's will was published, Moore arranged
for "a series of conferences" with McFadden family members.
Condolences were surely tendered. But more than likely—though
no fly-on-the-wall account exists—the mayor also lobbied for
a favorable outcome; even, perhaps, for setting aside the seven-
year deadline.[12] What Florence Bates McFadden, Philip Grandin
McFadden, Alice McFadden Brinton, and John Howard McFadden, Jr., made of the rough-and-tumble politician would be hard
to plumb. But a former newspaper hack turned political wheeler-dealer was not the element they usually consorted with.

Moore went on to hold "conferences" with trustees von
Moschzisker, Pepper, and Brinton. The three, in one way or
another, were all involved in Philadelphia's political hornet's
nest. All were Republicans, all had served in public office,
and all were as clean as a whistle. (To avoid any semblance of
conflict, Brinton, moreover, had resigned as a Pennsylvania
Museum trustee in 1917, the year McFadden's will was drafted.)
Still, Moore left the meetings thinking, erroneously, that he had
an "assurance"—however preposterous that might now seem in
hindsight—that the artwork could be displayed in Philadelphia
prior to 1928, even before construction on the new Pennsylvania Museum was "sufficiently advanced."[13]

The trustees had another idea, and John McFadden would
have approved.

THE TRUSTEES WERE as much "guardian angels" as legal guard-
ians. They realized the Wellington was hardly a safe site for the
multi-million-dollar collection. *The Philadelphia Inquirer* was
now speculating the artwork could be monetized for at least $4
million ($55.7 million today), twice its appraised value in Mc-
Fadden's will. Now widely publicized, the princely collection
also had a greater potential for theft, especially without the installation of security technology—much less a low-tech armed
guard. Fire was another threat. The destructive dining room
fire in 1916, which claimed Thomas Lawrence's *Miss Nelthorpe*,
was still fresh in mind. In addition, following Florence's death,
the McFadden children would not likely maintain their parents' Wellington penthouse at the yearly lease fee of $16,500
($228,500 today).

To the surprise of nearly everyone, the trustees turned to the
protective, and politically neutral, cocoon of the Smithsonian
Institution in Washington, where the artwork was to be exhibited in the U.S. National Museum, then Washington's premier art
showcase. (Andrew W. Mellon's National Gallery of Art was not
formally opened until 1941.) The trustees had chosen well. The
National Museum on the National Mall (the building would later
house the National Museum of Natural History) was a domed
colossus, the kind of structure that McFadden himself was hoping would rise on Fairmount Hill in Philadelphia.

Contrary to Mayor Moore's pipe-dream, no other exhibition
sites were contemplated.

By late 1921, "preliminary steps" were underway for the
loan. The Smithsonian's secretary, Charles D. Walcott, expressed some hesitancy, bemoaning "the fact that there is much
shortage of storage space in the halls occupied by the national
collections…." He also suggested a restriction to the exhibit's
duration.[14] "Notwithstanding," Walcott added, "…the acceptance
of this rich collection for a limited period is regarded with much
favor." And that period, presumably, extended for the next six

years. The collection would remain at the National Museum until its return to Philadelphia.

The trustees officially informed the City Council of the collection's departure to Washington several months later, in 1922. On September 7, the council notified Mayor Moore of the move. This exercise was a formality; the McFadden pictures had been hanging in the National Museum's two large, skylighted south rooms, prominently facing the National Mall, since July.[15] Frank Lynn Jenkins's bronze bust of McFadden was centered in one of the galleries, gazed upon by the beatific rendering of Little Bo-Peep in George Romney's idyll *The Shepherd Girl*. In the center of each gallery, according to photographs published at the time, additional, unidentified McFadden bibelots were encased in wood-framed glass vitrines.

The trustees' note to the City Council went beyond mere etiquette. Another motive emerged: would the city care to pay for "insurance against theft" while the pictures were in Washington? This payment, apparently, would not have been drawn from the $7,500 ($103,353 today) capital endowment McFadden had set aside for the collection's upkeep.[16]

DESPITE THE MCFADDEN Collection's almost semi-permanent residence in Washington, Mayor Moore, Pennsylvania Museum trustees, and other hometown stakeholders still had cause for optimism—despite the looming seven-year deadline. The terms of John McFadden's will had, against many odds, provided the leverage to tip the project's many participants into action. Local architects Charles L. Borie, Jr., Horace Trumbauer, and Clarence Zantzinger had put the finishing touches on the final look of the new museum. Some cheeky, viper-tongued critics were quick to dub the project as Philadelphia's "Greek Garage," as the monolithic, neo-Classical shape was visibly rising—however fitfully—at the former site of the city's reservoir on Fairmount Hill. Others said, dismissively, that Philadelphia was building its own "Quaker Acropolis."

Meantime, well underway was the new "Fairmount Parkway,"[17] a broad, connecting causeway from Center City to the museum. The expanse was designed by Parisian architect Jacques Gréber, whose selection prompted those with long memories to recall the controversy when another Frenchman, Philadelphia's wunderkind Paul P. Cret, revamped Rittenhouse Square in 1913. Fears that Cret would transform the square into an over-designed Parc Monceau-like space (he did not) were rekindled in a revised form. Now some wags wondered whether Cret's countryman would reimagine his venture as a bastardized version of the Avenue des Champs-Élysées. (He did.) Some may have appreciated the nativist pastiche of the Greek and French themes in the two new construction projects—an only-in-America dream come true.

What had been for many years a thicket of financial and bureaucratic twists and turns—and back-room cronyism—had finally narrowed to the final stages. In less than a decade, Philadelphia would undergo a momentous physical transformation, like none other in its history. How this rolled out on time—albeit over-budget—was the work and inspiration of mainly two men.

One was, incongruously, best known until then for a goat statue he had donated to Rittenhouse Square, that had been entertaining children and delighting their parents since 1917.

The other was America's gas meter king.

CHAPTER SEVENTEEN

Fairmount

1921–1928

BY THE EARLY 1920S, Eli Kirk Price II and John D. McIlhenny had forged an unusual partnership. Philadelphia insiders at first shook their heads, and then sighed with relief when they came to understand that the Pennsylvania Museum's fortunes were in such good hands. The relationship between the two civic leaders was informal, though still businesslike, given urgency by the knowledge that the fine art collections of George L. Elkins and his son George W. Elkins were, like the John H. McFadden Collection, also subject to an irrevocable deadline.

The Price-McIlhenny alliance was symbiotic. Price, known as resolute and imperious, pulled the levers of power. McIlhenny, of a more moderate disposition, had an eye for art. Their skills meshed. They were around the same age, both born in the 1860s. Both were also Proper Philadelphian snobs, though Price could snoot higher than McIlhenny, and he let it be known. Price's Quaker family had landed in Philadelphia in 1685. He was a Penn law graduate. McIlhenny's father was a nineteenth-century Protestant Irish immigrant. High school was the younger McIlhenny's highest academic achievement.

Comfortably rich and ensconced in the upper reaches of Proper Philadelphia, Price, a lawyer, rarely had the inclination, much less any need, to practice his profession. Rather, in civic circles, Price was known as a behind-the-scenes, sometimes shadowy figure called upon to dispel civic discord and promote community harmony. E. Digby Baltzell memorialized Price as the period's "foremost civic and cultural leader."[1] Notably, Price was also patient.

Nothing illustrated that trait better than the way Price went about donating *Billy*, a bronze rendition of a horned goat by Philadelphia sculptor Albert Laessle. The *Billy* saga began innocuously in 1915 when Price proposed that the Fairmount Park Art Association buy the near life-sized sculpture for $800 ($20,000 today). Amid grousing about its artistic merits and its siting in Rittenhouse Square, the proposal stalled, and in the end was turned down by an association sub-committee. Laessle garnered $25 ($600 today) for his trouble.[2]

The battle was lost. But not the war. Five years on, Price adopted a new *modus operandi*: anonymity. He purchased *Billy* on his own, and donated the work to the city, not to the association. The naysayers wound up with whiplash. Before they knew what had happened, Price had arranged for the statue to be sited in the square. Game, Price.[3]

Though wealthy like his social "better," McIlhenny slogged at a day job, heading Helme and McIlhenny, a gas meter manufacturing company founded by his father. He also maintained a lucrative sideline in the leveraged buyouts of distressed companies. Major layoffs usually resulted. His only son, Henry P. McIlhenny, would gloss over this unsavory aspect of the business, using the rather anodyne description, "buying up companies, putting them on their feet, and then selling them again at a profit."[4]

Unlike Price, McIlhenny was a collector, though his chosen field, textiles, had none of the panache and mass appeal of fine art collecting. Worse, McIlhenny was less a connoisseur than a gullible buyer, a victim of arts guru Wilhelm Reinhold Valentiner, who served up dubious advice and high commissions in the same measure.

What the two Philadelphians shared most was an unparalleled determination to bring the new Pennsylvania Museum to fruition. As museum trustees, both men were on an equal footing. But in a reversal of the pecking order that governed the city's body politic, McIlhenny had risen to the museum's presidency. Price served as vice president of the Fairmount Park Commission.

By 1925, with tacit trustee support, both men had established a bond that animated their joint mission. Personnel changes ranked high on their short list. Acting director Samuel W. Woodhouse Jr., despite accomplishments in fundraising and acquiring objects in his field of interest, was not going to be spared. McIlhenny might have viewed Woodhouse's departure as a kind of leveraged buyout—with a layoff of one.

WOODHOUSE HAD BEEN the Pennsylvania Museum's acting director since 1923, stepping in after the previous director, the feckless Langdon Warner, joined Harvard's Fogg Museum as curator of Oriental Art. By most measures, including temperament, training, and inclination, Woodhouse would never do as a transitional director. By training, he was a physician. By temperament, he was confrontational and egotistical—traits that the equally haughty Price could not countenance. And Woodhouse had little interest in championing the museum's expanded mission. He liked decorative arts: diamonds, jewelry, and Spode china, in the main. The Victoria and Albert was his kind of place.

Woodhouse's biggest black mark was indiscretion. He open-
ly criticized trustees as "hopeless." He then proceeded to wade
in on Price—a bad idea. He let slip, "Eli Price has saddled us with
a building that is far too big; it will require a much larger staff
and we cannot afford any more men than we have. We ought to
stick to Memorial Hall and specialize on the arts and crafts of
Philadelphia and take a worthy position in that field."[5]

ON PAPER, FISKE Kimball (1888–1955) would have been anyone's
ideal candidate. His education was a series of checks in all the
right boxes: bachelor's and master's degrees from Harvard, and
a doctorate from the University of Michigan. His subsequent
career was meteoric: heading the newly created department of
art and architecture at the University of Virginia and, only four
years on, plucked to be the first director of the Institute of Fine
Arts at New York University.

That was on paper. In person, Kimball struck another chord
entirely. Rather than the lean, urbane museum director from
Central Casting, he was big, bold, bullet-headed, and known for
the awkward contretemps. (Once attending a posh dinner party,
he splintered his hostess's Hepplewhite dining room chair—by
just sitting in it.) No amount of camouflage—even his ever-pres-
ent bowler hat and Brooks Brothers attire—was enough. Two
Kimball friends, George and Mary Roberts, provided a vivid visual: "He made a fine, upstanding figure, though his tall, thick
body looked as if it had been forcibly stuffed into his gray, dou-
ble-breasted suit. His head and face were big—indeed he seemed
a little more than life size....His hair was clipped very short
and the back of his short neck creased....He looked rather like a
wartime cartoon of a typical German."[6]

McIlhenny and Price, two of the most proper of Philadelphians, liked what they read in Kimball's *curriculum vitae*

and—providentially for the new museum's future—even liked what they saw. During a series of meetings, starting in 1924 in New York and winding up in the dark, inner recesses of the Art Club of Philadelphia, McIlhenny and Price also discovered Kimball's rich intellect, strong-willed commitment to scholarship, and, as important, his start-up management skills as demonstrated at UVA and NYU. He was hired on June 9, 1925.

Proper Philadelphians gasped. McIlhenny and Price might be willing to accommodate Kimball's diamond-in-the-rough demeanor. But Proper Philadelphia's imprimatur, admission to the holy ground of the Philadelphia Club, was another matter indeed. When a membership inquiry was made on Kimball's behalf, a friend's muted response was, "I have tried." Another Rittenhouse Philadelphian, who thought himself Kimball's better, declared, "I hate Fiske Kimball; he's always trying to get my mother to give our good furniture to that Museum of his!" Licking his wounds, Kimball wound up with a consolation prize, membership in the Rittenhouse Club.[7]

Charles Poore, a *New York Times* critic, noted that those around Kimball never knew when "he was going to blow his top; they were certain that at any gathering calling for suavity he might commit instead some egregious malaprop."[8] Kimball was bellicose. He was irascible. He was a force of nature.

FIVE MONTHS AFTER Kimball joined the museum, McIlhenny, then sixty, suffered a heart attack while in New York, and died three weeks later. Though it was ghoulish to dwell on, Price's recruitment of Kimball was all the more timely—given that McIlhenny's death destabilized the institutional equilibrium and momentum that the late president had set in motion. Kimball's management skills—those he had brought to bear at UVA and NYU—were immediately enlisted, and they proved invaluable: his commanding and steady presence filled the immediate administrative power vacuum. Though the challenge was of course unforeseen, Kimball prevailed in what had become a test in crisis management.

The new director's visible, steady hand was not unnoticed by Price. The pair almost immediately formed a new vanguard. What had been for Price and McIlhenny an association of social equals had now taken on the air of an odd couple. The sixty-five-year-old Price was slight and refined. The thirty-seven-year-old Kimball was cantankerous and blustering. Price moved up to museum president. With Kimball as director, it was a match made in heaven.

Their antagonist, Dr. Woodhouse, the museum's departing acting director, chimed in, "It will be a long, cold winter for the Museum."[9] As usual, he was wrong.

WHILE PRICE AND Kimball worked cooperatively, each had his own remit. Price was the "builder." His brief included paying the bills, and he pioneered then-modern forms of professional fundraising. He crunched numbers. He counted bricks.

Kimball was the artistic and cultural warrior. In stark contrast to Woodhouse, he saw the new museum breathing life into a unique, encyclopedic rendition of human experience—in fine arts, decorative arts, sculpture, and architecture. He made an exception. By casual agreement with Penn's University Museum—a gentleman's understanding, really—only Western post-Christian art and Oriental art after 500 CE would fall within the new museum's purview. The informal "non-compete clause" left ancient art, the art of other cultures, and anthropology (spears, arrows, mummies, and the like) to the University Museum.[10]

Kimball's vision for the new municipal museum shunted aside the model of the Metropolitan Museum of Art, then the unchallenged cynosure of America's high culture. Even the idea of a "Philadelphia Louvre," also on everyone's short list as a template, got shelved. Kimball's imagination was animated instead by Berlin's Kaiser-Friedrich-Museum, founded in 1904.[11] Arguably alone among prominent international museums, the Kaiser-Friedrich presented its collections geographically and chronologically, not segregated by similar themes and forms.

Architectural historian David B. Brownlee observed, "This 'cultural-historical' arrangement, Kimball recognized, offered a picture of human life and achievement that was far more appealing to the general public than the crowded galleries of most contemporary museums, with paintings organized by donor and the other arts grouped by material."[12]

Kimball's fertile mind conjured another form of staging coming into its own: "period rooms" that faithfully recreated historical living and working spaces. The idea was not new, but had not been widely adopted, nor heralded. The Met installed its first period rooms in 1924, a year before Kimball was hired in Philadelphia. Still, the idea had been clearly germinating in Kimball's imagination for some time. As the Philadelphia director fleshed out the concept just a year later, its genesis was arguably his to claim—or, at least, to share honorably with the Met.

Years later, a museum report expounded, "While 'period rooms' existed before, both at the Museum and elsewhere, Kimball's overarching vision and meticulous attention to authenticity were in many ways legendary. His integrated and contextual approach spurred the installation plan...."[13]

In time, Kimball would learn that institutional laurels such as this did not always fall equally, nor fairly.

———————✕———————

IN PROMOTING THE encyclopedic concept, with period rooms dotting a Kaiser-Friedrich-like landscape, Kimball had laid out the new Pennsylvania Museum's internal structure. In finely tuned public relations-speak, he spoke of how visitors would walk along the "Main Street of Art." Elsewhere, he adopted exquisite prose to further define the mission:

> The building of the new Museum by the public is a magnificent civic achievement. To fill it worthily will take the united labor of all. To assemble there the artistic riches of Philadelphia, and expand them by the united wealth and devotion of the community, would make a museum of which any city, any nation, might be proud—a source of delight and inner enrichment to every citizen. Let us dedicate ourselves to the task.[14]

Such lyrical, lofty rhetoric, ironically, sowed some fair-minded seeds of doubt. Skeptics wondered: Would the new museum "cater to high-brow taste exclusively" and emerge as "a club for the city's wealthy"?[15] Price had a ready response. Unfortunately, his approach was tone-deaf, patronizing, and jingoistic.

Taking his cue from Kimball's mission statement, Price went about crafting a fundraising program. In doing this, he explored still largely untilled ground in the latest solicitation techniques. Firstly, he hired a New York-based fundraising firm, John Price Jones Corporation, to oversee a community-wide appeal that would burrow into private, corporate, and governmental donor classes. The company's founder, Pennsylvania-born Jones, had pioneered the use of data mining. Fundraising had become a "science."

In its early stage—in 1922, before Kimball came on board—the effort wallowed in ethnic insensitivity. A thirty-four-page campaign brochure, "The New Museum and its Service to Philadelphia," produced in pocket-book-sized form, did make it clear the new museum would be no adjunct to the Philadelphia Club.

But, in targeting its potential middle- and upper-class donors,
the giving rationale took a curious turn: foreign-born Philadelphians were singled out as those most in need of the soothing,
civilizing benefits of art. Even more incongruous, given the social milieu of those who drafted the brochure, the appeal was
also laced with an overtly anti-clerical twist. "Art in the Service
of Americanization" was stressed:

> A large number of our visitors are foreign born or
> of foreign parents. To them the museum must take
> the place of the cathedral, the mediaeval church
> with its stained glass windows, its carvings and its
> brasses, or of the local manor house of ancient archi-
> tecture, which is part of everyday life of town and
> country-bred workers in Europe. We have come to
> understand that to rob such people of the things of
> the spirit and to supply them with higher wages as
> a substitute is not good economics, good patriotism
> or good policy.... To talk of the "Americanizing" of
> our citizens only by filling their bellies and teach-
> ing them the Constitution is folly. The most careful
> research has failed to find an individual possessed
> of his wits, who cannot be profoundly moved by
> the arts....

DURING THE NEAR two decades of the museum's gestation—from
a post-Centennial dream, to the missed opportunity of P. A. B.
Widener's promise to pay for the place himself (he died in 1915),
to the birth-pains of actual construction—how much money actually poured into the project was unevenly reported. Price had
initially started out with a paltry $200,000 ($2.5 million today),
begrudgingly doled out by the Philadelphia City Council. That

amount, it was understood, would be a down payment on the museum's full $3.5 million ($43.7 million today) price tag.

Through the years 1923 and 1924, scandal-ridden cost over-runs pushed the bottom line ever upwards. Finally, it came to rest with an eye-popping expenditure, in public money alone, of between $12 million ($175 million today)[16] and $13 million ($190 million today).[17]

All along, city paymasters were on the hook. Bringing his power-brokering skills to bear, Price knotted a financial noose on the newly elected mayor, W. Freeland Kendrick. The museum plan called for the multilevel structure to be three-sided, its three pavilions squared around a central courtyard facing Fairmount Parkway. Price cleverly decided to build the two outer wings first, and these were completed by 1925. Then he tightened the screws: by this formula, the main, connecting building would *have* to be built.[18] The plan was reminiscent of Price's end-run in siting *Billy* in Rittenhouse Square. Wheeler-dealer Kendrick—mayor, imperial potentate of the Shriners, and president of the scandal-plagued Sesquicentennial Exhibition in Philadelphia in 1926—was also no match for the museum president.

Private fundraising went on unabated. By 1927, Price had recruited a Museum Fund executive committee, including John McFadden's longtime associates Edward T. Stotesbury and John S. Jenks. He appointed the ubiquitous R. Sturgis Ingersoll as a committee member, and took a similar position for himself. Two other appointed members, George D. Widener, Jr., P. A. B. Widener's grandson; and William M. Elkins, son of George W. Elkins and grandson of William L. Elkins, had particular self-interests, as each held controlling stakes in their own and their family's art patrimonies. Most telling was who was *not* a committee member: P.A.B. Widener's son Joseph E. Widener, who alone would determine where father's vast art holdings would find permanent wall space.

The fundraising strategy used in 1924 had been revised from two years before. Instead of the previous, heavy-handed theme of lifting up immigrant classes, the Museum Fund now sought to arouse a cultural commitment, brandishing "Philadelphia's Opportunity" to showcase some of the world's greatest art. The appeal ventured into hyperbole. A 1924 brochure claimed that no other "museum or gallery in any European country [has] begun its life with such treasures in its possession."[19] Cited were the Wilstach Collection, long a mainstay at Memorial Hall; the John G. Johnson Collection, transferred to the museum's aegis following a court judgment; and the William L. Elkins and the George W. Elkins collections. (These, too, would be governed by Orphans" Court edict.)

Like the McFadden Collection, the now-paired Elkins collections of father and son were also restricted by a make-or-break construction deadline, imposed by William L. Elkins's 1919 will. (Unlike the McFadden will, which cited the Met as an alternative venue, Elkins did not propose a secondary repository.) By 1924, grandson and executor William M. Elkins had had enough, and released the collections by declaring that William L.'s five-year deadline had been met—by a completed basement corridor that had been quickly designated for the artwork.[20]

The Elkins pieces, including pictures by Gainsborough, Lawrence, Romney, and the like, significantly expanded the museum's holdings of important English works. But, as a whole, their collective strengths still fell short of the McFadden collection's potential for showcasing English art—that is, if its donation did not fall through. Of a total of 130 Elkins paintings, then valued at $2.5 million ($35.8 million today), only fifteen were by English practitioners collected by McFadden.

Whether the public noticed or not, museum officials were politic in not mentioning collections amassed by P. A. B. Widener and Edward T. Stotesbury.

In Peter Widener's case, his son and executor Joe Widener took a page from his father's playbook, and claimed he was ready to build his own eponymous museum. As an inducement, Mayor Kendrick had offered to give Widener a city-owned site on Fairmount Parkway. In a way, Joe Widener was toying with Kendrick and his fellow Pennsylvania Museum trustees. He also said about the same time that he might donate his father's collection to the Metropolitan, or, hmm—perhaps the Smithsonian. Fickle as he was, he finally adopted a third alternative: in 1939, he offered everything to the new National Gallery of Art in Washington, which officially opened in 1941. The municipal museum in Philadelphia lost more than 2,000 artworks. A true Philadelphian, Joe Widener had a long, unforgiving memory of how Proper Philadelphia had treated his father, a simple resident of North Broad Street.

Stotesbury's fine art collection, housed in his two Rittenhouse Square mansions and at his suburban Whitemarsh Hall, was also problematic. In 1927, Stotesbury was worth $100 million ($1.4 billion today). After the Great Depression, his holdings plummeted to $4 million ($70.8 million today), his estate's value at his death in 1938. His spendthrift widow, Eva, a fixture in Palm Beach, took care of the rest, deaccessioning art to make ends meet.

John McFadden trustees Robert von Moschzisker, George Wharton Pepper, and Jasper Brinton were not as forgiving, nor as pliable as William M. Elkins. In mid-1927, as proof of their uncompromising commitment to McFadden's wishes, they reaffirmed a specific date, February 16, 1928—seven years to the day from McFadden's death—to trigger the collection's removal from the Smithsonian, where it was being temporarily exhibited, to a permanent home at the Metropolitan.

Even at this late date, the McFadden collection's destiny was not certain. *The New York Times* headlined the concern: "FEARS ART TREASURE LOSS. Philadelphia Collection Will Come Here [New York] if Museum Wing Is Not Built."

The Times added, "Councilman Charles B. Hall tried in vain to obtain the assurance of Eli Kirk Price...that the collection would not be lost to Philadelphia. Mr. Price, however, refused to be definite, but said he 'thought the building would be ready for the collection if the Mayor and Council cooperated....'"[21]

Price knew Kendrick was jittery about the possible loss of the Widener Collection to New York or Washington—the reason behind his land offer to Joe Widener. Price played upon a similar sense of dread. Instead of tightening a noose, this time he drew a gun: "Mr. Price disclosed that an addition to the [building] fund must be made if the new museum is to be completed."[22] Done.

In July, Price was not as coy, nor bullying. Well before the February deadline, he announced that "contractors have agreed to complete the [McFadden] wing of the local Art Museum by next Jan. 1...."[23]

As promised, the builders delivered. Trustee von Moschzisker made it official. On January 1, 1928, Philadelphians had something more to celebrate than the New Year. They awoke to the headline: "Says Philadelphia Will Keep Art."[24]

CHAPTER EIGHTEEN

Inauguration

1928

FISKE KIMBALL WAS EAGER for the McFadden collection's quick return from the U.S. National Museum. The artwork had been at the museum, the Smithsonian Institution's principal art venue, for more than five years, a time span that edged closer to making the collection seem more like a permanent resident than just a long-term guest. Charles D. Walcott, the Smithsonian's secretary, had mixed feelings. On one hand, the much-prized collection was a featured draw. Yet he fretted about the open-ended "loan" that he knew would never become an outright gift. Removal of the McFadden pictures, he further reasoned, would free valuable presentation space.

Kimball had arranged with the Philadelphia offices of Davies, Turner & Co., an international freight forwarding company, to secure and crate the individual pieces. On January 24, the collection's forty-three pictures and one sculpture, Frank Lynn Jenkins's bronze bust of McFadden, set out from Washington. The heavily padded van assigned to the task took a full day for the 125-mile trip, and arrived in Philadelphia twenty-three days short of McFadden's deadline and two days shy—"no later" than January 26—of a transfer date set by Kimball himself.

Kimball feared the move might encounter some danger. The possibility of a hijacking en route prompted the director to assign armed guards during the trip north. Other rifle-bearing security personnel were deployed and patrolled when the collection was uncrated and stored overnight.[1]

Whether stationing the sentries was attributed to any real threat of theft, or whether the guards were part of a publicity stunt Kimball had cooked up has never been determined. *The Philadelphia Inquirer* reported the protective arrangements with a straight face—and in breathless detail.

PRICE SATISFIED THE most challenging part of John McFadden's will: a completed, fully formed new art museum manifest on Fairmount Hill. To be sure, its completion was, according to the will, just in the nick of time. It was also eerily similar to a make-believe structure on a Hollywood backlot—effectively, just a shell. Working at a breakneck pace, twenty upper-floor galleries had just been readied for the public.[2] They were empty.

Designing the interiors was up to Kimball, and he met this aspect of the McFadden directive with skill and wiliness, two of Kimball's emerging personal hallmarks. Less known than the date mandate, the McFadden will also demanded that the collection be hung in its "entirety" in a single, "dignified" gallery fit for "permanent maintenance." In turn, Kimball wanted as many as possible of his beloved period rooms—his personal embodiment of high culture as it meandered down the "Main Street of Art"—to be installed before opening day. In four second-floor galleries (277, 278, 279, and 280) in the Northeast Wing dedicated to the McFadden collection, Kimball combined both goals.

Kimball's reimagined settings were the former interiors of two eighteenth-century English country houses, Sutton Scarsdale Hall in Derbyshire and Wrightington Hall in Lancashire. Both had been torn down in the 1920s, and Kimball had picked up the paneled pieces at auction in New York in subsequent years. Three Sutton Scarsdale interiors (1724) and one from Wrightington Hall (1748) would house the collection. An accompanying curatorial description stated:

> In contrast to the early Georgian styles of [early eighteenth century English architects Christopher Wren and Richard Boyle, Third Earl of Burlington] in the rooms of Sutton Scarsdale, [Wrightington Hall] shows the airy and delicate carving, inspired by French work which we associate with Chippendale's name.[3]

The rooms were outfitted with "fine furniture" upholstered in period fabric, eighteenth-century metalwork in firebacks, and "superb old locks" on doors. Windows were adorned with draperies made from "antique Georgian damask." The fully dressed rooms, according to the museum, placed the McFadden pictures in what could be, in the mind's eye, "a gentleman's house," or that of "a great nobleman."[4]

If the period chambers also suggested a Hollywood film set, depicting a cliché of "gentleman's house," or that of "a great nobleman," there was good reason. In later years, other Sutton Scarsdale interiors made their way to movie companies for films requiring period environments. Additional interiors turned up at Hearst Castle, the California estate of newspaper baron and Hollywood tastemaker William Randolph Hearst.

McFadden trustees von Moschzisker, Pepper, and Brinton approved of the siting. Their preferences mirrored their times, and so too, seemingly, did Hearst's most arriviste instincts. McFadden's Anglophilia, the provenance of his artworks, and just the novelty of the interiors no doubt contributed to their appeal. In the event, Kimball's penchant for their adoption precluded any attempt at an alternative—say, a conventional bare-walled gallery with clean sightlines and proper lighting. The director's concept of "dignity," as he channeled McFadden in the Sutton Scarsdale and Wrightington rooms, was not questioned.

So favored were the rooms that even John H. McFadden, Jr., and Joseph E. Widener celebrated the collection's new habitat. On at least one day, February 13, just a month from the museum's opening day, the two millionaires donated something other than "treasure" to the museum: time, helping workmen install pictures.[5]

Until then, no one had decided what pictures would be hung where, and according to what plan, if any. Artist? Year? Theme? Ultimately, there was no plan. Placement was assigned by a picture's size and the contours of the oak and deal wall space. Needing to conform to an assigned space sometimes meant—at least, on the few occasions when the pictures adorned mantelpieces, or their surrounds—that the paintings themselves took a back seat, with a viewer's appreciation compromised by awkward angles and sightlines.

John McFadden's favorite, *Lady Rodney* by Thomas Gainsborough, was not spared. A place of pride in the second Oak Room (Gallery 279) had been set aside above a five-foot-wide marble fireplace. Though the attention-grabbing position was normally associated with a "clou," or anchor piece, the oil of Henrietta was well off the ground by seven feet, a difficult height for a clear view.

There was no mistaking the *Englishness* of the setting. Curators furnished Lady Rodney's salon abundantly with period pieces—none of which was from Sutton Scarsdale, nor necessarily consistent with the room's original purpose-built design. The result was a miscellany—interesting to be sure, but a distracting gallimaufry as well.

A museum bulletin offered a flavor of the layout: "...Queen Anne wing chairs in green damask; a bench and two stools of oak with old needlework, style of William Kent; four walnut side chairs, Queen Anne period, with needlework seats; a tall clock by Thomas Tompion; a large side table of the early Georgian period." And, "On the table there is a case of silver by Paul Lamerie, Charles Adam, William Fleming, George Beale and others working in the first quarter of the XVIII century....The curtains are of old green brocatelle, of a pattern identical with that of the hangings of the state bed of George I at Hampton Court Palace."[6]

Other McFadden galleries were similarly bedecked.[7]

Earlier in February, before the paintings were moved into their galleries, a curatorial memo for the "New Museum of Art Inaugural Exhibition" cited the pictures slated for display. Presumably Jack McFadden and Joe Widener, in their volunteer capacity, were taking their cue from these guidelines in hanging pictures. The roster was labeled "Confidential—not for publication. Copyright strictly reserved." It was a remarkable document—for being so incomplete. Thirty-nine paintings were named, four short of the collection's total.

As hands-on as he was, working in the newly installed galleries, and surely privy to the "confidential" memo, Jack must have been aware how Kimball was being less than careful in adhering to his father's demand that everything be hung in its "entirety." If the trustees expressed any displeasure, it went untold. Further, the search for clarity in how and where the paintings wound up has been muddied by the museum's records themselves.

The thirty-nine pictures cited in the "confidential" pre-opening memo left four missing, as noted, out of the collection's total of forty-three. They were *The Lock* and *Hampstead Heath*, both by John Constable; and *Mrs. Tickell* and *John Wesley*, both by George Romney.

The Pennsylvania Museum Bulletin of March 1928 detailed what is believed to be the first public accounting of which pictures were hung where in the period chambers.[8] Thirty-three pictures are accounted for, six *less* than those tallied in the curatorial memo and ten less than catalogued by William Roberts.

Oak Room, Sutton Scarsdale Hall I: *Lady Grantham* and *Mrs. Crouch*, both by George Romney; *Master Bunbury*, Joshua Reynolds; *Mrs. Hoppner*, John Hoppner; *Mrs. de Crespigny*, George Romney; *Alexander Shaw*, Henry Raeburn; *The Leader Children* and *The Misses Leader*, both by Henry Harlow; *Mr. Laurie of Woodlea*, Henry Raeburn; *Portrait of a Gentleman*, Henry Raeburn; and *The Fruits of Early Industry and Economy*, George Morland.

Deal Room,[9] Wrightington Hall: *Lady Belhaven*, Henry Raeburn; *Lady Hamilton*, George Romney; *Landscape*, Thomas Gainsborough; *The Fontaine Family* and *A Conversation at Wanstead House*, both by William Hogarth.

Oak Room, Sutton Scarsdale Hall II: *Lady Rodney*, Thomas Gainsborough; *Master Thomas Bissland*, Henry Raeburn; *Master John Campbell*, Henry Raeburn; *The Burning of the Houses of Parliament*, J.M.W. Turner; *The Dell at Helmingham*, John Constable; *Landscape*, George Stubbs; *Mrs. Weddell and her Children*, Henry Harlow; and *Lady Elibank*, Henry Raeburn.

Deal Room, Sutton Scarsdale Hall: *Little Bo-Peep*, George Romney; *Blacksmith's Shop, near Hingham, Norfolk*, John Crome; *The Lock*, John Constable; *Miss Finch*, George Romney; *John Wesley*, George Romney; *Sir Walter Scott*, John Watson-Gordon; *Edmund*

Burke, Joshua Reynolds; *Sir Charles Christie*, Henry
Raeburn; and *Miss West*, Thomas Lawrence.

Based on the *Museum Bulletin*'s listing, the following paintings were absent in the initial exhibit: *Coast Scene in Normandy*,
Richard Parkes Bonington; *The Lock* and *Hampstead Heath*, both
by John Constable; *Going to Hayfield, 1849*, David Cox; *Woody
Landscape*, John Crome; *The Storm, 1853*, John Linnell; *Old
Coaching Days* and *The Happy Cottagers*, both by George Morland; and *Mrs. Tickell*, George Romney.

A later reckoning by the museum, "First-Known Locations
for the McFadden Collection," cites museum registrar records
that cast doubt on the *Museum Bulletin*'s accuracy.[10] The missing pictures may have been hung, but mistakenly not listed; or
they may have been hung at an unrecorded later date.[11]

Registrar records also differ in indicating where the pictures were hung. *Mrs. Hoppner* was assigned to the Deal Room
of Sutton Scarsdale and *John Wesley* to the Sutton Scarsdale Oak
Room I. And the records tweak attributions. *Woody Landscape*
is "after" John Crome; *Mrs. Hoppner* was updated to "imitator"
of John Hoppner; *Portrait of a Gentleman* to "follower" of Henry
Raeburn; *Dell at Helmingham Park* to "imitator" of John Constable; *Coast Scene* to a "follower" of Richard Parkes Bonington;
Hampstead Heath to the "studio" of John Constable; and *Edmund
Burke* to a "follower" of Joshua Reynolds.

THE MUSEUM'S FIRST public launch, for the press, was on
January 3, 1928, one of four "rolling" openings. Adopting a
thoroughly modern technique in targeted marketing, Kimball
hosted—through to the museum's actual début in March—three
additional "soft" openings tailored to different constituencies
and donor classes.

A March 7 "opening" catered to those giving at least $1,000 ($15,000 today). Invitees to a third "opening," less than a week later on March 13, appealed to a wider audience of 1,000—those expected to pledge less. Each attendee was provided with two pledge cards: one for the invitee and another for a friend. Kimball believed that high volumes in pledges would offset lesser giving levels. French Ambassador Paul Claudel was on hand as a celebrity draw. Most memorable was a request by Joe Widener that everyone observe a moment of silence in tribute to his old friends and colleagues, William M. Elkins, George W. Elkins, and John H. McFadden.[12]

On March 26, Kimball once again flung open the doors. Six hundred of Philadelphia's "most prominent citizens" had received engraved invitations: "THE COMMISSIONERS OF FAIRMOUNT PARK and THE TRUSTEES OF THE PENNSYLVANIA MUSEUM request the honor of your presence at the official opening of the European and American Sections of the Pennsylvania Museum of Art...."[13] The afternoon inauguration was formal. Given the time of day, men likely wore morning dress; women, tea gowns.

The gala was ceremonious: museum president Eli Kirk Price presented the museum's "keys" to George Wharton Pepper, the Fairmount Park Commission's lawyer. Price returned to his seat, a folding chair. Pepper remained standing, tall and ramrod straight, a grey-haired figure of patrician Philadelphia. Proper Philadelphia sensed the moment: it was the sixty-eight-year-old Price's last hurrah, a milestone that Pepper, the McFadden Collection trustee, movingly recognized:

> ...I have met some faithful stewards, and from time to time I have viewed with admiration, the intelligence, the sanity and the patience with which a few great men have carried great enterprises to a successful conclusion; but I have never seen, and never expect to see, any measure of fidelity and in-

telligence and sanity and patience more noteworthy
than that which has characterized the work of the
man who has just taken his seat.

Among out-of-town luminaries at the inauguration were, in
a gesture of collegial goodwill, the director of the Metropolitan
Museum of Art, Edward Robinson; the vice-president of the
American Museum of Natural History, George Frederick Kunz;
and the director of the Brooklyn Museum, William Henry Fox.
Among a contingent of foreign dignities were French Ambassa-
dor Paul Claudel, on a return visit,[14] and Mme. Henri Lapauze, of
France's semiofficial Superior Council of Fine Arts.[15]

The ceremony encapsulated a dramatic break with the past:
symbolic, though palpably final. No British consular representatives, nor British museum administrators were present. Fifty
years previously, Sir Francis Philip Cunliffe-Owen, the South
Kensington Museum director, had attended the opening of Memorial Hall in an emblematic bonding of the two institutions.[16]

Mme. Lapauze declared that "the museum meant the beginning of a new era in Philadelphia's cultural life."[17] *The Burlington
Magazine for Connoisseurs*, England's cultural touchstone, stated
that the museum established Philadelphia as "one of our chief
centres of art."[18]

Fiske Kimball was emphatic, telling the press that the Cen-
tennial-era Memorial building would be abandoned after its
objets d'art were removed and reinstalled.[19]

"We no longer today," Kimball said, "dare take the view which
governed the International Exposition of 1851 and the creation
of the South Kensington Museum that technical conditions of
material and use are the primary aspect of the work of art, or the
aspect we wish chiefly to emphasize."[20]

With such unequivocal dispatch, Memorial Hall was uncere-
moniously tossed on the rubbish heap of history. From then on,
the prominent local arts patron and painter Albert Rosenthal

told the *Evening Ledger,* the Pennsylvania Museum "will be to Philadelphia what the Louvre is to Paris."[21] *The Burlington Magazine* announced, "Philadelphia looks up to [its 'splendid' new museum] as Athens looked up to its Acropolis."[22] Mme. Lapauze, the French representative, expressed a less extravagant approbation. Still, in an unctuous bow to Kimball, she attributed her presence "largely" to "her Government's interest in the manner of displaying art treasures in period settings...."[23]

STARTING PROMPTLY AT 10 o'clock on Tuesday, March 27, the day after the inauguration and its formalities, Philadelphians of all backgrounds started swarming to the majestic colossus on Fairmount Hill. Everyone was welcome seven days a week, and entry was free. There to greet them in Galleries 277, 278, 279, and 280, far from the confines of Proper Philadelphia below at Rittenhouse Square, were John H. McFadden's "Great Britons"— and the landscapes of his beloved "green and pleasant land."[24]

New Yorkers

FOLLOWING THE DEATHS OF their parents, both in 1921, the McFadden children, Philip, Alice, and Jack, cut short their time in Philadelphia. They went their separate ways, but their paths forward intersected through work and residence in New York. Moreover, each of their pursuits was sweetened by an individual combined inheritance of about $1.17 million ($22 million today) from their father and mother.[1]

The McFaddens' oldest child, Philip Grandin, was an established New Yorker. Even before marrying Manhattan socialite Annette Buckley in 1912, he plied nominal day work at the Geo. H. McFadden & Bro.'s Wall Street office at 56 Beaver Street. In later years, he expanded his personal business interests to trading in coffee and sugar, commodities beyond his family's traditional ventures in cotton.[2]

All along, commercial trading was secondary to Philip's ardor as a clubman, bon vivant, high-goal polo player, and lavish party-giver. He parlayed his Oxford University degree and his favorable marital alliance with Annette into quick entrée to

New York's 400. On their home ground. His address, 330 Park Avenue, could hardly have been better.

Philip and Annette had no children, but spent lavishly on Florence Pamela Brinton, Alice's daughter.[3]

While travelling on business, Philip died in Phoenix, Arizona, on February 8, 1949. He was seventy-one. No cause of death was given in newspaper reports.[4]

———×———

ALICE BATES MCFADDEN had no role in McFadden business affairs. Her main interest—indeed, passion—was the theater, and she had long dedicated herself to amateur theatrical presentations in Philadelphia.

After divorcing Jasper Yeates Brinton in Paris, she moved to New York to be closer to America's professional theater scene. There, in 1925, she married the playwright and actor Laurence Eyre.

Brinton and Alice had two children, the aforementioned Florence Pamela Brinton and John Brinton. Alice named her daughter for her mother Florence, but everyone knew the girl as Pamela. While Pamela continued to live with her mother in New York and Philadelphia, John moved to Alexandria, Egypt, where his father served as an American representative to an international court.

Even after Alice married Eyre, she maintained strong ties to the Pennsylvania Museum of Art and to its later incarnation as the Philadelphia Museum of Art. Overall, she donated more than 100 objets d'art, including the bronze bust of her father by Frank Lynn Jenkins.

Alice and Eyre were childless. She died in New York on March 19, 1973, six days short of her 90th birthday.

———×———

JOHN MCFADDEN'S YOUNGEST son, his namesake, John H. McFadden, Jr., or Jack, was most like his father—an ardent art collector, donor, and a committed member of the family firm. Like his father and Philip, he was a clubman, holding memberships in New York, Philadelphia, Paris, and Liverpool.

He also cultivated a maverick streak. After graduating from the University of Pennsylvania, he struck out to serve in the American Field Service in France—*before* the United States entered the Great War in 1916. He was among the founders of the Field Service's ambulance corps, serving with distinction under fire and rising to the rank of captain. He was a romantic, embracing an emotion that hardly ever stirred within his father. Jack was a rake. But never a bounder.

He later served as an assistant military attaché at the American Embassy in Paris, returning to the United States with an unusual souvenir—a tattoo of a bird that ran from his right shoulder to almost his right wrist.[5] While in Europe, he also developed a fondness for art collecting. Interestingly, his tastes were similar to his father's in eighteenth-century art by British masters.

Back in the United States, in 1921, Jack moved to New York, to a townhouse at 16 East 81st Street, and to work at the McFadden company's Wall Street branch. Ties to Philadelphia were not entirely severed. He maintained another townhouse there at 2123 Spruce Street. For a time, as a bachelor in New York, he also kept an apartment there at the Ritz-Carlton Hotel.

A year after resettling in New York, Jack became the last of the McFadden children to marry. His first wife was Florence Magee Ellsworth, a New York socialite. The marriage ended in divorce. In 1934, he married Marian Graham Williams, a divorcée and another well-known New York socialite.

Until 1936, he served as the president of the New York Cotton Exchange, remaining on its board—and those of the New Orleans and Liverpool cotton exchanges—until his death. About the time his term as president expired, Jack saw growth in "spot" cotton brokering, a form of trade then popular in Houston, Texas, and which he envisioned as a coming national trend. Following instinct, he moved to Houston to head the McFadden firm's local office. Later business dealings demanded another transfer—to Memphis, Tennessee, the very location of his company's founding by his grandfather in 1858.

Jack and Marian lived happily as transplanted Southerners, though their country life was a far cry from both Rittenhouse Square and Manhattan's East Side. Their new residence was, fittingly enough, an antebellum mansion set on thirty-eight acres near Memphis. Bracketed by pillars, it looked like a version of Tara in *Gone With the Wind*. They called it Croxteth Farm, undoubtedly in recognition of the neighborhood location of his father's house in Liverpool where Jack had been born. (The senior McFadden's residence, Worsley House, was also located on Croxteth Road.) During their years in Memphis, the McFaddens expanded their art collection and redesigned their mansion with imported English interiors.

Unlike his father, Jack was not loyal to a single art dealer. Thos. Agnew & Sons in London had been the senior McFadden's favored dealer. Jack also had an early association with Agnew's while still in Europe. Among his earliest acquisitions was from Agnew's in 1920, *The North Terrace at Windsor Castle, Looking East* by Paul Sandby.

After returning to America, he collected elsewhere, for a time with the famed Jacques Seligman & Cie., directly in Paris, and later with the firm's representatives in New York.

His actual purchases came mainly from M. Knoedler and Son, an equally high-end New York gallery. His scorecard resembled that of the senior McFadden. Among about fifteen artistic gems he acquired from Knoedler were works by George Romney, Henry Raeburn, and even a beach scene by Richard Parkes Bonington, the very artist (and the very kind of image) that had eluded his father.

While the senior McFadden had failed in acquiring a *genuine* Bonington, Jack in turn had bad luck with the authenticity of a work by eighteenth-century Italian artist Pompeo Girolamo Batoni, at the time hugely popular among the English élite. The putative Batoni, titled *A Conversation Piece: James Grant of Grant, John Mytton, Hon. Thomas Robinson, and Thomas Wynn,* was later credited, after Jack's death, to Nathaniel Dance-Holland, a founding member of the Royal Academy of Arts. Jack paid Knoedler $6,500 ($92,000 today) in 1928 for the "Batoni." Despite the mistaken attribution, he still probably got his money's worth.

Most of these and other paintings were over time donated to the Philadelphia Museum of Art. Jack had also arranged that the 1916 portrait of his father by Philip A. de László be another gift. Also bequeathed, according to Jack's will, was Croxteth Farm, which the museum quickly liquidated for the cash proceeds.

Jack died, in Doctors Hospital in New York, on August 17, 1955. He was sixty-five years old, and had been suffering from an "illness" for "several weeks," according to *The New York Times.*[6] Marian and Alice were the only immediate survivors.

Acknowledgments

THE INTRICACY OF this book, roaming over a period of almost a century, with most of its narrative played out in Liverpool, London, New York, and principally, of course, in Philadelphia, required much editorial advice, research assistance, and personal support from many quarters. Though these benefits were shared in different measures, I want to thank all those, whatever their role and contribution, who happily and willingly made their valuable impact on this book.

My onsite research in Liverpool and London involved forging new relationships with colleagues and sometimes making new friends. Two individuals in particular—Dr. Nigel Hall, most recently a research fellow at the University of Essex, and Ron Jones, of the Liverpool Athenaeum—gave of themselves selflessly.

Their tireless engagement was key to fleshing out John H. McFadden's life in his adopted English hometown, Liverpool. Nigel took his doctorate degree in the study of the British cotton trade at the University of Oxford, and is now one of the most eminent scholars of the subject during the period in question. He offered insight and diamond-bright detail. He is a brilliant conversationalist on a myriad of arcane topics, and I felt warmed by his erudition and scholarship.

Ron is the unofficial "keeper of the keys" to the Athenaeum's archives and library. He directed my research in that learned

ACKNOWLEDGMENTS

institution. His companionship when we visited the site of Mc-
Fadden's former residence, Worsley House, in Prince's Park, and
as we toured the grounds and surroundings of the "Flags," made
for many delightful hours of kinship. Two of Ron's books immediately grabbed my attention: one, *The American Connection*,
because it had direct bearing on the McFadden saga and the other, *The Beatles' Liverpool*, because I am, like many pilgrims to the
Beatles' Liverpool, a fan of the Fab Four.

I need to recognize Joan Hanford, the Athenaeum's *official*
librarian; Jim Powell and Andrew Popp, both at the University
of Liverpool; Sarah Heaps of the International Cotton Association; and Brian Kernaghan, who offered books and good cheer
in the bright confines of his eponymous bookshop, one of the
finest anywhere. The Liverpool Record Office and the Liverpool
Central Library were wonderful resources, and I am grateful to
the staffs at these fine institutions for making the tedious chore
of moldy research a delight. Well, almost.

In London, the book's manuscript, in several stages of development, received tender loving care from Raymond Chellel, a
scholar in English literature and an old hand at editing. Ray is a
good friend. His knowledge is boundless, and he was also able
to set me right more than once. I was in good hands.

Research help in London also came from Julie Carrington
of the Royal Geographical Society, Nickolaus Karlson of Thos.
Agnew & Sons, Alex Leigh of the Research Centre at the National Gallery, and the amazing staff at the Paul Mellon Centre
for Studies in British Art. I also received a warm welcome from
one and all at the National Arts Library at the Victoria and Albert Museum.

A special thanks also goes to Richard Dorment, the author
of the catalogue raisonné, *British Painting in the Philadelphia
Museum of Art*, which served as a guide and guiding light. Richard was well into a much-deserved retirement when I met him
at his London home for tea, and he was very gracious in re-

ceiving me, turning an otherwise unplanned disruption into a warm, inviting occasion.

I am indebted to an array of consummate professionals in Philadelphia. Among these are Lynn Dorwalt of the Wagner Free Library; Evan Peugh of the Academy of Natural Sciences at Drexel University; the Reverend John Gardner, the Reverend Rachel Gardner, and Margaret P. Dipinto, all of the Church of the Holy Trinity; Chip Seltzer of the Corinthian Yacht Club; Cassandra Keith and Nancy S. Taylor, both of Episcopal Academy; Pam E. Kosty of the Museum of Anthropology at the University of Pennsylvania; Cornelia King of the Library Company; Michael Schlesinger of Allan Domb Real Estate; Jennifer Johns and Hoang Tran, both of the Pennsylvania Academy of the Fine Arts; and Bruce Laverty and Jill LeMin Lee, both of the Athenaeum.

Staffs of the Philadelphia Athenaeum, Fisher Fine Arts Library of the University of Pennsylvania, Penn's Van Pelt Library, the arts collection at the Free Library, and at Laurel Hill Cemetery were energetic in responding to my entreaties.

Curators and other professional staff at the Philadelphia Museum of Art provided backbone to my research, with unswerving courtesy, generosity, and within a remarkably quick response time. In particular Miriam Cady, Emily Rice, Susan K. Anderson Laquer, and Angel González deserve special mention. Angel is a PMA security guard. Each time I visited the museum, I was met with Angel's warm greeting, "Welcome home!"

I want to express my gratitude to Jennifer Thompson, the PMA's curator of the John H. McFadden Memorial Collection and the John G. Johnson Collection. Jenny heartily shared her unique perspective on British painting of the period and also offered valuable pointers for my research in London.

Sara Noreika, an independent editor, was indispensable. So were Miriam Seidel and Holiday Campanella, my editors at Camino Books.

My thanks also go to René Corado of the Western Foundation of Vertebrate Zoology in Camarillo, California; Ellen Hampton of the American Cathedral in Paris; and Justin T. Carreño of Washington. John H. McFadden's great-grandson, Jasper Brinton of Phoenixville, Pennsylvania, was one of the most enthusiastic supporters of the project. He shared mementos and memories. How helpful and delightful these were! I also came away from Jasper's country house well fed. Out of the blue, he prepared a gourmet lunch, and I partook of the meal enthralled by Jasper's yarns and storytelling.

Two others stand out.

John H. McFadden of Philadelphia, McFadden's great-great-grandnephew, provided the grant that funded the project. Without his curiosity about his ancestor, this book would never have gone forward.

As always, my partner Joan T. Kane was my chief cheerleader. Her encouragement and forbearance when work compromised our time together made this book possible. It could only have happened with Joan by my side.

—Richard Carreño

Preface to Catalogue of the Collection of Pictures formed by John H. McFadden, Esq., of Philadelphia, Pa.

by William Roberts

WITH AN ADMIRABLE steadfastness of purpose, and in spite of the many natural temptations to branch out in other directions, Mr. John H. McFadden has adhered to his scheme of forming a collection of pictures exclusively by British artists. In doing this he has observed a restraint very unusual among collectors, and the sum total of his efforts is a collection sui generis; and not only this, but a collection of extraordinary beauty and interest. Variety is the mainspring of collecting, and the greater the variety the keener does the instinct of the collector become. It very frequently happens that a man begins to collect, and for some time confines himself to, one phase of art; but just as one book opens up many others, so the step from one branch of art to another is a matter of easy gradation. From engravings the collector naturally passes to drawings, thence to pictures in oils, and from one school of artists to another. The question of variety in art collecting is largely a personal matter; but those who have seen this collection when it was in Mr. McFadden's own home, or when it was on view in the public galleries in Philadelphia, Chicago [Pittsburgh], or New York, will agree that, though Mr. McFadden has confined himself to the Early British School, his collection is remarkable in its variety and in its interest.

Mr. McFadden began to collect a quarter of a century ago. As is the case with many other men who have developed into collectors, his object in purchasing a fine picture now and then was rather to adorn a vacant space on the walls of his dining or sitting room than to form the nucleus of what would someday become a collection. But *l'appetit vient en mangeant*; so in the course of time, during his frequent visits to England, one painting after another was added, and a few pictures developed into an imposing collection entirely different from any other in America.

It is interesting to note that Mr. McFadden's first purchase was Gainsborough's splendid portrait of Lady Rodney, which will always remain one of the gems of the collection, and which, it may be mentioned by the way, is now commercially worth at least five times as much as the owner paid for it. The same may be said, indeed, of the other pictures which were acquired before the great rise in prices of the last few years. Whilst no wise man buys pictures with the same motives as he buys stocks and shares—solely in the hope of profitable dividends—yet it is always a satisfaction to know that one's hobby is not an unprofitable one even in the mere matter of money. But the intellectual enjoyment afforded by a fine collection of pictures such as this has no money equivalent.

The dominating notes, if one may use the phrase, of Mr. McFadden's collection, are the fine series of portraits of women and men by Romney and Raeburn. Probably there is not anywhere in the United States another gallery in which either artist is represented by so many characteristic works. Most of these portraits are not only of people who were famous in their own day, but some of them have become part and parcel of British history, perhaps not a little with the aid of the artists to whom they sat for their portraits. Others, such as the Master Bunbury of Sir Joshua Reynolds's splendid portrait, died before his time, and he is known to posterity almost exclusively as the subject of Sir Joshua's famous picture. On the other hand, it might also be said that Sir John Watson Gordon, in spite of his high qualities as an artist, owes much of his celebrity with posterity on account of his portrait of the "Wizard of the North," Sir Walter Scott.

Hogarth hands down to us—after an interval of nearly two centuries—groups of two distinguished families, both long since extinct in the male line, but both of which contributed much to the making of English history when England was not much more than an island kingdom. By a happy coincidence Hogarth has in the Fountaine and the Castlemaine groups, bequeathed us exquisite miniature-like representations of the most eminent members of both families. An unfortunate fire completely destroyed Lawrence's portrait of Miss Nelthorp, but the beautiful Miss West is still present with us in all the loveliness of youth. Lawrence's most successful pupil Harlow—who would have become a serious rival but for his early death—is represented by two masterly groups of the Leader family, and by a charming one of Mrs. Weddell and her pretty children in all the frolicsomeness and abandon of the nursery.

Turner's magnificent view of the "Burning of the Houses of Parliament" may justly rank at the head of the pictures other than portraits. By a happy accident the picture which follows it comprises something of the same scene ninety years before by a man whom Turner may have met in his early boyhood, Richard Wilson. This is one of the earliest existing pictures of London by Wilson, and as a document in the history of the capital of the British Empire it is of the highest interest, apart from its importance as a very early work of one of the first and one of the greatest of English landscape painters. Constable, with his fine "Lock" and other pictures, Crome and Stark of the Norwich school, David Cox, John Linnell, George Morland with his three pictures of English rural life, George Stubbs, and that interesting figure in the history of Anglo-French art, Bonington, all contribute to the completeness of this collection.

A word of thanks, in conclusion, is due to Mr. McFadden's friend, Mr. Lockett Agnew, who has given the writer every assistance in the compilation of the following pages.

W.R.
London,
September, 1917

APPENDIX II

The John Howard McFadden Memorial Collection

HIGHLIGHTS

Total Paintings: 43

Earliest Painting: *The Assembly at Wanstead House*, William Hogarth, 1728

Latest Painting: *The Storm (The Refuge)*, John Linnell, 1853

Largest Painting: *The Leader Children*, George Henry Harlow, 94½" × 58¼"

Smallest Painting: *The Happy Cottagers (The Cottage Door)*, George Morland, 14½" × 18½"

Most Represented Artist: Henry Raeburn and George Romney (eight paintings each)

First: George Stubbs's painting, *Laborers Loading a Brick Cart*. The exhibition at the Pennsylvania Academy of the Fine Arts in Philadelphia is believed to be the first time the artist's work was displayed publicly in the United States.

Misattributions: 5 (12%)

THE COLLECTION

Richard Parkes BONINGTON (1802–1828)

A Coast Scene (c. 1828–1840)
oil on canvas, 24" × 33"
(Later credited as in the "style of Richard Parkes Bonington")

John CONSTABLE (1776–1837)

Sketch for "A Boat Passing a Lock" (1822–24)
oil on canvas, 50½" × 48"

Branch Hill Pond, Hampstead Heath (after 1825)
oil on canvas, 23" × 29½"
(Later credited as "John Constable and Studio")

The Dell Helmingham Park (after 1828)
oil on canvas, 30½" × 38½"
(Later credited to "imitator of John Constable")

David COX (1783–1859)

Going to the Hayfield (1849)
oil on canvas, 28" × 36"

John CROME (1768–1821)

The Blacksmith's Shop, Near Hingham, Norfolk (c. 1808)
oil on canvas, 60½" × 48"

Woody Landscape at Colney (late 19th century)
oil on canvas, 22½" × 17"

Thomas GAINSBOROUGH (1727–1788)

Lady Rodney (c. 1781–82)
oil on canvas, 50¼" × 39⅞"

*A Pastoral Landscape (Rocky Mountain Valley with Shepherd, Sheep, and
       Goats)* (c. 1783)
oil on canvas, 40⅛" × 50⅛"

John Watson GORDON (1778–1864)

Sir Walter Scott (c. 1831–35)
oil on canvas, 30" × 25"

George Henry HARLOW (1787–1819)

The Misses Leader (1813–14)
oil on canvas, 94¼" × 58"

The Leader Children (1813–14)
oil on canvas, 94½" × 58¼"

Mother and Children (c. 1816)
oil on canvas, 36" × 28¼"

William HOGARTH (1697–1764)

The Assembly at Wanstead House (1728–31)
oil on canvas, 25½" × 30"

Conversation Piece with Sir Andrew Fountaine (c. 1730–35)
oil on canvas, 18¼" × 23"

John HOPPNER (1758–1810)

Mrs. Hoppner (c. mid-19th century)
oil on canvas, 30¼" × 24⅞"
(Later "after the style" of John Hoppner)

Thomas LAWRENCE (1769–1830)

Miss Harriott West, Afterwards Mrs. William Woodgate (c. 1824–25)
oil on canvas, 30½" × 25⅛"

John LINNELL (1792–1882)

The Storm (The Refuge) (1853)
oil on canvas, 35½" × 57½"

George MORLAND (1763–1804)

The Stagecoach (1791)
oil on canvas, 34½" × 46½"

Fruits of Early Industry and Economy (1789)
oil on canvas, 30¼" × 25⅛"

The Happy Cottagers (The Cottage Door) (c. 1790–92)
oil on canvas, 14½" × 18½"

Henry RAEBURN (1756–1823)

Lady Belhaven (c. 1790)
oil on canvas, 36⅛" × 27⅞"

Master Thomas Bissland (c. 1809–10)
oil on canvas, 56½" × 44⅜"

John Campbell of Saddell (c. 1800)
oil on canvas, 49¼" × 39⅛"

Charles Christie, Esq. (c. 1800)
oil on canvas, 30½" × 25½"

Lady Elibank (c. 1805)
oil on canvas, 36" × 28"

Walter Kennedy Lawrie of Woodhall, Laurieston (c. 1815)
oil on canvas, 30" × 25"

Alexander Shaw (c. 1810–15)
oil on canvas, 30" × 25⅛"

Portrait of a Gentleman (19th century)
oil on canvas, 29¼" × 25¼"
(Later credited to a "follower of Sir Henry Raeburn")

Joshua REYNOLDS (1723–1792)

Master Bunbury (1780–81)
oil on canvas, 30⅛" × 25⅛"

Rt. Hon. Edmund Burke (c. 1756–60)
oil on canvas, 30¼" × 25⅛"
(Later credited to the "circle of Sir Joshua Reynolds")

George ROMNEY (1734–1802)

Mrs. Crouch (c. 1793)
oil on canvas, 50¼" × 39½"

Mrs. Crespigny (1786–90)
oil on canvas, 51⅛" × 40"

Mrs. Finch (1790)
oil on canvas, 35⅞" × 27¼"

Lady Grantham (1780–81)
oil on canvas, 46½" × 39"

Lady Hamilton as Miranda (1785–86)
oil on canvas, 14⅛" × 15½"

Mrs. Tickell (1791–92)
oil on canvas, 24" × 20⅛"

John Wesley (1788–89)
oil on canvas, 30" × 25"

The Shepherd Girl (Little Bo-Peep) (c. 1778)
oil on canvas, 46½" × 35½"

George STUBBS (1724–1806)

Laborers Loading a Brick Cart (1767)
oil on canvas, 24" × 42"

J.M.W. TURNER (1775–1851)

The Burning of the Houses of Lords and Commons, October 16, 1834 (exhibited 1835)
oil on canvas, 36¼" × 48½"

View on the Thames: Westminster Bridge under Construction (1745)
oil on canvas, 32⅛" × 54"

Titles in this listing are those adopted by the Philadelphia Museum of Art.

Chronology

1805
- Pennsylvania Academy of the Fine Arts founded in Philadelphia

1806
- George M. McFadden born in County Cavan, Ireland

1809
- James Madison becomes president

1817
- James Monroe becomes president

1820
- George M. McFadden and family immigrate to Philadelphia

1825
- John Quincy Adams becomes president

1829
- Andrew Jackson becomes president

1836
- Frederic Christian Zerega, JHM's future business partner, born in New York

1837
- Martin Van Buren becomes president

1841
- William Henry Harrison becomes president

- John Tyler assumes presidency

1845

- James Polk becomes president
- George M. McFadden weds Charlotte Elliot

1847

- George Henry McFadden born in Philadelphia

1848

- Florence De Witt Bates, JHM's future wife, born in Cincinnati, Ohio

1849

- Zachary Taylor becomes president

1850

- Millard Fillmore assumes presidency
- JHM born in Philadelphia

1852

- South Kensington Museum, London, founded

1853

- Franklin Pierce becomes president

1857

- James Buchanan becomes president

1858

- George M. McFadden moves to Memphis, Tennessee
- Geo. McFadden company established as dry-goods business
- The firm opens an office at 299 Main Street, Memphis

1861

- Abraham Lincoln becomes president
- Civil War starts
- George M. McFadden returns to Philadelphia
- George M. McFadden partners with Randolph & Jenks
- Geo. McFadden company reestablished in Philadelphia
- Family lives at 613 North 8th Street

1862

- James Franklin McFadden born in Philadelphia

1865

- Andrew Johnson assumes presidency
- Civil War ends
- JHM enters Episcopal Academy

1868

- George M. McFadden dies
- George H. McFadden establishes "Geo. H. McFadden, Cotton Merchant"
- JHM leaves Episcopal Academy

1869

- Ulysses S. Grant becomes president

1871

- George H. McFadden marries Emily Barclay Kennedy
- The couple moves to 2044 Chestnut Street

1872

- JHM joins brother in George H. McFadden cotton firm
- Geo. H. McFadden, Cotton Merchant, renamed "Geo. H. McFadden Co. & Bro., Cotton Merchants"

1876

- Centennial International Exhibition underway in Philadelphia
- Opening of Memorial Hall art gallery
- JHM and Florence Bates wed in Paris
- The newlyweds move to 506 North 18th Street

1877

- Rutherford B. Hayes becomes president
- Pennsylvania Museum and School of Industrial Art opens in Memorial Hall

1878

- Philip Grandin McFadden born (JHM's first child)
- The McFaddens buy a building at 121 Chestnut Street as their principal office

1879

- JHM and Florence move to the Aldine Hotel, in the 1900 block of Chestnut Street

1880

- Metropolitan Museum of Art opens
- JHM, Florence, and Philip move to 2107 Chestnut Street

1881

- James Garfield becomes president
- Chester Arthur assumes presidency
- JHM and family move to Liverpool to establish the firm's branch there

1883

- Alice Bates McFadden, JHM's second child, born in Philadelphia

1885

- Grover Cleveland becomes president

1887

- Art Club of Philadelphia founded

1888

- James Franklin McFadden weds Mary Adèle Lewis in Philadelphia
- Frank and Adèle move to a corner house at 19th and Delancey Streets
- JHM joins the Art Club of Philadelphia

1889

- Benjamin Harrison becomes president
- South Kensington Museum renamed Victoria and Albert Museum

1890

- John H. McFadden, Jr., known as "Jack," JHM's third child, born in Liverpool
- JHM launches District Messenger and News Company, Ltd., London

1892

- JHM purchases his first artwork, *An Alexandrian School* by J.C. Horsley, from Thos. Agnew & Sons, Liverpool

1893

- Grover Cleveland becomes president

- JHM acquires Thomas Gainsborough's *Lady Rodney*, the first piece in what would become the John Howard McFadden Memorial Collection

1897

- William McKinley becomes president

1901

- Theodore Roosevelt assumes presidency
- George H. McFadden creates the "McFadden Line" steamship company in Trenton, New Jersey

1902

- JHM moves from Liverpool to New York to open the firm's branch there
- JHM purchases a townhouse at the corner of 19th and Walnut Streets at Rittenhouse Square, Philadelphia, and, later, relocates there permanently

1903

- William L. Elkins dies in Philadelphia

1906

- JHM named trustee of the Pennsylvania Museum

1909

- William Taft becomes president
- Alice McFadden marries Jasper Yeates Brinton in Philadelphia

1910

- Ernest H. Shackleton visits Philadelphia as JHM's guest

1911

- JHM forms the Thompson-McFadden Commission, New York
- JHM named president of the Art Club of Philadelphia

1912

- Philip McFadden marries Annette Buckley in New York

1913

- Woodrow Wilson becomes president
- John H. McFadden Research Institute, Liverpool, established
- Ernest H. Shackleton returns to Philadelphia

1915

- Peter A.B. Widener dies in Philadelphia

1916

- JHM named a director of the Pennsylvania Academy of the Fine Arts
- PAFA displays McFadden collection
- Thomas Lawrence's portrait of *Miss Nelthorpe* lost in house fire
- The Wellington apartment house on Rittenhouse Square completed

1917

- United States enters World War I
- John G. Johnson dies in Philadelphia
- Ernest H. Shackleton attends fundraising event in Philadelphia
- JHM acquires *A Coast Scene* by Richard Parkes Bonington, designated the last picture in his collection
- William Roberts compiles his catalogue raisonné of the McFadden collection
- McFadden collection displayed at Carnegie Institute, Pittsburgh
- Metropolitan Museum of Art displays McFadden collection
- JHM drafts will, bequeathing his art collection to Pennsylvania Museum under restrictive conditions

1918

- Ernest H. Shackleton, in last visit to city, speaks to Philadelphia Geographical Society
- The Spanish Flu ravages Philadelphia

1921

- Warren G. Harding becomes president
- JHM hospitalized in Philadelphia
- JHM dies in Atlantic City, New Jersey
- Florence McFadden dies in Upper Saranac Lake, New York
- Details of JHM will made public, revealing a seven-year deadline for the completion of the Pennsylvania Museum on Fairmount Hill
- McFadden collection moved to the Smithsonian Institution for exhibition and safekeeping

1923

- Calvin Coolidge assumes presidency

1924

- Alice McFadden and Jasper Brinton divorce in Paris
- William M. Elkins donates the collections of his father and grandfather to the Pennsylvania Museum

1925

- John D. McIlhenny, president of Pennsylvania Museum, dies
- Eli Kirk Price II named the museum's president
- Fiske Kimball appointed Pennsylvania Museum director

1928

- McFadden collection moved from Smithsonian Institution to Pennsylvania Museum
- Pennsylvania Museum opens, meeting JHM's seven-year deadline

Endnotes

ABBREVIATIONS

In citing works in the endnotes, works frequently cited have been identified by the following abbreviations:

American Art Annual (AAA)
American Art News (AAN)
American Magazine of Art (AMA)
American Wool and Cotton Reporter (AWCR)
Art in America (AiA)
Brinton (Jasper) Archives (Brinton)
Commerce and Finance (CaF)
McFadden (John H.) Last Will and Testament (Will)
New York Times (NYT)
Pennsylvania Academy of the Fine Arts (PAFA)
Philadelphia Inquirer (PI)
Philadelphia Museum of Art (PMA)
Philadelphia Telegraph (PT)
Public Ledger (PL)

ENDNOTES

Preface

1. For a time, under ten years, McFadden's collection was also the largest assembly of British art on public display in America. From 1921 to 1928, the Smithsonian Institution exhibited the collection. In 1927, after Henry E. Huntington's death, the Californian's collection, newly opened in its self-named museum, instantly became the largest

collection of British art outside the United Kingdom. The Yale Center for British Art, founded by Paul Mellon in 1974, subsequently claimed that distinction.

PART I

Prologue: Will

1. Will, December 2, 1917.
2. Will.
3. Will.
4. Despite the arcane spelling of the company name and its distinct Dickensian flavor, it was the form favored in newspaper advertising and in public documents. The name has been cited as "George H. Mc-Fadden and Brother."
5. PI, March 2, 1906, 6.
6. Will. Exact values for artwork, be they individual pieces or collections, are impossible to determine unless the marketplace "speaks" when the art is sold and a price is affixed. The figure here is based solely on inflation, from 1917 to 2018.
7. AiA, vol. 6, 1918, 108. William Roberts mentioned how prices could spiral out of control. In the preface (Appendix II) to his catalogue raisonné, he calculated that *Lady Rodney* by Thomas Gainsborough, acquired by McFadden in 1893 for the equivalent of $469,425 today, was "commercially" worth about $2.4 million (in today's dollars) fifteen years later. "The same may be said, indeed, of the other pictures which were acquired before the great rise in prices of the last few years," he added. "Whilst no wise man buys pictures with the same motives as he buys stocks and shares—solely in the hope of profitable dividends—yet it is always a satisfaction to know that one's hobby is not an unprofitable one even in the mere matter of money."
8. James Gibbons Huneker, *The Pathos of Distance: A Book of a Thousand and One Moments* (New York: Charles Scribner's Sons, 1913).
9. Richard Dorment, *British Painting in the Philadelphia Museum of Art* (Philadelphia: Philadelphia Museum of Art, 1986), xiii.
10. Ella L. Browning, "Incidents" (unpublished memoir), 1954.

Chapter One: Philadelphia

1. Henry James, *The American Scene* (New York: Penguin Books, 1994), 203.

2. Charles Dickens, *American Notes* (New York: St. Martin's Press, 1985), 89.
3. Richard Reeves, *American Journey* (New York: Simon and Schuster, 1982), 252.
4. PAFA restricts its permanent collection to works by Americans.
5. This figure represented an astonishing fifth of all Americans.
6. NYT, June 27, 2017, 2.
7. Calvin Tomkins, *Merchants and Masterpieces* (New York: E.P. Dutton & Co., 1970), 21.
8. Stephen May, *An Enduring Legacy: The Pennsylvania Academy of the Fine Arts, 1805–2005* (Philadelphia: Pennsylvania Academy of the Fine Arts, 2005), 21.
9. E. Digby Baltzell, *Puritan Boston and Quaker Philadelphia* (New York: The Free Press, 1979), 46.
10. John A. Lukacs, *Philadelphia: Patricians and Philistines 1900–1950* (New York: Farrar, Straus & Giroux), 1981.
11. Archives, PMA.
12. "Our Story," PMA website: https://www.philamuseum.org/information/45-19.html (retrieved January 6, 2020).
13. S. N. Behrman, *Duveen* (New York: Vintage Books, 1952), 21.

Chapter Two: Cotton Man, 1820–1881

1. The building, now addressed as 299 South Main Street, is still there. It houses a restaurant.
2. Janie V. Paine, *Memphis Cotton Exchange…One Hundred Years* (Memphis: Memphis Cotton Exchange, circa 1982), 1–2.
3. The early years of the George M. McFadden narrative rely on a collection of ephemera compiled by Ella Browning (1877–1965), one of George's grandchildren. Included in her cache are biographical sketches, letters, and travelogues, some of which recount her journeys with her father George Henry to Liverpool and beyond.
4. Among Central's alumni are such prestigious Philadelphians as P. A. B. Widener, John G. Johnson, and Dr. Albert C. Barnes, the legend behind the Barnes Foundation.
5. *Gopsill's Philadelphia Business Directory* (Philadelphia: James Gopsill's Sons, circa 1865).
6. Charles Latham, Jr., *The Episcopal Academy 1785–1984* (Devon, Pennsylvania: William T. Cooke Publishing Inc., 1984), 74.
7. Ibid.
8. Ibid.

9. Ibid.
10. Ibid., 73.
11. Ibid.
12. Ibid., 85.
13. Ibid., 81.
14. Ibid., 85.
15. *The National Cyclopaedia of American Biography*, undated, circa 1875.
16. In McFadden's will, the building was appraised at $42,000 ($592,315 today).
17. This building is still standing.
18. The church was not consecrated as a cathedral until 1923.
19. PI, April 18, 1881.
20. Sources differ regarding this departure date. Some cite 1883. This date is almost surely erroneous. Based on consensus and McFadden's work history in Liverpool, 1881 emerges as the most reliable date.

Chapter Three: Liverpudlian, 1881–1902

1. Hugh Hollinghurst, *Liverpool* (Stroud, Gloucestershire: Amberley Publishing, 2018), 1.
2. Daniel Allen Butler, *The Age of Cunard* (Annapolis, Maryland: Lighthouse Press, 2003), 45–46.
3. H. C. Ross, *The Lancet* (London: March 5, 1921), 511.
4. Trevor May, *The Victorian Domestic Servant* (Oxford, Oxfordshire: Shire Publication, Ltd., 1998), 4.
5. NYT, December 24, 1888.
6. McFadden's strong kinship with Zerega was such that at least one report, a court document of the New York State Surrogate Court, identified the Philadelphian as the "sole acting executor" of Zerega's estate when the latter died around 1915.

Chapter Four: Trader, 1881–1902

1. NYT, January 13, 1901.
2. Baring Brothers, Liverpool, in a letter to Baring Brothers (London: ING Baring, The Baring Archive, March 15, 1894) (Citation provided by Nigel Hall).
3. *Liverpool Mercury*, October 23, 1891.
4. "Summary History of Geo. H. McFadden & Bro., Raw Cotton Merchants" (Philadelphia: Geo. H. McFadden Bro., 1991), 5.

5. Nigel Hall, "The Liverpool Cotton Market: Britain's First Futures," *Transactions of the Historical Society of Lancashire and Cheshire*, vol. 149, 2000, 100.
6. Hall, email to author, August 2018.
7. Kleinwort, Sons & Co., London: United Kingdom Information Book No. 2, manuscript, London Archives 58. (Citation provided by Hall.)
8. Hall, "The Liverpool Cotton Market," 100. Kleinwort, Sons & Co., London: United Kingdom Information Book No. 2, manuscript, London Archives 58. (Citation provided by Hall.)
9. Hall, 112.
10. Joseph Jacobs, *Jewish Encyclopedia: A Descriptive Record of the History, Religion, Literature, and Customs of the Jewish People from the Earliest Times to the Present Day* (New York: Funk & Wagnalls, 1906), 315.
11. Bruce E. Baker and Barbara Hahn, *The Cotton Kings* (New York: Oxford University Press, 2016), 50.
12. NYT, January 14, 1892, 3.
13. Ibid.
14. NYT, June 16, 1912.
15. "Whinfad cables" refers to an unidentified McFadden office or operative.
16. Hall, email to author, August 2018.
17. NYT, April 15, 1913.
18. NYT, January 13, 1901. Many years later, by 1918, George further expanded the firm's portfolio to include coffee imports in a partnership with Prado Chaves, one of Brazil's top growers of the crop. See *Spice Mill*, March 1921, 484.
19. Baker and Hahn, 47.
20. PI, March 20, 1904, 1.
21. Ibid.
22. A German U-boat torpedoed and sank the *Oriel* in 1916.
23. Seymour Taylor, *Bulls and Bears* (Liverpool: C. Tingling & Co., Limited, 1908), unpaginated.
24. George Bigwood, *Cotton* (London: Constable & Co., 1918), 114–115. (Citation provided by Hall.)
25. Taylor, unpaginated.
26. The family name was intentionally misspelled. In 1906, the Liverpool Cotton Association Ltd. built its enlarged third and last exchange building in Old Hall Street, adjacent to the Albany.
27. *Liverpool Mercury*, undated.
28. Ibid.
29. Taylor, unpaginated.

Chapter Five: Connoisseur, 1892–1902

1. Will.
2. David Watkin, et al., *Grand Hotel: The Golden Age of Palace Hotels, an Architectural and Social History* (Secaucus, New Jersey: Chartwell Books, 1984), 148.
3. PI, March 2, 1906, 6.
4. Geoffrey Agnew, *Agnew's, 1817–1967* (London: The Bradbury Agnew Press Ltd., 1967), 41.
5. Ibid., 42.
6. Stock Books, Archives of Thomas Agnew & Sons, Research Centre, National Gallery, London.
7. Agnew, 44.
8. Later, 43 Old Bond Street. At the time, art savant Bernard Berenson lived at 14 Old Bond Street.
9. Agnew's referred to prints, watercolors, and sketches as "drawings," according to Alex Leigh of the National Gallery's Research Centre.
10. Also known as *Manchester Coach.*
11. Titles are those cited in *British Painting in the Philadelphia Museum of Art*, not necessarily those listed in the Agnew's Stock Books.
12. H.M.W. (Harvey Maitland Watts), *The John Howard Collection of Portraits and Landscapes of the British School, An Appreciation and Interpretation with Catalogue* (Philadelphia: Pennsylvania Museum and School of Industrial Art, 1923). Watts is one of three McFadden Collection cataloguers. The others are William Roberts (1917) and Richard Dorment (1986).

Chapter Six: Collectors

1. Behrman, 16.
2. Huneker, 202.
3. P.A.B. Widener had his own Sargent, a portrait commissioned in 1902.
4. George Roberts and Mary Roberts, *Triumph on Fairmount: Fiske Kimball and the Philadelphia Museum of Art* (Philadelphia: J.B. Lippincott Company, 1959), 230.
5. Jennifer Thompson, "The 'Raeburn Craze' in Philadelphia," in *Making for America: Transatlantic Craftsmanship, Scotland and the Americas in the Eighteenth and Nineteenth Centuries* (Edinburgh: Society of Antiquaries of Scotland, 2013), 190.
6. AAN, May 4, 1912, 4.

Chapter Seven: Anglomane, 1902–1913

1. Lukacs, 27.
2. Edwin Wolf 2nd, *Philadelphia* (Harrisburg, Pennsylvania: Stackpole Books, 1975), 279.
3. E. Digby Baltzell, *Philadelphia Gentlemen* (Chicago: Quadrangle Books, 1971), 92
4. Scheduled service between Philadelphia and Liverpool began as early as 1850, instituted by the Philadelphia and Liverpool Steamship Company, an English enterprise. The service was the first to carry immigrants in steerage, according to Liverpool historian Ron Jones. Jones, *The American Connection* (Moreton, Wirral: Ron Jones, 1986), 63.
5. Lukacs, 8.
6. Ibid., 9.
7. CaF, February 23, 1921, 308.
8. PI, January 1, 1901.
9. Charles J. Cohen, *Rittenhouse Square: Past and Present* (Philadelphia: Privately printed, 1922), 190.
10. PI, March 2, 1906, 6.
11. Butler, *The Age of Cunard*, 167–168.
12. Lucius Beebe, *The Big Spenders* (Garden City, New York: Doubleday & Company, 1966), 156.
13. Butler, 239.
14. Beebe, *The Big Spenders*, 154–155.
15. Correspondence, to Edwin AtLee Barber, June 24, 1913.
16. *The Wall Street Journal*, January 13–14, 2018, C10.
17. Thompson, 192.
18. NYT, March 29, 1913.
19. Baltzell, *Philadelphia Gentlemen*, 345.
20. Ibid., 347.
21. Ibid., 351.
22. The now-defunct "junior" club was associated with the Conservative Party, as was the "senior" Carlton Club which still flourishes. Back home, McFadden was a Republican. Brother George was a Democrat, according to his daughter Ellie Browning
23. One would have supposed the yacht's berth would have been at the Corinthian Yacht Club of Philadelphia, given that it fulfilled all the necessary social markers. The club was founded on the Delaware by the senior Drexel himself. A slew of Rittenhouse Sunday sailors followed in his wake. The club has no record of a John McFadden membership.
24. In later life, McFadden established friendships with the explorer Sir Ernest H. Shackleton and the London art dealer Lockett

Agnew. These relationships involved a one-way exchange of money—
McFadden to them.

25. PI, December 24, 1911.
26. The hotel was built in 1911 by Peter A. B. Widener's elder son George
    D. Widener out of spite after his wife was chastised for smoking in
    public at the nearby Bellevue-Stratford Hotel.
27. PI, July 31, 1910.
28. *Science*, May 29, 1914, 794.
29. Kumaravel Rajakumar, "Pellagra in the United States: A Historical Per-
    spective," *Southern Medical Journal*, vol. 93, no. 3 (March 2000), 252–257.

Chapter Eight: Philadelphian, 1902–1918

1. Decision by the New York Appellate Division, First Department, December 7, 1906.
2. PI, March 2, 1906, 1.
3. Ibid., 6.
4. Decision by the New York Appellate Division, First Department, December 7, 1906.
5. Cohen.
6. Later, Brown Brothers, Harriman & Co.
7. AAN, May 4, 1912, 6.
8. Art reviewers were fond of terming *Lady Rodney* as the collection's "clou,"
   an arcane usage from the French meaning "cornerstone," or "keystone."
9. AAN, May 4, 1912, 8. The picture was not otherwise identified. Doughty was known for scenic renderings, including an 1824 view of the
   Fairmount Park Waterworks.
10. Huneker, *The Pathos of Distance*.
11. H.M.W. (also known as Harvey Maitland Watts), p. 23. Watts used a
    "signature" byline. The local author was not otherwise shy in using his
    full name in other works.
12. The book was still in print in 1922.
13. Presumably, Jack.
14. AAN, May 4, 1912, 6.
15. Ibid.
16. Ibid.
17. Ibid.
18. The Van Rensselaer family lived at the west corner of 18th and Walnut
    Streets, and did so until 1942. Their house still exists, now occupied
    by a retail shop, but has been heavily modified.
19. These numbers have been extrapolated from contemporary census
    data. An exact Center City population in 1900 was not available.

20. Baltzell, *Philadelphia Gentlemen*, 182–183. Whether other early twentieth-century urban power centers like Washington Square in New York and Louisburg Square in Boston met this test is debatable.
21. Ibid., 189.
22. Ingersoll, 100–101.

Chapter Nine: Pater Familias, 1909–1917

1. PI, December 29, 1909.
2. Ibid.
3. Cohen, 303.
4. PI, August 9, 1914.
5. PI, March 23, 1916, 12.
6. *Old Penn Weekly Review*, March 25, 1916.
7. *Old Penn* (Philadelphia: University of Pennsylvania, April 13, 1917).

Chapter Ten: Hero

1. PI, January 18, 1914.
2. Brinton.
3. Hugh Robert Mill, *The Life of Sir Ernest Shackleton* (Boston: Little, Brown & Co., 1923), 249.
4. Ibid., 175.
5. The Lippincott Company attributed the suicide to a "temporary aberration."
6. Brinton.
7. Ibid.
8. *Philadelphia Geographical Society Bulletin*, 1913, 130.
9. PI, January 17, 1913.
10. Ibid. The Wellington had not yet been constructed.
11. Ibid., January 25, 1913.
12. The unconventional spelling of Barber's middle name was a family quirk.
13. In subsequent correspondence, he corrected "donation," an apparent error, to "loan."
14. Correspondence, March 18, 1913.
15. "Bombs" are small bits of molten lava. Mt. Erebus is an Antarctic volcano.
16. J. St. George Joyce, editor, *Story of Philadelphia* (Philadelphia: Harry B. Joseph, Publisher, 1919), 386.
17. The Academy of Natural Sciences deaccessioned the eggs and the rocks in 2000. The eggs were "transferred" to the Western Foundation

of Vertebrate Zoology in Camarillo, California; the rocks, to the Wagner Free Institute of Science in Philadelphia. The whereabouts of the other items are unknown. *The Philadelphia Inquirer* reported on April 30, 1913 that it was "understood" that some of the collection would be donated to the University of Pennsylvania Museum. Penn Museum officials have no record of any such donation.

18. PI, May 11, 1913.
19. Ibid., January 25, 1914.
20. Correspondence, to Barber, September 25, 1914.
21. This was the expedition that McFadden claimed he had not funded.
22. PI, April 22, 1917.
23. Robert Peary, a Philadelphia Geographical Society member, was a previous Kane medalist.
24. Brinton. McFadden was referring to Shackleton's "suffering" during the 1915 expedition.

Chapter Eleven: Builder, 1913–1920

1. PT, February 24, 1913.
2. PI, December 30, 1915, 11.
3. Ibid., April 30, 1916, 26.
4. Dorment, xv.
5. PI, April 30, 1916, 26.
6. Will.
7. George also died at Barclay Farms, at 79 in 1926. His brother, J. Franklin, who divided his time between Philadelphia and New York, died at 73 in 1936 while vacationing on Nantucket, Massachusetts.
8. "Resolution Honoring Mrs. George McFadden," Historical Society of Pennsylvania, Digital Library Permanent ID 8155, https://digitallibrary.hsp.org/index.php/Detail/objects/8155 (Retrieved January 10, 2020).
9. Nancy M. Heinzen, *The Perfect Square: A History of Rittenhouse Square* (Philadelphia: Temple University Press, 2009), 113.
10. Including The Wellington.
11. NYT, February 6, 1927.

PART II

Chapter Twelve: Trustee, 1910–1921

1. The club was dissolved in 1940. Its building was razed in 1976.
2. *Annual Report*, The Art Club of Philadelphia (privately printed), 1911, 53.

3. PI, February 1, 1911.
4. *Annual Report*, The Art Club of Philadelphia, 1912, 54.
5. PI, February 26, 1911, 19.
6. Ibid., April 30, 1916, 26.
7. Leo J. Harris, *Before the Museums Came: A Social History of the Fine Arts in the Twin Cities* (London: Versita, 2013), 44.
8. AAN, November 9, 1918, 6.
9. Ibid.
10. Ibid.
11. Mary Ann Meyers, *Art, Education & African-American Culture: Albert Barnes and the Science of Philanthropy* (New Brunswick, New Jersey: Transaction Publishers, 2004), 157.
12. Edwin A. Barber was either the museum's fourth or fifth director, depending on how one accounts for William Platt Pepper, who served twice, as the first director from 1877 to 1879 and again from 1899 to 1907. William W. Justice was the second director, from 1879 to 1880.
13. Bertha Adams, editor, *An Enduring Legacy: The Philadelphia Museum of Art and its Benefactors*, http://philamuseum.org, retrieved 2018.
14. AAA, 1917, 33.
15. May, 22.
16. https://cabinetcardgallery.wordpress.com./ The specific web page is no longer available.
17. Eugène Castello, *The American Magazine of Art*, June 1916, 335–336.
18. Ibid., and AAN, December 23, 1916.

Chapter Thirteen: Exhibitor, 1916

1. Though no image of Lawrence's Lady Anna Maria Nelthorpe has been found, a catalogue describes a seated figure wearing a black, short-sleeved dress, with a shawl draped over her right arm. For most of the twentieth century, the painting was known as *Miss Nelthorp*. Kenneth Garlick, author of *Sir Thomas Lawrence: A Complete Catalogue of Oil Paintings* (Oxford: Phaidon Press Limited, 1989), set the record straight.
2. No record of an insurance value, nor a reimbursement from a claim has been found.
3. *The Spectator*, March 2, 1916, 99. In fact, McFadden had probably under-insured the rest of the collection, as well. Its total insurance declaration in 1916 was $1 million ($23 million today).
4. *Arts and Decoration*, May 1916, 350–351; PI, April 28, 1916, 8. Neither cataloguer Roberts nor cataloguer Dorment refer to this painting's damage. A visual inspection shows no evidence of damage, nor repair.

5. W. (William) Roberts, *Catalogue of the Collection of Pictures formed by John H. McFadden, Esq., of Philadelphia, Pa.* (London: Chiswick Press, 1917), vii.
6. No purchase date, nor a price are listed in Agnew's Stock Books. McFadden paid £5,650 ($1,014,000) for another Turner, *The Nore*, acquired on December 3, 1895 and later sold.
7. PI, April 30, 1916, 26.
8. Ibid., April 28, 1916.
9. Ibid., April 30, 1916, 26.
10. Castello, AMA, June 1916, 336. McFadden's second purchase of a Gainsborough, another landscape titled *View Near Ipswich*, bought on February 12, 1900, had already been sold.
11. Ozias Humphry and John Mayer, *A Memoir of George Stubbs* (London: Pallas Athene, 2005), 78.
12. No Stock Book records exist.
13. AAN, May 4, 1912, 8. An oil representation of *The Horse Fair* was an 1887 gift from Cornelius Vanderbilt to the Metropolitan Museum of Art. Another version of the 1885 work was bequeathed to the National Gallery, London.
14. Huneker, 206.
15. PI, April 30, 1916, 26. The Dobson pictures were also memorable because they were never seen again.
16. NYT, May 7, 1916, 18.
17. Ibid., October 24, 1916.
18. Ibid., November 18, 1916.

Chapter Fourteen: Curator, 1917–1920

1. Roberts, William, AiA, vol. 6, 1918, 108.
2. Agnew's Stock Book entries show sales directly to John H. McFadden. Many years after his father's death, Jack donated *The North Terrace*; *David Hartley, M.P.*; and *Thomas Payne, His Family, and Friends* to the renamed Philadelphia Museum of Art in his own right. Daughter Alice sold *Gainsborough Dupont, Esq.,* at auction.
3. Dorment, 36.
4. Dorment has reported that McFadden never bought a painting sight unseen. Dorment, xiv.
5. Roberts, *Catalogue*, v.
6. Ibid., 1.
7. Roberts, AiA, vol. 6, 1918, 117. Roberts also committed some finicky spelling errors. The sitter in Lawrence's work *Miss Nelthorp*, as he called it, was actually Miss *Nelthorpe*. In Lawrence's *Miss West* (*After-*

wards Mrs. Woodgate), as Roberts fashioned the title, he referred to the sitter as Harroit West. Dorment references the painting as *Miss Harriott West, Afterwards Mrs. William Woodgate.*

8. PL, February 17, 1921.
9. Dorment, xiii. Also Agnew's Stock Books.
10. The picture appeared in the collection's Pittsburgh show in April 1917.
11. The 30-inch-by-25-inch oil of Beaumont had an appraised value in 1908 of $380 ($8,000). There is no way of understanding McFadden's enduring affection for the watercolor of Bonheur's *The Horse Fair,* a work that he had been displaying at 19th and Walnut through 1916. Other than, as previously mentioned, he was just fond of it. He was not alone in this appreciation. The picture, in its different forms, was immensely popular—in America and in Europe.
12. Handwritten aide-memoire drafted by Fiske Kimball, the museum director hired in 1925 and who helped define the McFadden collection. PMA Archives, April 2, 1946.
13. The will makes no mention of this purchase option.
14. Telephone conversation between Jack McFadden and Kimball. PMA Archives, April 2, 1946.
15. A De Lázló picture, depending on size and subject, today sells for up to $200,000, or more. Jack donated his father's portrait to the Philadelphia Museum of Art in 1956. It is now, from time to time, shown with the permanent works of the John Howard McFadden Memorial Collection.
16. The portrait is in a private collection.
17. The bronze version débuted during the collection's loan from 1921 to 1928 at the Smithsonian Institution in Washington. It later became a temporary adjunct to the permanent installation at the Pennsylvania Museum. All along, the bust was owned by Alice McFadden Brinton Eyre, who officially loaned it to the new museum in 1928. She gave it outright to the rechristened Philadelphia Museum of Art in 1940. It remains in storage.
18. PAFA cannot provide additional details.
19. *Pennsylvania Society Yearbook,* 1913, 207.
20. PI, June 9, 1918, 35.
21. Aline Saarinen, *The Proud Possessors* (New York: Random House, 1958), 93.
22. *The International Studio, An Illustrated Magazine of Fine and Applied Art,* vol. 61, June 1917.
23. The paintings were signed and dated in Bath in 1786. PI, June 9, 1918, 36.
24. PI, June 9, 1918, 36.

25. The Williams pictures last appeared in the McFadden collection in the Pittsburgh show. Since then, the paintings have been sold several times at auction in London.
26. It was closer to twenty-five years.
27. *Metropolitan Museum of Art Bulletin*, June 1917.
28. Bryson Burroughs, *Catalogue of Portraits and Landscapes of the British School Lent by John H. McFadden* (New York: Metropolitan Museum of Art, 1917), iii–viii.
29. Author's italics.
30. H.M.W. (Harvey Maitland Watts), 22.
31. John H. McFadden, Jr., correspondence to Fiske Kimball, PMA Archives, June 11, 1946.

Chapter Fifteen: Founder, 1920–1921

1. Correspondence, PMA Archives, January 10, 1912.
2. Ibid.
3. Ibid., December 23, 1913.
4. Ibid., January 3, 1914.
5. *American Wool and Cotton Reporter*, February 24, 1921, 671.
6. PI, February 17, 16.
7. Ibid.
8. AWCR, February 24, 1921, 35.
9. PI, February 20, 1921, 16.
10. AAN, February 19, 1921, 4.
11. H. C. Ross, *The Lancet*, March 6, 1921, 511.
12. Joyce (ed.), *Story of Philadelphia*.
13. PL, February 17, 1921.
14. The family name was intentionally misspelled.
15. Undated correspondence, PMA Archives.
16. These values were conservative estimates. City officials put the collection's worth "far" into the millions of dollars. PI, March 1, 1921, 1.
17. Will.
18. The Mixed Courts was an international legal system, akin to the international court at The Hague, in The Netherlands. Its rulings were recognized by the United States. Jasper Yeates Brinton, *The Mixed Courts of Egypt* (New Haven, Connecticut: Yale University Press, 1930), 367.
19. Will.
20. Ibid.
21. Ibid.
22. NYT, March 24, 1921.
23. PI, January 15, 1921, 1.

24. Ibid., April 27, 1921, 5.
25. Michael Haag, *Alexandria: City of Memory* (New Haven, Connecticut: Yale University Press, 2004), 126.

PART III

Chapter Sixteen: Aftermath, 1921–1928

1. PI, August 14, 1921, 18.
2. *New York Tribune*, August 21, 1921.
3. Ibid.
4. Ibid.
5. PI, October 25, 1921, 4.
6. Ibid., March 1, 1921, 13.
7. NYT, March 1, 1921.
8. Ninety years later, this technically remains the case. The prefix "M" in citations and labels of objects in the McFadden collection indicates city ownership.
9. McFadden never had a role in fighting hookworm and scarlet fever. Moore failed to mention McFadden's actual efforts in pellagra prevention.
10. PI, March 1, 1921, 13.
11. Robert E. Drayer, *Hampton Moore: An Old-Fashioned Republican* (Doctoral dissertation, University of Pennsylvania, 1961).
12. The Orphans' Court can revise or nullify wills. Such actions are rare.
13. PI, March 1, 1921, 13.
14. Charles D. Walcott, "Report of the Secretary of the Smithsonian Institution." Washington: Smithsonian Institution, for the year ending June 30, 1922, 48.
15. H.M.W. (Harvey Maitland Watts).
16. No record is known regarding the insurance payment.
17. Renamed the Benjamin Franklin Parkway in 1937.

Chapter Seventeen: Fairmount, 1921–1928

1. Baltzell, *Puritan Boston and Quaker Philadelphia*, 436.
2. Heinzen, 110–111.
3. Ibid., 111–112.
4. Rishel, Joseph J., *The Henry P. McIlhenny Collection: An Illustrated History* (Philadelphia: Philadelphia Museum of Art, 1987), 10.
5. Roberts and Roberts, *Triumph on Fairmount*, 55.

6. Ibid., 27.
7. Ibid., 61–62.
8. Charles Poore, NYT, November 12, 1959.
9. Roberts and Roberts, 58.
10. This agreement was formalized in 1941. Evan H. Turner, *Treasures of the Philadelphia Museum of Art* (Philadelphia: Philadelphia Museum of Art, 1973), unpaginated introduction.
11. It was renamed the Bode Museum in 1956 to honor its first curator, Wilhelm von Bode.
12. David B. Brownlee, *Making a Modern Classic: The Architecture of the Philadelphia Museum of Art* (Philadelphia: Philadelphia Museum of Art, 1997), 99.
13. "About Us: Our Story 1920–1930," Philadelphia Museum of Art website, https://www.philamuseum.org/information/45-227-23.html (retrieved January 18, 2020).
14. Roberts and Roberts, 54.
15. Steven Conn, *Museums and American Intellectual Life, 1876–1926* (Chicago: The University of Chicago Press, 1998), 223–224.
16. Price Family Papers. Collection 3690, The Historical Society of Pennsylvania, Philadelphia, Pennsylvania.
17. Conn, 223.
18. Brownlee, 81.
19. The British Museum, established in 1753, was largely endowed with collections donated by Sir Hans Sloane.
20. Brownlee, 82. That corridor was recently refurbished and reopened to the public
21. NYT, February 10, 1927.
22. Ibid.
23. Ibid., July 14, 1927.
24. Ibid., January 1, 1928.

Chapter Eighteen: Inauguration, 1928

1. Roberts and Roberts, 88.
2. Brownlee, 82.
3. Curatorial document, PMA, circa 1928, 4.
4. Ibid., 3.
5. Roberts and Roberts, 89.
6. *The Pennsylvania Museum Bulletin*, Pennsylvania Museum, March 1928, 21.
7. Since 1928, McFadden's paintings and the interior décor of the period rooms have been rearranged many times. *Lady Rodney* is now

located in Gallery 277, in a position that in 1928 was home to *Master Bunbury*.

8.   *The Pennsylvania Museum Bulletin*, March 1928, 19–23.
9.   Deal is a form of softwood.
10. Curatorial document, "First-Known Locations of the McFadden Collection," PMA, 2018.
11. One citation indicates that *Portrait of a Gentleman* and *Miss West* may have been hung as late as January 1929.
12. Brownlee, 104.
13. Roberts and Roberts, 92. Note that the invitation did not actually announce the "opening" of a new home for the Pennsylvania Museum. Rather, "sections."
14. Conn, 225.
15. NYT, March 27, 1928, 16.
16. Conn, 225.
17. NYT, March 27, 1928, 16.
18. *The Burlington Magazine for Connoisseurs*, London: The Burlington Magazine for Connoisseurs, May 1928, 254.
19. NYT, March 27, 1928, 16.
20. Conn, 225.
21. Ibid.
22. *The Burlington Magazine for Connoisseurs*, 254.
23. NYT, March 27, 1928, 16
24. The Pennsylvania Museum was renamed the Philadelphia Museum of Art in 1938.

Epilogue: New Yorkers

1.   Will.
2.   NYT, July 1, 1931.
3.   NYT, December 18, 1936.
4.   NYT, February 11, 1949, 46.
5.   Victor J. Lang, Jr., letter, July 12, 1978. Lang reminisced about Jack, based on his conversations with friends of McFadden.
6.   NYT, August 18, 1955.

Some citations are incomplete. When data is missing (page number, publication date, etc.), these details were unavailable. Though infrequent, this was particularly the case for research obtained online.

Bibliography

Aldrich, Jr., Nelson W. *Old Money*. New York: Alfred A. Knopf, 1988.

———. *Tommy Hitchcock, An American Hero*. London: Fleet Street Corporation, 1984.

Alsop, Joseph. *The Rare Art Traditions*. New York: Harper & Row, Publishers, 1982.

Armory, Cleveland. *The Trouble with Nowadays*. New York: Arbor House, 1979.

———. *Who Killed Society*. New York: Harper & Brothers, Publishers, 1960.

Aspin, Chris. *The Cotton Industry*. Oxford, Oxfordshire: Shire Publications Ltd., 2012.

Baker, Bruce E.; Hahn, Barbara. *The Cotton Kings*. Oxford: Oxford University Press, 2016.

Baltzell, E. Digby. *Philadelphia Gentlemen*. Chicago: Quadrangle Books, Inc., 1971.

———. *Puritan Boston and Quaker Philadelphia*. New York: The Free Press, 1979.

———. *Puritan Boston and Quaker Philadelphia*. Boston: Beacon Press, 1982.

Basbanes, Nicholas A. *A Gentle Madness*. New York: Henry Holt and Company, 1995.

Bearden, William. *Cotton*. Charleston, South Carolina: Arcadia Publishing, 2005.

Beebe, Lucius. *The Big Spenders*. Garden City, New York: Doubleday & Company, Inc., 1966.

Behrman, S.N. *Duveen*. New York: Vintage Books, 1952.

Bennett, Shelley M. *The Art of Wealth. The Huntingtons in the Gilded Age*. San Marino, California: The Huntington Library, Art Collections, and Botanical Gardens, 2013.

Birmingham, Stephen. *The Right People*. Boston: Little, Brown and Company, 1968.

———. *The Right Places*. Boston: Little, Brown and Company, 1973.

Browning, Ella L. "Incidents." unpublished typescript, 1954.

Brownlee, David B. *Building the City Beautiful. The Benjamin Franklin Parkway and the Philadelphia Museum of Art.* Philadelphia: Philadelphia Museum of Art, 2017.

——. *Making a Modern Classic, The Architecture of the Philadelphia Museum of Art.* Philadelphia: Philadelphia Museum of Art, 1997.

Burroughs, Bryson. *Catalogue of Portraits and Landscapes of the British School Lent by John H. McFadden (1917).* New York: Metropolitan Museum of Art, 1917.

Butler, Daniel Allen. *The Age of Cunard.* Annapolis, Maryland: Lighthouse Press, 2003.

Carreño, Richard. *Museum Mile: Philadelphia's Parkway Museums.* Philadelphia: WritersClearinghousePress, 2011.

Cohen, Charles J. *Rittenhouse Square, Past and Present.* Philadelphia: Privately printed, 1922.

Colby, Reginald. *Mayfair.* London: Country Life Limited, 1966.

Conn, Steven. *Museums and American Intellectual Life, 1876–1926.* Chicago: The University of Chicago Press, 1998.

Dickens, Charles. *American Notes.* New York: St. Martin's Press, 1985.

Dorment, Richard. *British Painting in the Philadelphia Museum of Art.* Philadelphia: Philadelphia Museum of Art, 1986.

Duveen, Bt., Sir Joseph. *Thirty Years of British Art.* New York: Albert & Charles Boni, Inc., 1930.

Egerton, Judy, editor, et al. *George Stubbs 1724–1806.* Salem, New Hampshire: Salem House, 1985.

Greenfield, Howard. *The Devil and Dr. Barnes.* New York: Viking, 1987.

Haag, Michael. *Alexandria.* New Haven, Connecticut: Yale University Press, 2004.

Hall, Nigel. "The Liverpool Cotton Market: Britain's First Futures Market." *Transactions of the Historical Society of Lancashire and Cheshire,* volume 149, 2000.

Harris, Neil. *Capital Culture.* Chicago: The University of Chicago Press, 2013.

Heinzen, Nancy M. *The Perfect Square.* Philadelphia: Temple University Press, 2009.

Hildebrandt, Rachel. *The Philadelphia Area Architecture of Horace Trumbauer.* Charleston: Arcadia Publishing, 2009.

Hill, Edwin Charles. *The Historical Register.* London: Forgotten Books, 2015.

Hollinghurst, Hugh. *Liverpool.* Stroud, Gloucestershire: Amberley Publishing, 2018.

Humphry, Ozias; Mayer, Joseph. *A Memoir of George Stubbs.* London: Pallas Athene, 2005.

Huneker, James. *The Pathos of Distance*. New York: Charles Scribner's Sons, 1922.

Ingersoll, R. Sturgis. *Recollections of a Philadelphian at Eighty*. Philadelphia: National Publishing Company, 1971.

James, Henry. *The American Scene*. New York: Penguin Books, 1994.

Jenkins, Alan. *The Twenties*. New York: Universe Books, 1974.

Jones, Ron. *The American Connection*. Moreton, Wirral: Ron Jones, 1986.

Konolige, Kit; Konolige, Frederica. *The Power of their Glory*. New York: Simon and Schuster, 1978.

Latham Jr., Charles. *The Episcopal Academy 1785–1984*. Devon, Pennsylvania: William T. Cooke Publishing, Inc., 1984.

Layton, J. Kent. *Transatlantic Liners*. Oxford: Shire Publications, 2012.

Loebl, Suzanne. *America's Art Museums*. New York: W.W. Norton & Company, 2002.

McKown, Robin. *The World of Mary Cassatt*. New York: Thomas Y. Crowell Company, 1972.

May, Trevor. *The Victorian Domestic Servant*. Oxford: Shire Publications Ltd., 1998.

Master Builders. Maddex, Diane, editor. Washington: The Preservation Press, 1985.

Metropolitan Museum of Art Guide, The. Howard, Kathleen, editor. New York: Metropolitan Museum of Art, 1987.

Miller Jr., William H. *The Fabulous Interiors of the Great Ocean Liners*. New York: Dover Publications, Inc., 1985.

Morton, Brian N. *Americans in London*. New York: William Morrow and Company, Inc., 1986.

Paine, Janie V. *Memphis Cotton Exchange*. Memphis, Tennessee: Memphis Cotton Exchange, circa 1974.

Noreika, Sarah, editor. *Philadelphia Museum of Art Handbook*. Philadelphia: Philadelphia Museum of Art, 2014.

Philadelphia Museum of Art Handbook of Collections. Babbitt, Sherry, editor. Philadelphia: Philadelphia Museum of Art, 2008.

Philadelphia's Best Buildings. Philadelphia: The Foundation for Architecture, 1994.

Pye, Ken. *Liverpool at Work*. Stroud: Amberley Publishing, 2017.

Reeves, Richard. *American Journey*. New York: Simon and Schuster, 1982.

Rishel, Joseph J. *The Henry P. McIlhenny Collection, An Illustrated History*. Philadelphia: Philadelphia Museum of Art, 1987.

Roberts, George and Mary. *Triumph on Fairmount: Fiske Kimball and the Philadelphia Museum of Art*. Philadelphia: J.B. Lippincott Company, 1959.

Roberts, W. *Catalogue of the Collection of Pictures formed by John H. McFadden, Esq., of Philadelphia, Pa.* London: Chiswick Press, 1917.

Rybczynski, Witold. *Urban Expectations in a New World.* New York: Scribner, 1995.

Saarinen, Aline B. *The Proud Possessors.* New York: Random House, 1958.

Secrest, Meryle. *Duveen.* Chicago: The University of Chicago Press, 2004.

——. *Kenneth Clark, A Biography.* New York: Holt, Rinehart and Winston, 1984.

Shand-Tucci, Douglass. *The Art of Scandal: The Life and Times of Isabella Stewart Gardner.* New York: HarperPerennial, 1998.

Sharples, Joseph. *Liverpool.* New Haven: Yale University Press, 2004.

Skaler, Robert Morris; Keels, Thomas H. *Philadelphia's Rittenhouse Square.* Chicago: Arcadia Publishing, 2008.

Spaeth, Eloise. *American Art Museums.* New York: Harper & Row, Publishers, 1975.

Summary History of Geo. H. McFadden & Bro., Raw Cotton Merchants. Anonymous, unpublished typescript, 1991.

Sutton, Peter C. *Northern European Paintings in the Philadelphia Museum of Art.* Philadelphia: Philadelphia Museum of Art, 1990.

Thompson, Jacqueline. *The Very Rich Book.* New York: William Morrow and Company, 1981.

Tomkins, Calvin. *Merchants & Masterpieces.* New York: E.P. Dutton & Co., Inc., 1970.

——. *Merchants & Masterpieces.* New York: Henry Holt and Company, 1989.

Treasures of the Philadelphia Museum of Art. Marcus, George H., editor. Philadelphia: Philadelphia Museum of Art, 1973.

Watkin, David, et al. *Grand Hotel.* Secaucus, New Jersey: Chartwell Books, Inc., 1984.

Waterhouse, Ellis. *Gainsborough.* London: Spring Books, 1958.

Webster, Richard. *Philadelphia Preserved.* Philadelphia: Temple University Press, 1981.

Willis, Abigail. *Museums & Galleries in London.* London: Metro Publications, Ltd., 2016.

Wilton, Andrew. *Five Centuries of British Painting.* London: Thames & Hudson, 2001.

Wolf 2nd, Edwin. *Philadelphia.* Harrisburg, Pennsylvania: Stackpole Books, 1975.

Woodman, Harold D. *King Cotton and His Retainers.* Washington: Beard Books, 2000.

Index